From Tejano to Tango

From Tejano to Tango

Latin American Popular Music

EDITED BY

WALTER AARON CLARK

Routledge
New York and London
OCM 47689767

Published in 2002 by
Routledge
29 West 35th Street
New York, NY 10001

Published in Great Britain by
Routledge
11 New Fetter Lane
London EC4P 4EE

Routledge is an imprint of the Taylor & Francis Group.

Printed in the United States of America on acid-free paper.

10 9 8 7 6 5 4 3 2 1

Library of Congress Cataloging-in-Publication Data

From tejano to tango : Latin American popular music / edited by Walter Aaron Clark.
    p. cm.
    Includes bibliographical references and index.
    Contents: Politics and identity, Argentina and Central America — Locality and interlocality, North America and Cuba — Globalization and mass mediation, Peru and Brazil.
    ISBN 0-8153-3639-X — ISBN 0-8153-3640-3 (pbk.)
    1. Popular music—Latin America—History and criticism. I. Clark, Walter Aaron.

ML3475 .F76 2002
781.64'098—dc21

2001048174

To the Memory of
Carmen Miranda

O que é que a carioca tem?
Tem graça como ninguém!

["Oh, what does a girl from Rio have?
She has grace like nobody else!"]

Paraphrase of a stanza from the samba
"O que é que a baiana tem?"
by Dorival Caymmi

Contents

III
Globalization and Mass Mediation
Brazil and Peru

Preface

The most prominent feature on the twentieth-century musical landscape is the rise of popular music of the western hemisphere to a preeminent position in global culture. This trend will no doubt continue well into the twenty-first century. *From Tejano to Tango* contributes to our knowledge of Latin American popular music in particular and the important role it has played in the development of the contemporary musical landscape. Over the centuries, and especially today, numerous Latin American songs and dances (*chacona, habanera,* rumba, samba, tango, bolero, *danzón,* bossa nova, etc.) have exercised a profound influence on Western classical music as well as U.S. pop and jazz; in addition, they have become ballroom favorites and staples of Broadway musicals, Hollywood films, and television. Given the increasing Hispanic population in the United States, this influence will also continue into the foreseeable future. Of course, the popular music of Latin America, in all its diversity, possesses intrinsic aesthetic value transcending its influence or dissemination.

The alliterative title of this book suggests that between its covers lies an encyclopedic taxonomy of musical styles, carefully laid out in alphabetical order, a sort of "A to Z" of Latin American popular music. Nothing could be further from the truth. Consider what is *not* treated within, for example, mariachi, mambo, bossa nova, salsa, and that soon becomes clear. And though our subject matter appears to stretch from the Río Bravo to the Río de la Plata ("From Tejano to Tango"), many important nations, such as Colombia and Venezuela, are not represented. I have become attached to the title because of its catchy quality, but I readily concede that its appeal is purely meretricious. Nonetheless, despite some gaps, this collection manages to cover a very wide range of topics, and it achieves broad geographic representation, including North and Central America, the Andes, Argentina,

Brazil, and the Caribbean. The contents have been organized along general thematic lines, with emphasis on the crucial issues of politics and identity, locality and interlocality, as well as globalization and mass mediation.

Given the manifold ramifications of popular music in the wider sphere of culture, society, and politics, it is inherently an interdisciplinary area of study. That is why this collection is not the domain of only one brand of "-ologist." The subject requires the interpenetration of expertise and perspectives from several disciplines, including ethnomusicology, historical musicology, sociology, and anthropology. All of these are represented by the contributors to this volume. Balancing breadth and depth, quantity and quality is always a delicate task. I believe that the contributors and I have succeeded in providing insights into a wide, if not exhaustive, range of styles and issues, and that the succeeding chapters will be of interest not only to specialists but general readers as well.

It is unlikely that any one person could ever have written this book. It was a necessarily collaborative effort, and though I had toyed with the idea years ago, the impetus to begin bringing it together was provided in 1998 by Soo Mee Kwon, then music editor at Routledge/Garland. I would like to express my sincere appreciation to Soo Mee's successor, Richard Carlin, for his ongoing faith in the project and editorial suggestions, as well as to Gage Averill, series editor, for his encouragement and invaluable counsel. Of course, I have been sustained by the magnificent exertions of my contributors, to whom I am deeply grateful.

Finally, my wife and son, Nancy and Robert, merit kudos for their tolerance and patience in dealing with a husband and father often distracted by his work and fluctuating between the editorial ecstasy of timeliness and accuracy, and the agony of delays and revisions. Om, Shanti, Om.

Part I

Politics and Identity
Argentina and Nicaragua

1

The Popularized Gaucho Image as a Source of Argentine Classical Music, 1880–1920[1]

Deborah Schwartz-Kates

Between 1880 and 1920 in the city of Buenos Aires, classical and popular music stood worlds apart. The classical milieu was dominated by a small but influential group of composers who identified with the European "high art" tradition. Out of necessity, this group came from the ranks of the elite because Argentina at the time lacked the infrastructure to support professional development of the fine arts. These composers scorned an emergent group of working-class musicians who grew up in Argentine slum regions known as the *arrabal* and who created popular forms such as the urban *milonga* and early tango. When the socially prominent writer Leopoldo Lugones (1874–1938) decried the tango as obscene and pornographic, he spoke for many members of the intellectual and artistic elite (Novati and Cuello 1980, 40). Yet, despite the seemingly unbridgeable gulf that separated classical and popular musical traditions, at a certain critical moment in their history, their paths intertwined.[1]

This chapter focuses on this critical stylistic juncture, which occurred at the precise moment the popular and classical repertoires assumed definitive shape. Specifically, the chapter examines the earliest group of professionally trained classical composers, who appropriated symbolic resources derived from popular traditions to create a sense of *argentinidad* (or "Argentineness") in their works. In previous studies, the majority of scholars have emphasized rural folk music as a primary source of Argentine national art music (Kuss

3

1976; Veniard 1986; Plesch 1998). My own writings have followed down this path by exploring the symbolic role that the gaucho (or native horseman) played in forging a distinctive national identity (Schwartz-Kates 1997 and 1999). The present chapter both supports and expands upon these findings by demonstrating how the *gauchesca* tradition proved inseparable from the urban popular milieu through which the rural horseman's folk culture was mediated.

The Musical Actors

The classical composers active between 1880 and 1920 came of age during a dynamic period in Argentine history. The country achieved unprecedented wealth as it emerged as a world exporter of leather, beef, wool, and grains. As the nation fulfilled its dreams of progress and prosperity, its creative artists sought to transform Buenos Aires, the capital city, into a magnificent cultural showplace. The composers of this generation perceived Europe (particularly Paris) as a model of artistic emulation. They therefore based their aesthetic ideals on external models, and, prompted by the desire to master an art largely defined in foreign terms, identified with the European classical tradition. Yet, in this age of self-conscious nation building, the composers also aimed to create something uniquely representative of their culture that could be understood alongside the prestigious foreign "masterworks" of the day. Out of these competing and contradictory cultural claims emerged the earliest art music of a definitively national character.

To express their veneration for foreign culture and overcome ostensible feelings of native backwardness, Argentine composers traveled to Europe, where they fulfilled the social expectations of their class and secured the technical foundations of their art.[2] Ironically, once these composers arrived on foreign soil, they encountered the doctrine of musical nationalism, which, by the late nineteenth century, had earned widespread currency throughout Europe and which prompted them to turn toward their own cultural heritage as a source of inspiration. The principal composers associated with this generation encountered European musical nationalism in various ways. Yet, by the time they returned to Buenos Aires, they identified with the unique musical resources of their nation and began writing in a distinctively Argentine style.

As the basis of their nationalist conception, these composers embraced the *tradición gauchesca*: a potent aesthetic movement that extolled the native horseman as the embodiment of the national essence. During this period, political statesmen, cultural architects, and intellectual leaders used the gaucho figure as the personification of the rich heartland of the nation, upon which its future prosperity was based. They endowed the native horseman with noble attributes such as courage, individualism, machismo, and independence, which they promoted as the basis of national values, traditions, and beliefs. Eloquent writers established the practice of idealizing the heroic lifestyle of the gaucho in first-rate works of Argentine literature. These literary figures set a valuable precedent for classical composers by showing how Argentine nationality in the arts could meaningfully be portrayed.

Urban Transmission

On the surface, it would appear that the *gauchesca* basis of Argentine classical music derived exclusively from rural sources. Yet, the urban transformation and popularization of this repertoire also formed a significant part of composers' nationalist representations. One reason for this development stemmed from the gaucho's changing position in Argentine society. During the late nineteenth century, a radical transformation of the countryside uprooted the native horseman's lifestyle on the plains. New technologies in refrigerating, preserving, and shipping meat allowed ranchers to reap handsome profits from the export of quality livestock products. They rejected previous methods of selling the hides of native animals and instead raised superior grades of cattle that commanded competitive prices. They therefore bred, selected, and branded their animals with care and protected them in pens enclosed with barbed-wire fencing. These changes led to the commercialization of the Argentine ranch (or *estancia*) and eliminated the open range. Fencing eradicated the traditional lifestyle of the gaucho by imprisoning him inside, or marginalizing him outside, the new borders.

The Argentine horseman now faced difficult choices as he was forced to adapt to a modern system that no longer valued his work. Sadly, many gauchos were unable to make the change and were forced to live on the margins of society, where they robbed and scavenged for food. Others remained on the *estancia* but were relegated to menial tasks, working as servile peons ruled by the overseer of the ranch. Still others migrated to the outskirts of Buenos Aires, where they found new employment in industries such as slaughterhouses, refrigeration plants, and meat-packing factories. Highly characteristic of the age were the transplanted gauchos or *compadres* who earned a living by traversing the borders between the countryside and the city. A typical occupation was that of a *carretero*, or wagon-driver, who transported commercial goods between rural regions and Buenos Aires. As he sold his wares in city plazas, train stations, and fruit markets, the *carretero* mingled with a new group of immigrants, who were also socially marginalized and economically displaced. Out of the resulting mixture between native and foreign, on the meeting ground between urban and rural, a syncretic process took place. Ultimately, it was the music product resulting from this cultural synthesis that classical composers associated with the *gauchesca* tradition.

New Performance Contexts

During the last two decades of the nineteenth century, new performance contexts arose that facilitated the integration of rural and urban traditions. Many of these contexts involved spectacles and performers that moved from place to place, thus fostering the diffusion and intermixture of Argentine vernacular forms. Within these new contexts, musicians sought to intensify audience identification with their works by creating fresh styles, forms, and genres and by revitalizing traditional modes of expression that suited their artistic purposes. Both individually and in conjunction, these contexts thus fostered great innovation during the period. In particular, the professional *payador*, circus, and theater emerged as three central means of performance that influenced classical composers and their stylization of Argentine music.

The Professional Payador

Prior to the urbanization of Argentine rural life, the *payador* figured as a gaucho singer and guitarist, who improvised, composed, and memorized music. He was regarded as an essential member of traditional gaucho society, and no rural gathering was complete without him. The *payador* appeared as a musician in local *fiestas* and performed in *pulperías* (bars and stores), where anyone who sang could drink for free. There he played music for his own enjoyment, providing an accompaniment for dancing and improvising songs. The *payador* was most known for his improvised duels known as *payadas*, which were performed in competitions with other gauchos. These contests demonstrated his verbal dexterity, as he contrived clever poetic responses in the form of riddles, puns, and double entendres to counter, challenge, and defeat his opponents.

Beginning in the 1880s, a new type of musician emerged, still known as a *payador*, who affected a markedly urban style. Instead of singing exclusively at local gatherings, he performed throughout Argentina. He traveled by train, slept in comfortable hotels, and dressed in modern clothing. He was treated like a professional musician and reaped substantial economic benefit from his work. While his music still referred to old gaucho song types, it increasingly emphasized the new styles of the day. The urban *payador* helped transmit these musical changes because he took the old gaucho repertoire out of the countryside and brought it into the city, which led to the urbanization of rural forms. Later he reversed this process by reintroducing the urbanized repertoire back into provincial regions, where it invigorated the existing musical culture. In addition to his activities as a solo singer, the professional *payador* appeared in popular entertainments such as the circus and theater.

The Circus

The *circo criollo*,[3] or native circus, emerged as another central context that contributed to the popularization of rural forms. It drew extensively upon Argentine characteristics and placed special emphasis on the gaucho. Fostered by an emergent spirit of Romanticism and its emphasis on popular values, the *circo criollo* retained close ties to the masses. While other musical settings (such as the urban salon) appealed exclusively to the elite, the circus was for everyone. It maintained a strong core of popular support, and, unlike the theater, which was concentrated in the cities, circulated widely throughout the interior of the nation. Because of its broad range of appeal, the *circo criollo* proved invaluable in transmitting new forms of music throughout Argentina.

The earliest national circuses, which began in the late eighteenth century, differed little from their foreign counterparts. They were simple and modest affairs that entertained the public with jugglers, acrobats, dancers, and mimes. Yet by the 1880s, Argentines had endowed circus performances with a distinctive national flavor. José Podestá (1858–1937), the leader of a prominent circus family, instituted many changes. He created the unforgettable character of Pepino 88, a *criollo* clown, who delighted audiences with his picaresque sense of humor. Later, he exploited the a priori triumph of *gauchesca* literature by dramatizing works that glorified the Argentine horseman and by incorporating them into his productions. He transformed the entire structure of the circus by restricting its traditional entertainments to the first half of the show, where they were performed in the circus ring. He then reserved the second half of the performance for the more substantial *criollo* drama, which was produced on stage. Podestá's *circo criollo* also incorporated the professional *payador*, whom the public viewed as the apotheosis of the gaucho. Almost immediately, audiences required the *payador*'s presence in the circus, refusing to accept a production of a *gauchesca* drama without his participation in the event.

Within the *circo criollo*, the urbanized repertoire of gaucho music emerged as a vital means of celebrating Argentine customs. It provided a strong sense of local color, imbued performances with traditionalism, and satisfied public tastes. Many of the gaucho genres that the circus incorporated (such as the *gato, huella, pericón, cielito,* and *media caña*) had previously reached the point of near extinction in rural regions, and it was only through their revival in the circus that they have survived to this day (Vega 1981, 49–51). Clearly, these song and dance types differed markedly from their folkloric originals in their greater degree of stylization. Nevertheless, these popularized musical genres played a fundamental role in shaping Argentine perceptions of vernacular music by exposing audiences to folkloric customs at the same time that they displaced traditional rural forms with urbanized revisions of the gaucho past.

The Theater

Podestá's incorporation of native *criollo* dramas within the circus ultimately led to the creation of an Argentine national theater. Shortly after the landmark *gauchesca* work *Juan Moreira* triumphed in the circus (1890), it premiered on the stage of the Politeama Theater of Buenos Aires. Other theatrical productions soon followed, with their number and popularity increasing after the turn of the century, when the Podestá circus disbanded and several of its members formed theatrical companies of their own. The most innovative form of national theater that developed during the period was the *sainete nacional*, which depicted local personages, aesthetic forms, and customs. Performed in large cities, this genre revealed marked cosmopolitan influences. While it still referred to old gaucho characters, it focused greater attention on new urban personages such as the *cocoliche* (Neapolitan immigrant who spoke broken Spanish) and the *compadrito* (insolent bully and dancer of the tango). In addition to popularizing rural folk genres, the *sainete nacional* presented modern music of the city, particularly the early tango. By juxtaposing rural and urban stylistic sources, this repertoire attested to the presence of new gaucho and immigrant groups within the city, and effected their integration. The theatrical music of the time thus reflected, inscribed, and articulated prevailing social currents. It formed a critical part of the context through which classical composers filtered their perceptions of Argentine music and thus shaped the transformation of the gaucho repertoire within their works.

The Urban Perspective of Classical Composers

Argentine composers of the period not only witnessed the dissemination of an urbanized gaucho repertoire but adapted it as the basis of their own compositions. It was natural to appropriate these sources, because the majority of composers were *porteños* (residents of Buenos Aires) and cultivated a sophisticated lifestyle, remote from rural experience. Classical musicians of the period had little opportunity to acquaint themselves with rural folk music firsthand. Alberto Williams (1862–1952), a paradigmatic elite composer of the day, exemplified these tendencies. Williams was known for his luxurious lifestyle, and it was said he lived in a "crystal paradise" (Williams and Cimaglia Espinosa 1990).[4] Yet, despite his lack of actual folk-music exposure, he acquired a working knowledge of Argentine musical idioms within his *porteño* milieu. As the distinguished musicologist Carlos Suffern (1990) explained, "Popular music existed everywhere. It was not necessary to go to a determined place in the mountains or *pampas* to have Argentine music. . . . It had already spread in its popular form in Buenos Aires."

Williams and other composers identified gaucho music with the new popularized forms they heard in the city. On purely musicological grounds, this association could be disputed as erroneous, but at the time it was accepted as legitimate. The lack of precise ethnographic information, the urgent need to construct a national style, and the cultural confusion created through the urbanization process itself led composers to overlook mislabelings and contradictions that today would be evident. Even as early as the 1930s, when Carlos Vega pioneered Argentine ethnomusicology, he complained that classical composers mistakenly equated urbanized forms with rural *criollo* music. He observed that:

> The lack of good [folk music] collections did not permit a correct discrimination of styles, and in this way the music of the . . . minuet, *media caña*, and *pericón*, which was of an entirely distinct origin and character from the old *criollo* repertoire, was arranged and "stylized," resulting in total confusion. (Vega 1937, 4)

Vega's assumption that classical composers would automatically consult folk-music collections (rather than observe rural performances firsthand) reveals the extent to which they remained isolated from the very traditions they sought to portray.

The appropriation of transformed *gauchesca* imagery fundamentally shaped the nationalist works of the period. Argentine classical composers drew upon musical references, themes, and genres popularized by the circus and theater. They gave emphatic weight to the musical song and dance type known as the *milonga*, whose rural/urban duality exemplified the syncretism of gaucho and immigrant characteristics. Within the *milonga* context, they emphasized familiar urbanized features that helped bridge the gap between gaucho folk music and cultivated Argentine expression. They also called upon popular musical resources to represent the fate of the "disappearing gaucho" as a discursive nationalist trope.

The Centrality of the Circus and Theater

Alberto Williams creates vivid musical tableaux that portray the circus in works such as his "Tightrope Walker's Milonga" (1916) and "Acrobat on Bottles" (1912).[5] In the first piece, he uses vacillating right-hand chords to evoke the precarious balance of the tightrope walker, whose final somersault he depicts with a concluding glissando gesture. In the second piece, he relies on similar evocative techniques, presented within a simpler musical setting. Williams also composed a suite of piano pieces entitled *Clowns* (1918),[6] in which he paid tribute to the circus and specifically recalled Frank Brown, who was one of the most popular clowns of his day. The seven short pieces of this collection bear the following characteristic titles: 1. "Greeting of the Clowns," 2. "Frank Brown Dancing," 3. "The Clown Is Sad," 4. "Somersaults on the Ground and in the Air," 5. "The *Milonga* of the *Criollo* Clown," 6. "Clowns on Horseback," and 7. "Slaps, Kicks, Blows with a Cane, and a Terrible Fight."[7] These titles indicate the significance that the circus held within the nationalist conception of Williams's day.

The *porteño* theater also influenced Argentine classical composers, who borrowed, assimilated, and adapted the popular works they heard on stage. They stylized and transformed modest song and dance types associated with the *sainete nacional*. Occasionally, they quoted theatrical melodies directly within their works. One composer associated with this practice was Julián Aguirre (1868–1924), an exquisitely talented musician, who was known for his imaginative recreation of *criollo* expressive forms. According to Jorge Novati and Inés Cuello (1980, 16), Aguirre based the third piece of his *Creole Airs* on a theatrical *milonga*, "Dúo de los compadres" ("The Duo of the Compadres"), which Eduardo García Lalanne composed for Eduardo Rico's 1890 play entitled *El estado de un país, o La nueva vía* (*The State of a Country, or The New Way*).[8]

A second example of theatrical borrowing involves a popular *milonga* that appeared within several *sainetes* of the day. According to Novati and Cuello (1980, 17), this charming piece was sung with the following words:

No me tire	Don't throw
con la tapa	the lid
'e la tinaja,	of the jug at me
porque se raja,	because it will crack,
doña Tomasa.	Doña Tomasa.

Later, another textual variant of the piece appeared (Novati and Cuello 1980, 17):

No me tires	Don't throw
con la tapa	the lid
de la olla,	of the pot at me
porque se abolla,	because it will get dented,
porque se abolla.	because it will get dented.

The Argentine classical pianist and composer Ernesto Drangosch (1882–1925) incorporated this theme into his *Criolla Overture* (1920). Later, Alberto Williams, who had previously taught Drangosch piano, made his own arrangement of the piece, which he entitled "Popular Milonga" (1941).[9] Although the documentary evidence that supports this direct borrowing of theatrical themes is currently confined to a small number of isolated cases such as these, additional research on this little-studied practice may yield further results.

Genre was a vital means through which classical composers drew upon the popular resources of the circus and theater. To understand this connection, it is essential to realize that nationalist composers constructed a distinctive form of Argentine musical identity by communicating through symbolic codes of discourse. The most vital aspect of this codified system was the recreation of folkloric genres, which both contained and *in themselves* constituted codes through which Argentine musical identity was articulated and expressed.[10] The performance of popular music played a vital role in this process because it was precisely the revitalized gaucho genres that classical composers imaginatively recreated in their works. For example, the *huella*, *vidalita*, and *milonga*—all of which were popularized by the circus—emerged as three fundamental genres of the period. According to Carlos Suffern, Williams produced masterful stylizations of these song and dance types (1977, 2); Emma Garmendia Paesky found them so significant that she focused her entire doctoral research (1982) on their incorporation within Williams's work.

In the music of Julián Aguirre, popularized Argentine genres also played a central role. Undoubtedly the work that earned Aguirre the greatest recognition was his *Huella* for piano (1917), which was frequently performed in its orchestral version, arranged by Ernest Ansermet. Outside of the *huella*, Aguirre was also known for his eloquent version of the *vidalita* for voice and piano. Although he failed to label any of his pieces a *milonga*, works such as his *Criollo Airs* and *Popular Argentine Airs* (1897)[11] bear the unmistakable imprint of the genre. Indeed, the impact of the *milonga* on Argentine musical creation was so significant that it needs to be be examined separately here.

Expressive Weight of the *Milonga*

Classical musicians accorded the *milonga* a dominant role in their compositions because the genre encoded the nation's sociodemographic transformation within a potent expressive form. As the Argentine musical type that best exemplified the dominant rural/urban duality, the *milonga* stood at the crossroads of gaucho and immigrant cultures. It developed during the late nineteenth century as a response to the confrontation between Buenos Aires and outlying rural regions. In 1883, Ventura Lynch, the first serious observer to study gaucho music, documented the presence of the Argentine *milonga*. In his historical treatment of the Unitarian and Federalist gaucho (1829–50), Lynch failed to mention the genre, but instead classified it as "contemporary." He described the typical performer of the *milonga*, not as the Argentine horseman, but rather as the *compadre* who navigated the boundaries between the provinces and the city and whose assimilated characteristics displaced the rural folk culture of the gaucho (Lynch [1883] 1953, 49–53).

Lynch included musical transcriptions in his study to enhance his description of gaucho culture. Even though he was an amateur musician and his notations contained frequent errors, they nevertheless established the Argentine genres and practices that were in place during his day. One of his transcriptions (see ex. 1.1, page 15) illustrates the combination of rural and urban features that conjoined within the *milonga* ([1883] 1953, 50). The rhythmic relationship of the two guitar parts can best be described as disjunctive. The first guitar plays in a *punteo* ("plucked") style; it is based on patterns of six eighth notes per measure (arranged in two groups of three). Its rhythmic organization characterizes many *criollo* folk genres such as the *gato*, *malambo*, and *huella* that were traditionally performed by the rural gaucho. In contrast, the second guitar part introduces *rasgueo* ("strummed") patterns derived from the *habanera*, which was a dance form promoted in South American cities and whose features were also associated with the urban *milonga* and early tango. In Lynch's transcription, the *criollo* and *habanera* rhythms appear in vertical juxtaposition, thus forming an iconic image of the colliding urban and rural cultures that coalesced in the formulation of the genre.

Other features of the *milonga* embody rural/urban distinctions. Sung versions of the genre frequently employ lyrics that express the pervasive duality between the country and the city. Some *milongas* glorify extinguished gaucho heroes or lament a lost sense of tradition. Others use textual themes that portray the stunned reaction of rural *criollos* when confronted with modern technological developments such as trains, automobiles, and movie houses. This style of *milonga* found its way into a relatively recent collection of folk music from La Pampa, compiled by Ercilia Moreno Chá (1975). Her recording of "The Light" humorously recounts the story of a rural *criollo*'s first encounter with electricity. In the following translation of the opening three stanzas, one observes an ironic mixture of emotions, ranging from perplexity and bemusement to frustration with the inevitability of change and its encroachment on a traditional way of life:

La pucha con los inventos	To hell with inventions—
el criollo más preparado	the most prepared *criollo*
debe quedar azonzado	must be dumbfounded
al ver cosas que al momento	when he sees things that
parece que fueran cuento,	seem as if they were make believe.
pero bien lo he comprobado	I have proven it well;
jamás me hube imaginado	never would I have imagined
que al dar vuelta un botoncito	that on turning a little button,
diera luz un vidriecito	a little piece of glass hanging
que había en el techo colgado.	from the ceiling would give out light.
En un viaje realizado	On a trip I took
que en cuyo hotel yo paré.	I stayed in a hotel.
casi una caja gasté	I wasted almost a box
de fósforos pa'encender	of matches to light
un vidrio que al parecer	a lamp that to all appearances had
forma de bolsa tenía	the shape of a purse;
y yo realmente creía	and I really believed
que era fácil de prender.	that it was easy to light.
Sobre una silla parado	Standing on a chair
para alcanzar donde estaba	to reach where it was,
los fósforos arrimaba	I held the matches next to it
pero sin ni un resultado	but got not a single result,
hasta que por fin cansado	until finally I got tired
fui a llamar al hotelero	and called the hotel manager,
que se me vino ligero	who quickly came to me
y al oído me gritó—	and shouted in my ear:
Este botón túerzalo	"See this button, turn it,
y tendrá luz, caballero.	and you'll have light, *caballero*."

The *milonga* not only integrated common characteristics of urban and rural regions, but it articulated their differences. As evidence of this distinction, the genre is divided into several subcategories that are determined by geographical setting, performance context, social function, and musical differentiae. In a recent publication, Moreno Chá categorized the *milonga* into four basic types: 1. instrumental pieces performed on guitar; 2. vocal music with composed poetry; 3. vocal music with improvised poetry; and 4. dances for embracing couples.[12] While the first three categories were associated with rural repertoires and guitar performance, the fourth was affiliated with Buenos Aires and Montevideo as well as with the instruments and repertoire of the early tango (Moreno Chá 1999, 265–66). The *milonga* thus connoted both rural and urban performance contexts, and *porteño* composers strategically invoked its dual identity to navigate the two worlds.

Argentine musical discourse has frequently referred to the rural/urban dichotomy inherent in the *milonga* when describing the nationalist content of classical works. Carlos Suffern has provided a penetrating analysis of this phenomenon in the compositions of Alberto Williams by observing that:

> With the *milonga*, Williams not only typified a sense of the countryside and the suburbs that border upon it, but he also established the psychological duality of this typology: that of the gaucho and of the *compadre*. He wrote a great number of *milongas* for piano, voice, and orchestra, establishing a vast gallery of types that go from the modest ranch to the nomadic circus and that constitute the richest in their category that we have. (1977, 2)

Similarly, composer Alicia Terzian communicated that:

> In the music of Julián Aguirre . . . the two expressive modes of Argentine feeling—the folkloric and the *porteño*—unite as a corollary of the sensibility of their age. (1963, 19)

I believe that the inherent dualism of the *milonga* perfectly suited the contradictory nationalist position of Argentine classical composers. Williams and Aguirre faced a unique aesthetic dilemma: they aimed to create a distinctive style of Argentine music based on the overarching *gauchesca* tradition, but they lacked the requisite knowledge of rural idioms upon which this style would presumably be based. For these composers, the *milonga* presented an ideal solution. Because certain forms of the genre developed in provincial regions among the Argentine horseman's descendents, the word *milonga* itself evoked potent *gauchesca* imagery. Yet, while acknowledging the rural significance of the *milonga* by name, composers still felt free to draw upon the more familiar popularized strands of the genre with which they were conversant. Reference to the *milonga* thus allowed them to affiliate with the *gauchesca* tradition and still utilize the urban musical resources that they knew. Moreover, because the urban *milonga* was sufficiently compatible with the polished style of music they aimed to create, their cultivation of the genre perfectly suited their goal of writing sophisticated classical music for elite *porteño* consumption. The *milonga* therefore emerged as a primary inflected genre within their works because it posed an effective resolution to the rural/urban polarity that they, as musical architects within the culture, faced.

The *milongas* of Alberto Williams reveal the composer's remarkable ability to blend rural and urban characteristics within his works. His twelve-part piano series, *Airs of the Pampa* (1893–1919),[13] contains many exceptional stylizations of the genre. The general title of this collection evokes an unmistakable *gauchesca* ambience, with its reference to the *criollo* horseman's

Ex. 1.1. Rural and urban features in the traditional *milonga*.

location on the Argentine *pampas,* or plains. Each individual piece also bears a separate title, and many designations allude to the classical imagery associated with the *gauchesca* tradition. Williams represents the equestrian pleasures of gaucho life with titles such as "My Horse's Prancing" (1913), "Galloping on the Pampa" (1916), and "The Joy of Horseback Riding" (1916).[14] Other evocative designations refer to gauchos immortalized in Argentine literature, such as: "Martín Fierro in the *Pulpería"* (1912) and "Santos Vega under a Weeping Willow Tree" (1913).[15] At times Williams supports the *gauchesca* implications of his titles by basing his music on rural folk sources, particularly the instrumental version of the *milonga* performed by the guitar (Moreno Chá's category 1). Yet just as frequently, he draws upon musical resources of the urban popular dance form (Moreno Chá's category 4). His pieces in the latter category display a remarkable admixture of Argentine imagery that projects rural images of the gaucho through a predominately urban musical means.

Williams's piano piece "Together around the Fireside" (1913)[16] demonstrates the latter approach to *milonga* composition. The title of the work refers to a typical scene from Argentine rural life, in which gauchos cook their meals, play their guitars, and recount daily events from their lives on the plains. "Together around the Fireside" contains musical features that support such a rural performance tradition (see ex. 1.2, page 16). The piece begins with a left-hand pattern that imitates a style of *punteo* guitar accompaniment found in typical rural settings of the genre. Its rhythms resemble the *habanera,* an urban popular dance whose characteristics also permeated the countryside—as evidenced by Lynch's inclusion of such patterns within his *milonga* transcription of the "contemporary" gaucho (ex. 1.1). Williams's piece follows simple patterned harmonies that adhere to a familiar folk progression: I-V⁷-V⁷-I. Such features reinforce the rural connotations of the composer's *gauchesca* title.

15

Ex. 1.2. Alberto Williams, "Together around the Fireside."

Beyond these characteristics, however, the remaining musical features reveal a thoroughly urban orientation. The style and contour of the melody (which appears in the upper voice of the right-hand piano part) calls to mind the urban instrumental dance form (Moreno Chá's category 4). Williams's use of three simultaneous parts as the musical norm for the piece suggests the typical trio ensemble consisting of violin, harp, and guitar (or flute) that frequently performed *milongas* in their popular settings (Novati and Cuello 1980, 17). While Argentine folk renditions of the genre generally remain within the main scale of the piece, Williams's work adds melodic alterations (indicated by sharps and flats) that derive from urban sources. The incorporation of these characteristics allows the composer to close the gap between Argentine folk forms and foreign classical influences. They provide him with an ideal meeting ground that allows him to mix Argentine "nativism" and European "sophistication." By creating classical music based on urban popular forms, Williams appropriates the gaucho legacy and transforms the Argentine rural heritage into something he legitimately claims as his own.

"The Disappearing Gaucho"

Williams's *Airs of the Pampa* contains pieces that nostalgically evoke images of the forsaken gaucho who tragically "disappeared" from the Argentine plains.

Works such as "Nostalgia for the Pampa" (1912), "Good-bye to the Deserted Village" (1913), and "Far from the Ranch" (1916)[17] all suggest these sentiments. These pieces resonate with a dominant trope of nationalist discourse that mourns the fate of an oppressed gaucho victim, whom progress eliminated from the plains. Numerous Argentine literary works embellish this central *gauchesca* theme. José Hernández's masterful two-part poem *Martín Fierro* (1872, 1879) delivers a searing social indictment against the dislocation, dispossession, and persecution of the Argentine gaucho. Hernández's epochal work inspired subsequent literary classics, such as Rafael Obligado's *Santos Vega* (1887), which tolled the death knell for a gaucho allegorically defeated by progress in a *payada* or song contest. Yet, even though such authors extolled idealized images of the gaucho on the plains, the outcome of their narratives seldom changed; it was writers such as Obligado, after all, who destroyed their own rural protagonists. Musical works that identified with this nationalist trope likewise exemplified the elite's paradoxical value system. While upholding romanticized images of the past, composers' works contributed to the gaucho's veritable demise by supplanting his expressive culture with urbanized musical resources and by imparting a discursive narrative that promoted the "progressive" agenda of the elite.

From an early point in his musical career, Williams's works reveal a close identification with the "disappearing gaucho" trope. The title of his first nationalist composition, "The Abandoned Ranch" (1890),[18] typifies this association. According to popular belief, Williams composed "The Abandoned Ranch" after a trip he took to the Argentine *pampas*, where he received his musical inspiration from a deserted shack that once belonged to Santos Vega (Suffern 1990). The composer also claimed that he visited a man well acquainted with the popular Juan Moreira (Williams [ca. 1890] 1951, 16–19),[19] whose life was portrayed in the acclaimed *gauchesca* drama performed by the circus and theater.

While listening to "The Abandoned Ranch," Williams's audience readily made these referential connections. A lecturer who described the work prior to its public performance mentioned Santos Vega by name, stating, "There, refreshed by the breezes of the *pampa*, in this ambience of sentimental traditions, the *maestro* [Williams] set out to evoke the *criollo* drama par excellence: the evolution of progress displacing the age-old ranch of Santos Vega" (Medina 1945, 35).

Similar referential statements lead us to conclude that listening to a performance of "The Abandoned Ranch" immersed Williams's listeners in *gauchesca* imagery that formed an essential part of their imaginative experience.[20] It is safe to assume that Williams's *porteño* listeners had a unique way of experiencing the work based on their enculturation within the composer's nationalist setting. One could further suppose that Williams communicated his sonic representation of Argentina through encoded forms of discourse that were shared by "insiders" within his musical milieu. Because these representations cannot necessarily be understood by those incognizant of the sociocultural matrix through which these meanings were conferred, I will offer an interpretation of the work, based on my own understanding of Argentine cultural aesthetics.

"The Abandoned Ranch" communicates essential elements of the "disappearing gaucho" trope through a discursive narrative that navigates between the Argentine present and the past. Williams develops this narrative within successive large sections of an ABA form that is readily discernible to his listeners. One might surmise that the opening A section portrays the musical "present." In this section of the work, Williams relies on specific devices that distance his audience from the abandoned gaucho ranch of the past. He achieves this effect by calling upon musical materials that retain a wholly European character and that are remote from native folkloric experience. He also portrays the desertion of the ranch and the desolation it engenders by drawing upon musical resources connoting "sadness" within the European classical tradition. Temporal stasis, the use of a minor key, the prevalence of descending melodies, and the reduction of sonic volume all enhance his musical representation.

In the B section of "The Abandoned Ranch," the composer calls to mind the prosperous life that once reigned in the now deserted village. He signals a musical flashback to the past by increasing the speed and by shifting his harmonies into the major key. In this section, Williams evokes imagery associated with the gaucho past by using a typical Argentine rhythm that he identifies with the *huella* (Williams 1913, 355). This term refers to a rural folk genre that was closely associated with the Argentine *pampas* and its gaucho inhabitants. As Williams builds his *huella* to a climax, he evokes the resurrected image of the gaucho at the height of his existence on the plains. He later returns to the A section and reestablishes the Argentine present by recalling the original music associated with the deserted ranch. During the last six bars of his piece, he diminishes the volume until the sound is barely audible. His final chord fades into silence as the lingering image of the ranch disappears.

Williams concludes "The Abandoned Ranch" in a major key. His transformation of the music from the minor to the major mode resolves the aesthetic tensions of the work and advances its narrative program. To understand the referential significance of his final harmonic gesture, one must realize that during Williams's lifetime, the *porteño* elite viewed the gaucho with ambivalence. While literary works such as *Martín Fierro* and *Santos Vega* awakened sympathy for the Argentine horseman's plight on the plains, the elite still favored policies such as immigration and the construction of railroads that automatically led to the gaucho's decline. Thus, at the same time that upper-class *porteños* nostalgically lamented the loss of traditional rural culture, they knew that change was inevitable and promoted new forms of progress.

By resolving the musical tensions of "The Abandoned Ranch" in a major key, Williams symbolically reconciles his listeners to the gaucho's tragic fate. Through ending his piece with a soothing harmonic gesture, he offers a mitigating sense of closure to any feelings of sorrow, guilt, or discomfort they might have experienced while listening to his work. By representing the gaucho's tragedy within a carefully controlled musical setting, Williams shelters his listeners from the harsh reality of the Argentine horseman's demise, and he absolves them of any guilt for complicity in the process. His piece thus inscribes the nation's changing social circumstances and favors the elite performer and consumer for whom his music was intended and conceived.

Further corroboration of the idea that Williams sonically promoted the elite's positivistic agenda is provided by an analysis of his piano composition "Good-bye to the Deserted Village" (1913). As in "The Abandoned Ranch," Williams divides this piece into multiple large-scale sections based on temporal states, whose narrative progression advances his ideological argument. In this case, "Good-bye to the Deserted Village" is based on the binary opposition of two musical sections (AB), which form an antithesis based on the Argentine past and future. In the first section, Williams presents a musical theme in the minor mode, with a static repetitive melody marked *andante mesto* ("slowly mournful"). The sorrowful sentiments associated with these features call to mind the dominant trope of the "disappearing gaucho" and reinforce the work's title that bids farewell to a deserted rural village of the past.

The A section of "Good-bye to the Deserted Village" communicates such sentiments by drawing upon key elements of traditional Argentine music. It is based on the Hispanic performance practice of singing in doubled thirds, and it relies upon the *criollo* scale system that Carlos Vega identified with the provincial Argentine interior (1944, 156–61).[21] Yet Williams casts the first section of his work as a *milonga*, which, as we have seen, embodies the Argentine rural/urban duality and substitutes for the traditional expressive forms of the gaucho. Interestingly enough, he employs a form of rhythmic disjunction between the melody and accompaniment that parallels Lynch's hybridized *milonga* (see ex. 1.1, page 15) and illustrates the composer's approach of representing old images of the gaucho past with popularized musical resources of the present.

At the end of the A section, Williams signals his farewell to the forsaken gaucho village by diminishing the sound, reducing the speed, and marking his music with the indication *perdendosi* ("dying away"). As the narrative perspective shifts into the future, the mood of the B section grows animated and triumphant. Williams increases the speed of the music to *Vivace* ("Lively"), transforms the minor harmonies into the major key, and reconciles the metrical disjunction of the preceding section. His sharply profiled rhythms create the impression of a horseback rider galloping away from the deserted gaucho village of the past. While such equestrian images may sound fanciful, Williams in fact renders them explicit through yet another reference to genre. Although previously the composer had relied upon folk and popular expressive forms to represent Argentine nationality, here he substitutes a European dance to fulfil his aesthetic requirements. Specifically, he bases the B section of "Good-bye to the Deserted Village" on a galop, a popular ballroom dance of European origin. The galop formed the musical basis of such fashionable works as Rossini's Overture to *William Tell*, which achieved widespread popularity within European and South American musical cultures. The choreography of the dance features rapid springing steps that imitate the galloping motions of a horse. Such gestural imagery, as well as the name "galop" itself, reinforces the equestrian implications of Williams's musical text.

The composer's substitution of a European dance form for Argentine rural resources advances his ideological argument that favors European modernity over ostensible native "backwardness." The languid inertia of Williams's A section resolves into the purposeful movement toward progress as the European galop overtakes the native *milonga*. Hopeless melancholy turns to rosy optimism as the composer bids farewell to the empty gaucho past and embraces the future promise of modernity. Viewed from this perspective, "Good-bye to the Deserted Village" encodes *porteño* values and socializes Williams's listeners to the role they must play within modern Argentine society. The composer's representation of the "disappearing gaucho" trope advances the elite's ideological agenda. One of the central ways his work articulates this stance is by promoting Europeanized popular music in lieu of traditional gaucho genres of the past.

The *Gauchesca* Tradition in Perspective

This chapter has illustrated the vital role that urban popular music has played in shaping Argentine classical works of the period. Although it is commonly believed that elite *porteño* composers based their nationalist conceptions on traditional rural genres, more often their representations stemmed from an imaginative recreation of the *gauchesca* tradition, as mediated by the popular culture of the city. Instead of drawing upon inaccessible rural sources, Argentine elite composers identified with familiar urbanized forms that were popularized by the professional *payador*, the circus, and the theater. Their reliance on syncretic resources such as the *milonga* allowed them to compose music that was polished, modern, and sophisticated at the same time that it conveyed a profoundly Argentine essence. Indeed, these composers never abandoned the *gauchesca* tradition, but they strategically selected the symbolic strains of this heritage that resonated within their own urban milieu. In opting for the resources of innovation over tradition, they articulated the values of their own social class and advanced the elite *porteño* agenda for building a modern nation.

Notes

1. For the sake of convenience throughout this essay, the terms "classical," "popular," and (later) "folk" music will be used in accordance with the meaning they have in common parlance.
2. Argentine leaders realized that the nation lacked the requisite infrastructure to provide young composers with professional music training. In 1882, the Provincial Legislature of Buenos Aires initiated the first in a series of government grants designed to nurture native musical talent. That year, Alberto Williams (1862–1952) received the first Argentine stipend to study in Paris; subsequent nationalist composers who benefited from this program included Constantino Gaito (1878–1945) and Felipe Boero (1884–1958) (Risolía 1944, 55–59; García Morillo 1984, 157, 191).
3. The word *criollo* has a unique significance in Argentina. In addition to its traditional meaning, i.e., the offspring of Spaniards born in the New World, it is also used to denote any native settler of the land, whether of pure Spanish extraction or of *mestizo* (mixed Spanish and indigenous) stock. In a broader sense, the term *criollo* thus roughly connotes "native," which is the meaning applied here and elsewhere throughout the chapter.
4. I would like to thank Dr. Janet Spinas for her invaluable assistance with Spanish translations here and elsewhere throughout the chapter.
5. "La milonga del volatinero," op. 72, no. 6, and "Equilibrista sobre botellas," op. 63, no. 2 (Williams n. d., 9–10).
6. *Payasos*, op. 77 (Williams n. d., 10).
7. 1. "Saludo de los payasos," 2. "Frank Brown bailando," 3. "El payaso está triste," 4. "Vueltas de carnero y saltos mortales," 5. "La milonga del payaso criollo," 6. "Los payasos a caballo," and 7. "Cachetadas, puntapiés, bastonazos, y bochinche mayúsculo" (Williams n. d., 10).
8. The Spanish title of Aguirre's collection is *Aires criollos* (García Muñoz 1986, 27). The publication date of its fifth edition is 1897; its composition date is unknown.

9. Drangosch's work, entitled *Obertura criolla*, is discussed by García Morillo (1984, 297–98). Williams's piece, "Milonga popular," op. 113, no. 8, forms a part of his collection *Para la gente menuda* ("For Young People") (Williams n. d., 13; Novati and Cuello 1980, 17).

10. Further discussion of the issue appears in Schwartz-Kates (1997, 328, 462, 638–40, 807–8, 906–7). For a similar application of this concept in which the rural *huella* is interpreted as an Argentine musical *topos,* see Plesch (1994).

11. *Aires criollos* (cited previously) and *Aires populares argentinas.* The publication date of the latter piece is listed in lieu of the date of composition, which is unknown (García Muñoz 1986, 27).

12. Other scholars have proposed alternative classificatory schemes. Lauro Ayestarán refers to three types of *milongas*: 1. an instrumental or vocal work used to accompany a dance; 2. an improvised *payada*; and 3. a sentimental *criollo* song (1967, 66–69). Carlos Vega speaks of: 1. an instrumental guitar form known as the *milonguita*; 2. a song genre performed by either a solo vocalist or two competing *payadores*; and 3. an urban popular dance (1965, 310–11). Aretz proposes two categories: 1. a rural song type of old Spanish derivation; and 2. an urban dance form that emerged around 1880 (1965, 157–59). Of these typologies, Moreno Chá's offers the clearest delineation of the *milonga* and proves the most valuable in establishing which version of the genre classical composers appropriated in their works.

13. *Aires de la pampa.* This collection represents one of the composer's most significant contributions to Argentine musical nationalism. It consists of twelve separate opus numbers, each containing three to ten pieces that stylize Argentine genres, particularly the *huella, vidalita,* and *milonga* (Williams n. d., 7–10).

14. "Escarceos de mi pingo," op. 64, no. 4; "Galopando por la pampa," op. 72, no. 2; and "La alegría de jinetear," op. 72, no. 5 (Williams n. d., 9–10).

15. "Martín Fierro en la pulpería," op. 63, no. 10, and "Santos Vega bajo un sauce llorón," op. 64, no. 7 (Williams n. d., 9).

16. "Junto al Fogón," op. 64, no. 2 (Williams n. d., 9).

17. "Nostalgia de la pampa," op. 63, no. 8; "Adiós a la tapera," op. 64, no. 6; and "Lejos del rancho," op. 72, no. 8 (Williams n. d., 9).

18. "El rancho abandonado," op. 32, no. 4, from the composer's piano suite *En la sierra* (1890) (Williams n. d., 7).

19. This testimony comes from the composer's essay "Origins of Argentine Musical Art" ("Origenes del arte musical argentino") that was first published in *La Quena* 13/64 (1932): 6–7 and was later reprinted in his collected works (1951). It appears that Williams penned this account shortly after he returned from the *pampas* and composed "The Abandoned Ranch" (1890). The exuberant youthful style of the essay, its statement that the composer deals with the genesis of Argentine music for the first time, and its wealth of detailed description suggest that he completed the account shortly following his return from the trip. Yet, neither the family guardians of his estate nor the Instituto Nacional de Musicología (which houses a substantial collection of his works) has thus far been able to locate a manuscript copy of the essay to verify its dating.

20. For example, one of Williams's biographers, Vicente Risolía has commented: "Whoever has read . . . [the composer's narrative of his pampean excursion], with

the picturesque details that are transcribed . . . and later listens to the celebrated composition . . . cannot fail to evoke the effigy of Julián Andrade and the group of *payadores* in front of the run-down shack that overlooks the immensity of the *pampa*" (1944, 148).

21. Carlos Vega's work is flawed by a Darwinist bias that causes him to assemble South American music into historical strata that represent "progressive" layers of musical evolution (arranged in *cancioneros*). Nevertheless, some of the stylistic features he assembles aid in the classification and analysis of Argentine repertoires. The exposition of this classificatory system appears in Vega's 1944 publication, *Panorama de la música popular argentina*.

References

Aguirre, Julián. [1897] 1953. *Aires criollos*. Rev. ed. Buenos Aires: Ricordi Americana.

———. [ca. 1897] 1955. *Aires populares argentinos*. Rev. ed. Buenos Aires: Ricordi Americana.

Aretz, Isabel. 1965. *El folklore musical argentino*. 2d ed. Buenos Aires: Ricordi Americana.

Ayestarán, Lauro. 1967. *El folklore musical uruguayo*. Montevideo: Arca.

García Morillo, Roberto. 1984. *Estudios sobre música argentina*. Buenos Aires: Ediciones Culturales Argentinas.

García Muñoz, Carmen. 1986. "Julián Aguirre (1868–1924)." *Revista del Instituto de Investigación Musicológica Carlos Vega* 7: 19–43.

Garmendia Paesky, Emma. 1982. "The Use of the *milonga*, *vidalita*, and *huella* in the Piano Music of Alberto Williams (1862–1952)." Ph.D. diss., Catholic University.

Kuss, Malena. 1976. "Nativistic Strains in Argentine Operas Premiered at the Teatro Colón (1908–1972)." Ph.D. diss., University of California, Los Angeles.

Lynch, Ventura R. [1883] 1953. *Folklore Bonaerense*. Buenos Aires: Lajouane.

Medina, Francisco. 1945. "Palabras alusivas a Alberto Williams." *Homenajes a Alberto Williams*. Amalia del Real, comp. Buenos Aires: Talleres Gráficos Garrot, 32–37.

Moreno Chá, Ercilia. 1975. *Documental folklórico de la provincia de La Pampa*. Qualiton recording and liner notes QF-3015/16.

———. 1999. "Music in the Southern Cone: Chile, Argentina, and Uruguay." In *Music in Latin American Culture: Regional Traditions*. Edited by John Schechter. New York: Schirmer Books, 236–301.

Novati, Jorge, and Inés Cuello. 1980. "Aspectos histórico-musicales." In *Antología del tango rioplatense*, vol. 1: *Desde sus comienzos hasta 1920*. Edited by Jorge Novati. Buenos Aires: Instituto Nacional de Musicología, 1–45. Liner notes for multi-volume recorded collection.

Plesch, Melanie. 1994. "Folklore para armar: la huella y la construcción de un *topos* musical argentino." Paper read at *Il Congreso Internacional Literatura y Crítica Cultural*, November 14–18, Buenos Aires.

———. 1998. "The Guitar in Nineteenth-Century Buenos Aires: Towards a Cultural History of an Argentine Musical Emblem." Ph.D. diss., University of Melbourne.

Risolía, Vicente Aníbal. 1944. *Alberto Williams*. Buenos Aires: La Quena.

Schwartz-Kates, Deborah. 1997. "The *Gauchesco* Tradition as a Source of National Identity in Argentine Art Music (ca. 1890–1955)." Ph.D. diss., University of Texas, Austin.

_____. 1999. "Argentine Art Music and the Search for National Identity Mediated through a Symbolic Native Heritage: The *tradición gauchesca* and Felipe Boero's *El Matrero* (1929)." *Latin American Music Review* 20/1: 1–29.

Suffern, Carlos. 1977. "Imagen de Alberto Williams." *La Nación* (Buenos Aires) (November 13): 4a/2.

_____. 1990. Interview by the author, August 4, in Buenos Aires.

Terzian de Atchabahian, Alicia. 1963. "Julián Aguirre." *Clave* (Montevideo), no. 51 (May-June): 19–20.

Vega, Carlos. 1937. "La creación en estilo popular." *La Prensa* (Buenos Aires) (July 18): 2/4.

_____. 1944. *Panorama de la música popular argentina con un ensayo sobre la ciencia del folklore*. Buenos Aires: Editorial Losada.

_____. 1965. *Las canciones folklóricas argentinas*. Buenos Aires: Instituto Nacional de Musicología.

_____. 1981. *Apuntes para la historia del movimiento tradicionalista argentino*. Buenos Aires: Instituto Nacional de Musicología.

Veniard, Juan María. 1986. *La música nacional argentina*. Buenos Aires: Instituto Nacional de Musicología.

Williams, Alberto. 1913. "Música argentina." *Atlántida* 12: 353–87.

_____. 1947. *Album de composiciones selectas para piano*. Buenos Aires: La Quena.

_____. 1951. *Aires de la pampa*. Buenos Aires: La Quena.

_____. [ca. 1890] 1951. "Orígenes del arte musical argentino." *Literatura y estética musicales: obras completas*. Vol 4: *Estética, crítica y biografía*. Buenos Aires: La Quena, 15–19.

_____. n. d. *Catálogo de sus obras*. Buenos Aires: La Quena.

Williams, Pablo, and Pablo and Lía Cimaglia Espinosa. 1990. Interview by the author, September 1, in Buenos Aires.

2

The Tango, Peronism, and Astor Piazzolla during the 1940s and '50s

María Susana Azzi

The nexus at which the careers of Juan Perón and Astor Piazzolla intersect is the tango. Indeed, there is an intricate sociohistorical connection between the ascent to power of Perón, the widespread dissemination of the tango, and the appearance of a musician such as Piazzolla. To be sure, there was no cause-and-effect relationship between *Peronismo* and the *piazzollista* phenomenon, but they are interwoven. This chapter will flesh out their relationship on political, cultural, and personal levels, relying in part on previously unpublished material gleaned from many hours of interviews with musicians from that era who were familiar with both figures. These two men continue to cast a long shadow over the political and cultural life of Argentina, and no study of the present situation there can afford to overlook the role they played in shaping it.

The Tango

The tango is a complex popular genre that involves dance, music, poetry, philosophy, narrative, and drama. It also unites African, American, and European cultural and aesthetic elements. This diversity of influences has its roots in Argentine history. Argentina was the second largest recipient of immigration in the Americas between 1821 and 1932, the United States of America being the first and Canada, the third. Immigrants have been assimilated into Argentine society, and the tango itself symbolizes the acceptance of diversity and the inclusion of marginality within the system. The tango is not only an informal institution but also a vehicle for accelerating multi-cultural integration (Azzi 1996).

From its roots in the lower classes of Buenos Aires in the late nineteenth century, the tango has evolved and metamorphosed dramatically through time. Rejected at home, it was adopted by Parisian high society in the 1910s, from whence it traveled to other capital cities in Europe and to New York. *Tangomanía* conquered London, Berlin, and Rome, but it came to a halt in 1914 when World War I broke out. The Hispano-American community left Paris; tango dancers, teachers, and musicians returned to South America. The context of the tango moved from Europe to the Río de la Plata region. Legitimated by European elites, the tango was accepted by the *porteño* (citizens of the port city of Buenos Aires) upper classes. It was only in the 1920s that the middle class took to this "lascivious" dance, now cleaned up by the Italians and the Spaniards: the *tango con cortes* ("with sexy choreography") became the *tango liscio* or *liso* ("plain") and needed "decent" dancing venues. The tango was soon to become the national music of Argentina, a metaphor and a metonymy, a shaper of identities, an umbrella for diverse sonorities and plural vocalities, and the expression of a profoundly emotional repertoire.

Peronism

Indeed, the Buenos Aires of the 1940s and '50s had changed dramatically from the *pequeña aldea* ("little village") it had once been to a modern metropolis fully integrated into the global village. The most momentous political development of the 1940s was the rise of Juan Domingo Perón (president, 1946–55), and this was the capital of which he became the master. As Tulio Halperín Donghi describes it:

> Once in office, Perón used the power of the state to consolidate his political supremacy and meld together an increasingly disciplined following. He nationalized the Central Bank, created a public corporation to oversee Argentina's foreign trade, restaffed the university and the judiciary with loyal personnel, and established nearly exclusive control over the press and the radio. (1993, 263)

World War II affected the Argentine economy and daily life. Oil, chemical, and medical products were scarce. By contrast, Argentine raw materials sold well in Europe, while imports were replaced by Argentine production. There was full employment and salaries were high. Holdings accumulated in the Central Bank, and Perón spent huge sums to buy foreign-owned public services, such as trains, gas, and telephones. Also, by expropriating industries and land from private owners and institutions, Peronists provided a unique opportunity for social and labor gains that gave the regime long-lasting popularity. Flimsy unions now became powerful organizations. But this was accompanied by the decay of infrastructure (railways and roads), which the state neglected. Without any technical improvement in the areas of agriculture and cattle breeding, the condition of the countryside deteriorated, which meant catastrophically lower exports. Consequently, Central Bank reserves that accumulated during the war were soon exhausted.[1]

The economic dislocations and movement of people from the countryside to the city would have far-reaching cultural ramifications as well. In the words of Alain Touraine:

> The main feature of the authoritarian state is that it speaks in the name of the society, a people or social class from which it has taken its voice and language. Totalitarian regimes are not reduced to the image they project, but there is a perfect relationship between the leader, the party and the people. These totalitarian regimes . . . can achieve positive economic and cultural results for a period of time. (1998, 145, 148–49)

Political, cultural, and economic isolation from Europe and the United States during Perón's government may indeed have had its positive effects in the short term, but those effects were devastating in the long term. Peronism was a nationalist and populist movement, and it used the interests of the popular classes. It took its voice from marginal sectors of society, and from migrants of the interior, the so-called *cabecitas negras* ("little blackheads").

Peronism and Culture

Attempts to create an alternative Peronist culture failed due to Perón's own inconsistencies and ideological limitations, plus the faux pas of attempting to attract intellectuals and scholars capable of creating the Peronist message. In fact, the intellectual establishment in general remained staunchly anti-Peronist. Only a few well-known intellectuals and popular artists, such as Enrique Santos Discépolo, Homero Manzi, Cátulo Castillo, "Tita" Merello, Lola Membrives, César Tiempo, and León Benarós, tilted to Peronism.

Perón thought it desirable to create an Undersecretary of Culture, which in fact would function within the Ministry of Education; thus, arts and literature would also "belong" to the state. But the "national revolution" was not restricted to the sphere of "high culture"; existing political myths, symbols, mass rituals, and traditions were reconstructed, and efforts were made to create an "everyday-life Peronist culture." Peronist mythology turned into a symbolic universe. Peronists promulgated the notion that national culture should resist every kind of foreign influence, an attitude that resulted in cultural isolation. In the words of Plotkin:

In early 1948, Oscar Ivanissevich, who would be highly influential in the construction of the political symbolic system, was named Secretary of Education. He converted Peronism into a true political religion; Peronist rituals would rapidly monopolize the public symbolic space. (1994, 126)

Still, "the Peronist state was unable to establish a structured system for the political organization of youth, and neither could it create formal mechanisms for the organization of workers' free time" (Pujol 1999, 179). But Perón did find good uses for the tango.

Peronism and the Tango[2]

Perón's rise to power had a somewhat diffuse impact on the tango story. With a few possible exceptions, there are no "Peronist tangos" as such. A number of tango artists openly supported him, most notably Enrique Santos Discépolo, who gave some memorable radio talks on his behalf. Later on, Discépolo stopped writing tangos, in order to dedicate himself to theater, cinema, and union activities. But political events attracted him to the point that he decided to gather actors into an organization, the purpose of which would be to promote the government's cultural project.

Hugo del Carril, the great popular singer and realist-cinema director, made numerous films and sang the *milongas* "Eva Perón" and "Juan Perón." He also recorded the "Marcha peronista" (with lyrics by the aforementioned Secretary of Education, Oscar Ivanissevich). While Alberto Castillo made the people dance and sing, Nelly Omar sang and praised Peronism. Composer and conductor Francisco Lomuto as well as singers Rosita Quiroga, Héctor Mauré, Carlos Acuña, and "Charlo" (Juan Carlos Pérez de la Riestra) were strong backers of the regime. The lyricist Homero Manzi was expelled from the Radical Party because of his undue enthusiasm for the general: "Homero Manzi, unlike Discépolo, left little written material to explain why he supported Perón, except for the following: 'Perón is the continuance of the work started by Yrigoyen'" (Castro 1991, 235). (Hipólito Yrigoyen was a populist political leader in the early twentieth century.)

By contrast, some artists were victims of political censorship, while others were harassed for more personal reasons. For example, the singer-actress Libertad Lamarque, who had once quarreled famously with Perón's all-powerful wife, Evita, found it advisable to pursue her successful career in Mexico, where she was already famous and where she became a national treasure. Most musicians, in traditional show-business fashion, avoided adopting unduly specific attitudes about the government. Some bandleaders were annoyed by the new rules on hiring and firing imposed by Perón's labor laws. Ángel D'Agostino, Carlos Di Sarli, Horacio Salgán, and Ricardo

Tanturi dissolved their bands. Anti-Peronism caused difficulties for Raúl Kaplún, and his refusal to join the Peronist Party resulted in the exclusion of his tango band from the radio. "If I were to blame someone for the tango's decay, I would blame Juan Domingo Perón," says Nicolás Lefcovich (Azzi 1991, 212–13). However, Víctor Sasson sees it differently:

> Perón favored the tango a lot, and not only because Evita was a friend of most tango-related people. The tango found an excellent platform in Peronism and *used* it [emphasis original]. That's beyond dispute. But I do believe that orchestras went through a crisis, due to copyright issues. Conductors organized small groups, quintets or trios, instead of large bands of ten or twelve people, and as a result, *orquestas típicas* diminished. (1992)

Gabriel "Chula" Clausi came back from Chile in 1954, after a ten-year absence, and confronted a dramatically altered musical landscape. To get a job, he *had* to belong to the Peronist Party. He vividly recalls the time a government officer curtly demanded to know if he was a Peronist:

> I was duly prepared, as my mother had described the political atmosphere to me and had implored me to join the Peronist Party. I followed her advice, and consequently got a job at the Río Hondo casino. I was lucky: my orchestra was a great success. Today, I feel really sad; never before (or later) had any employer ever asked me about my political affiliation. I joined the Peronist Party because my mother had asked me that very specially. I've never been a Peronist, but, unfortunately, to get a job, you had no choice. Aníbal Troilo [bandoneonist, composer, bandleader; see fig. 2.1] was never a Peronist, [but] he agreed to perform at the President's residence at Olivos, and his band was very active in those years. (1997)

The great Osvaldo Pugliese was thrown into prison several times during Perón's first government. He was seen by Peronists as a dangerous River Plate Bolshevik. He had joined the Communist Party in 1936, at the age of thirty-one, and he believed in "a more democratic and just society where work is part of human dignity, and not a punishment." When Pugliese could not play, because he was locked up or banned, his band played on, with a single red carnation laid on the piano to symbolize the presence of the maestro. Pugliese composed 150 themes, ranging from waltzes to *rancheras* and *milongas*, and even one "shimie." But he was best known for his tango compositions. Among the finest and most-played of them were "Negracha," "La Yumba," and "Malandraca" (three titles referring to the roughest segments of society).[3]

Despite these vicissitudes, and regardless of the various points of view, Castro is no doubt correct in asserting that:

Fig. 2.1. Aníbal Troilo, the celebrated bandoneonist, composer, and conductor, was never a Peronist, despite the pictures of Juan and Evita Perón in front of which he proudly stands.

the most transcendental factor in support of the tango as a generic part of *porteño* (and by extension Argentine) culture was the Peronist leaders themselves, Juan and Evita Perón. They were the tango. The theme of their government and political mission was the tango. Perón's image as the comrade of workers, coatless among the multitude, while at the same time champion of the industrialist, dressed in a smoking jacket, conjures up the image of Carlos Gardel. The rags-to-riches story of Perón's success, from a poor boy in the provinces to President of Argentina, is Gardelian in its scope. (1991, 234)

The economic bonanza induced by the government (and rapidly rising wages) undoubtedly contributed to the brilliant fortunes of the tango during its last classic decade. In effect, migrants from the interior then living in Buenos Aires were a major factor in this economic dynamism: they spent money attending theaters and other entertainment venues. The popular euphoria of the first Perón government showed itself always, not only on Labor Day or October 17 (Peronist Loyalty Day). The government not only broke with traditional labor politics and social practices, but promoted Peronist entertainment and a different nightlife. Juan Carlos Copes, dancer and choreographer, has revealed to this author that:

> In my club [late 1940s and '50s], one side of the dance floor was called "the capital," and the other side was called "the provinces." The girls from the provinces were on one side, the girls from the capital were on the other. We, the *milongueros*, were in the center of the floor. We observed the following ritual: the beginner—myself, for example—had to dance with girl number one, then girl number two, and so on. The girls from the provinces were ranked from one to fifty, and the girls from the capital were ranked from fifty-one to a hundred. The girls from the capital were prettier and were all accompanied by their mothers. The girls from the provinces were by themselves (they were somehow unprotected). But I had to dance with number one first. The *milongueros* watched you and would either approve of you or not. This was an unwritten law. This was the university where I got my Ph.D. as a *milonguero*. (Azzi 1995, 152)

The bandoneonist, arranger, and composer Ismael Spitalnik recalls that "farmers who left the countryside in the forties lacked the idea of class. But they were dazzled by Perón's politics. They jumped from under-consumption to the possibility of having extra money to buy records and record players. This fact supported the national music and entertainment industry" (1992). Moreover, "Workers literally 'took over' the urban public space for the first time ever in the history of the country. Public demonstrations had in many cases a festival-carnival character—people danced and drank in the streets" (Plotkin 1994, 93). Sergio Pujol, in his thorough history of dance, tells us: "Even in 1954, when the years of bonanza had been left behind, waves of people filled up the streets. Economic possibilities allowed that small amount of money for Saturday outings. Cinemas, theaters, *confiterías*, bars, and dancing venues were crowded" (1999, 216–17). Dancing couples shortened their tango steps, in order to share the floor with thousands of other dancers. Perón, indisputably a popular figure himself, was well aware of the tango's popularity, and he was more than happy to be photographed in the company of musicians and to attend the occasional tango festival.

Of course, there was a dark side to all of this. Perón's regime harbored Nazis who arrived in Argentina in the 1940s (mainly through Patagonia). When the war was over, the American government confirmed the sale—on behalf of Perón—of eight thousand blank passports. Hugo Wast (pseudonym of Gustavo Martínez Zuviría, 1883–1962), the greatest literary exponent of anti-Semitism, was also the greatest tango scourge. The fascist military coup of June 4, 1943, imposed censorship. Jews and the tango, joined by terror, shared a common enemy. In public schools, religious teaching was upheld and non-Catholic students were segregated from their schoolmates and made to attend classes on "morality" (Nudler 1998, 21).

Freedom of speech as well as religion came under attack. Lunfardo is a largely Italian-derived popular vocabulary that originated in Buenos Aires in the late nineteenth century and was later assimilated into daily speech and used in tango lyrics. Discépolo was a strong supporter of popular language, and he found that Lunfardo provided incredible phonetics for the tango. But tango language now had to be "national"; it was cleaned up by the authorities, and Lunfardo was suppressed. Lunfardo tango titles and lyrics were changed in ludicrous ways. In March 1949, after receiving a delegation of leading tango figures—Alberto Vacarezza, Manzi, and Discépolo—Perón lifted the absurd censorship of lyrics instituted by the military regime in 1943. In the event, Perón and Discépolo formed a lasting friendship.

Los Muchachos Peronistas

Los muchachos peronistas, a *marcha* that the crowds sang in the streets, became a symbol that anti-Peronists could hardly tolerate. In the catalogs of the Society of Authors and Composers of Music (SADAIC), it is attributed to an "anonymous" author. In fact, according to Hugo Gambini, the music was born in the old Barracas Juniors Club to accompany the performances of a powerful amateur soccer team. Juan Raimundo Streiff, a bandoneonist who lived just in front of the barracks, wrote the music. Old members of the club remember singing this *marcha* in their *barrio* ("neighborhood"). The president of Barracas Juniors, Baltasar Radetic, confirms that a rogue stole the 78 r.p.m. *marcha* recorded by Streiff. Streiff's children recall with nostalgia that "papa composed the *marcha* in the vestibule of our house, with the 'Turk' Mufarri, who was a singer. During carnivals, both went out in the streets, with the *bandoneón*, and two hundred people gathered and all sang the Barracas Juniors *marcha*." Streiff never registered the score of his *marcha* (cited in Gambini 1992). Its plagiarized version has become a powerful Peronist identity symbol.

Peronism and the Media

President Ramírez created the Undersecretary for Information and the Press on October 21, 1943; he could not have imagined that this would become one of the best tools available to Perón for building his political base. Even less could he have supposed that such an organ would become, over time, one of the basic pillars of the Peronist platform, with characteristics similar to those of a Ministry of Propaganda. The information provided to the media was "constructed by the Undersecretary" (Gambini 1999, 408).

National radio networks were Peronized: not only were Perón and Eva constantly on the radio, but union leaders gave frequent speeches. Eva opened a series of popular events at the Colón opera house, which was another symbol of the middle and upper classes now used for the benefit of the party in attracting the lower classes. After one popular demonstration at the Plaza de Mayo, the crowd attended *bailes populares* ("popular dances"), organized in the streets under the auspices of the municipal administration of Buenos Aires: "The image of workers dancing in the streets traditionally monopolized by the upper classes served as a symbolic recreation of the 'take over' of the city and its symbols of power, which the *descamisados* ["shirtless ones"] had carried out some time before" (Plotkin 1994, 109). The underlying political dynamics of these demonstrations were clear to many observers:

> The ideological weakness of Peronism continues and except for Perón's speeches, the national movement seems a blind giant that never strikes at the right place. Peronist publicity becomes more intense, and the bourgeoisie rejects Perón even more. (Galasso 1973, 189)

With the purchase of British railway companies on February 12, 1947, Perón started a series of acquisitions, which included the radio stations. The government bended the radio to its own will, since all broadcasters were part of the national radio network. The series *Pienso y digo lo que pienso* ("I Think, and I Say What I Think") began on the national radio network in October 1951, and it was part of the electoral campaign when Perón ran for a second presidential term (Gambini 1999, 411). Lola Membrives, "Tita" Merello, Pierina Dealessi, Juan José Míguez, and Enrique Santos Discépolo all participated. Another program organized by the undersecretary was a musical show that began airing in 1950 on radio El Mundo, every Sunday at 12:30 P.M. The program was called *Estrellas a mediodía* ("Stars at Noon"). Four *orquestas típicas* and eight jazz bands performed (Gambini 1999, 413). Carlos Ulanovsky sheds light on the musical fare:

> As far as the tango is concerned, the offerings were varied: Astor Piazzolla, Juan D'Arienzo, Virginia Luque, Héctor Mauré and Alberto Castillo. Radio programs were real shows where the *orquesta típica* was always present, jazz bands, the soloist in fashion (a bolero or folksong singer), *varieté*, a reciter, and a master of ceremonies. In an interview in 1995, Ben Molar admits that in

those days, the whole year was—or seemed to be—a carnival. "I worked in a music publishing company, and I knew how important it was for an artist to work in *confiterías* or in dancing venues, but I also knew that without the radio it was impossible to make a success. Only those who worked in the radio were hired by the clubs," says Ben. (1995, 169–70)

The radio was indeed an enormously powerful force at the time. Ismael Spitalnik recalls that when he arrived in a small town after a radio performance, "people would look at us as if we were demi-gods." Tango magazines, which included full tango lyrics and articles on the tango, were also popular. The revival of the tango as a dance had an unavoidable impact on the structure of tango ensembles, and consequently on orchestration. The larger the orchestras grew, the more need there was for arrangers. Spitalnik explains the changes that became necessary:

We had to study harmony and counterpoint and apply the new knowledge to enrich the interpretation of the tango . . . The demand for greater responsibility and the discipline imposed by the music stand—the need to be able to read music—raised the average professional capacity of the musicians. It was very different work from thirty years earlier, when there would be a trio or a quartet *a la parrilla* [improvising the arrangement], with only one score on the piano. The arranger and the music stand disciplined the musicians. From a musical point of view, we stood in opposition to the so-called classical musicians who looked down on us and despised us like rats. But later on the violinists who had mastered the tango played in symphony orchestras—the professional quality had improved that much.[4]

It is no coincidence that TV started in Argentina in 1951 on the day of "Peronist loyalty." Perón governed through the radio during the period 1946 to 1951, and with the radio and television between 1951 and 1955.

The economy decayed slowly, but few people worried. There was money, and it was spent joyfully. But the party would not last long. Perón was ousted from power in September 1955, and efforts were made to "deperonize" Argentina. The departure of Perón had an immediate impact on Peronist musicians. As Daniel Castro has observed:

While both Manzi and Discépolo were active Peronists, their deaths protected them from the retribution of the triumphant anti-Peronists in 1955. Discépolo was symbolically punished with the redesignation of the theater originally named after him. Cátulo Castillo, however, lived beyond the fall of Perón in 1955, and he suffered for his loyalty to Perón. As head of the National Commission on Culture, the Municipal Conservatory of Music, and the Society of Authors and Composers of Music [SADAIC], he was vulnerable to attack. He was fired from the Conservatory, fired as head of the Commission, and the SADAIC not only expelled him but kept him from collecting money owed him as part of his author's rights. Cátulo was able to salvage a large portrait of Perón from the SADAIC but was not able to save the bronze bust of Eva Perón, which was destroyed. (1991, 245)

Astor Piazzolla during the Peronist Epoch

Astor Piazzolla (1921–1992), the revolutionary tango master, was a prolific composer who wrote more than 3,000 works, an arranger, a unique bandleader, and a virtuoso instrumentalist. He played the *bandoneón*, a squeezebox of German origin, which has become the quintessence of the tango sound. Piazzolla used to say that he had had three teachers: Alberto Ginastera, Nadia Boulanger, and the city of Buenos Aires. His music reflected and spoke to one's deepest feelings. Although he kept the tango's essential spirit, he played tangos for listening and not for dancing. He did not follow the tango tradition, and for that he was rejected by conservative *tangueros*. Piazzolla was controversial and his audience was heterogeneous: jazz fans, classical-music lovers, rock musicians, university students, youth. He fought not only against the establishment by creating the "new tango," but he came to represent a new Argentina with new sounds, needs, and resources.

However, by mid-1949, Astor Piazzolla was ready to call it quits. Running a tango orchestra at the time was not without its headaches. Argentina was living through the euphoria of Juan Perón's first presidency, which, among other things, encouraged the spectacular growth of trade unionism (under Perón's own control). The atmosphere had its impact on musicians. Piazzolla ran his band on principles he always maintained: equal rewards for all members, with a double share for himself as bandleader and arranger. He certainly made enough to live on from his work with the band. Though there were evidently a few union-style demands from the musicians, much more serious was the pressure exerted on Piazzolla to perform and record suitably patriotic material and to play free for government-sponsored functions. In November 1948 he did record a couple of numbers, one of which was the rather harmless patriotic waltz *República Argentina*. But he never played it again. In a moment of weakness and at the behest of a poet with Peronist connections, he composed a *Hymn to Perón* that he promptly destroyed. Piazzolla and his wife, Dedé Wolff, were strongly anti-Peronist. His parents Vicente and Asunta Piazzolla, by contrast, favored the Perón government. After July 1952, like many loyal *peronistas*, they kept one of their clocks permanently set at 8:25 P.M., the official time of Evita Perón's death.

Although the band was still performing at a variety of venues in the city and suburbs, Peronist pressure was almost certainly the main reason why

Fig. 2.2. Astor Piazzolla playing the bandoneón in the early 1960s.

Piazzolla dissolved his band in mid-1949. Dedé remembers a phone call from the actress Fanny Novarro, one of the numerous lady-friends of Juan Duarte, brother of the formidable Evita and President Perón's private secretary. She relayed what amounted to an order for Piazzolla to play at a lavish benefit for Evita's powerful Social Aid Foundation. The show was to be held at Luna Park, Buenos Aires's main indoor sports stadium, on Thursday,

September 22, 1949, with several leading *orquestas típicas* on hand. "If there isn't a band, it can't perform," he told Dedé. Over the phone, Piazzolla informed Novarro that he could not attend: he had just dissolved his band!

Piazzolla held a farewell dinner for the musicians, and his first band simply melted away—not with a bang but a whimper. A few months later he managed to reassemble some of its members to record four tangos with a string orchestra for the TK label. But that was the end, and the 1946 band passed into history.[5]

The Relationship between Peronism and Piazzolla's *Nuevo Tango*

Astor Piazzolla is tango *contreculture*. Certain times allow *contreculturel* phenomenona, while others do not. In the Peronist age, however, traditions were defied constantly. Argentina was closed to the world, but opened up inside its borders, particularly in the case of popular culture. Piazzolla was able to take advantage of this because he had no frontiers: he felt as comfortable living in Mar del Plata as in Buenos Aires, Rome, Paris, Milan, New York, or Punta del Este. He was cosmopolitan. Traditional tango emanated from the *barrio*, but Buenos Aires's identity had changed, and Piazzolla was the expression of a new metropolis.

While Astor Piazzolla represented a paradigmatic change in the tango, Juan Domingo Perón posed a paradigmatic change in the politics of Argentina. Both changes, in the tango and in Argentine political history, were simultaneous. Perón broke with traditions of every kind, started a new historical epoch, and was the driving force behind a new period in music. Like most populists, Perón was an authoritarian and cheating transgressor. In a sense, he had an opportunity to reshuffle the political deck of cards. Perón was part of a political renovation, and his demagoguery made possible the inclusion of marginalized people within the political sphere. He definitely included more Argentines in politics, and more citizens were entitled to political rights, including women (on September 7, 1947, the law of *voto femenino* was passed). In short, Perón was an authoritarian social integrator.

For better or worse, Perón also promoted the industrialization of the country. Under Perón, the traditional Argentine economic model of an agricultural-exporter country was abandoned. To make possible the incorporation of the working class and internal migrants into the political system, industrialization was necessary. It was a historic modernization in economic, political, and social terms, and Perón established a new paradigm. On the other hand, the Peronist totalitarian regime had the enormous advantage of the *compre nacional* (a politics that favored the manufacture of Argentine products, with a subsequent ban on imports). In August 1953, *números vivos* ("live performances") were mandated in every cinema. The performance of foreign musicians was severely limited. Seventy-five percent of the members of any group of more than three had to be Argentine, and an equal percentage of the artists on each radio station had to be Argentine. As far as records were concerned, an old regulation was enforced, which restricted to 30 percent the amount of recorded music that could be broadcast. Thus, jobs were created for musicians and singers, and the business of recording companies was limited.

In this atmosphere of innovation, not only was the traditional tango reinforced, but a new tango found its place: Astor Piazzolla's *nuevo tango*. Despite the fact that Piazzolla was a confessed anti-Peronist, we can hardly imagine that Piazzolla's music could have existed in a non-populist context. Piazzolla's art was not a purely individual creation, but the product of collective social events and of collective work. The 1940s were the tango's golden decade, and Piazzolla was largely the product of that decade. Besides, Piazzolla wrote his music for a different audience. He never changed his essence for money. He wrote and played *his* music; he never sold himself. The original tango emerged from the lower classes, and the upper bourgeoisie embraced it; later on, the middle classes adopted it as their own. Such is the social itinerary of the tango and its cultural traffic: social-class barriers disappeared on dance floors and stages. Piazzolla's music, however, is different. It is a fusion of jazz and classical music with sounds and musical practices that come from traditional tango and the lower classes. As Pablo Ziegler explains:

> Tango is the music that represents us, and it is also humor, play, dance, roguishness. It is our *canyengue* ["street language"], equivalent to swing plus slang. Defiant and exhibitionist, the authentic tango expresses *mugre* ["filth"] and *roña* ["fight"]. It is provocation, sensuality, ease, and a quarrelsome temper. The dialect of a *porteño* is boastful and humorous. A *compadrito* [young hoodlum of the slums] is a daring man. Coming from the marginal origins of tango dancing, the *mugre* and the *canyengue* turned into music. They became a note, an inflexion, a challenge, and a provocation. No matter the context, tango must express *camorra* ["provocation"], which is how its roots are preserved.
>
> Piazzolla wrote very sophisticated compositions, and at the same time, they are *mugrosas*. Such *mugre* can be felt in spite of the intricacy with which those tangos were written or whether the language was contemporary, impressionist, or expressionist. Tango has always been related with fighting, with *roña*, with guys breaking the law. One plays this music on the borderline between tango and chamber music. This is perceived through the accents and the manner in which it is played. Piazzolla's music was taken toward more refined levels, keeping a hard-hitting, provoking edge; whether it is transformed strictly into chamber music or a reminiscence, you can hear something more solemn and distant. (1998)

Violin effects, percussion, and improvisation come from the lower classes, but the music writing is bourgeois. There is a synthesis of classes. Piazzolla is the product of a tradition and the rupture of that tradition.

To summarize, Piazzolla's tango came out of the *porteño* scene that was dependent upon Peronist support and patronage. But it engaged an internationalist musical culture (jazz, classical, etc.) that was anathema to Perón and his xenophobic following. Thus, it was created by the Peronist aesthetic but transcended it at the same time. To be sure, Astor Piazzolla never saw himself as a political animal, and he never was in any traditional sense. But he did speak to new audiences in a new language. He was a breaker of paradigms. In the event, Evita was also a natural breaker of paradigms, while Perón was deceitful in his conflation of the nation and the state. One may question his kind of modernization, but it became a driving force that changed the nation forever.

In Argentina, political revolutions have been varied and frequent. Perón's was very particular: "My policies," he declared, "were always directed at wages and living conditions rather than toward moral values" (Rock 1993, 155). But all dictators make political use of popular art, and Perón was no exception. Piazzolla's concern was either "Do you like my music?" or "Don't you like my music?" If he aspired to conquer in the manner of a Perón, it was only within the context of his art: "My dream is to impose my music, my country's music, all over the world."[6]

Notes

1. See Félix Luna, "Con sello *peronista,*" *La Nación* (Buenos Aires), December 31, 1999.
2. See María Susana Azzi, 1995, 114–60 (for a brief description of the Peronist phenomenon, see 155–57).
3. See Andrew Graham-Yooll, "Osvaldo Pugliese" (obituary), *Independent* (London), July 31, 1995.
4. This quote and the material in the preceding paragraph come from Azzi (1995, 150).
5. For an in-depth treatment of the life and career of Piazzolla, see Azzi and Collier (2000).
6. Astor Piazzolla quoted in *Clarín,* December 1, 1974.

References

Azzi, María Susana. 1991. *Antropología del Tango. Los Protagonistas.* Buenos Aires: Ediciones Olavarría.

———. 1995. "The Golden Age and After." *Tango.* London and New York: Thames and Hudson.

———. 1996. "Multicultural Tango: The Impact and the Contribution of the Italian

Immigration to the Tango in Argentina." *International Journal of Musicology* 5: 437–56.

Azzi, María Susana, and Simon Collier. 2000. *Le Grand Tango: The Life and Music of Astor Piazzolla*. New York: Oxford University Press.

Castro, Donald S. 1991. *The Argentine Tango as Social History 1880–1955*. San Francisco: Mellen Research University Press.

Clausi, Gabriel "Chula." 1997. Interview by the author, October 1, in Buenos Aires.

Gambini, Hugo. 1992. "La verdadera historia de la *Marcha peronista.*" *La Nación*. Buenos Aires (October 17).

———. 1999. *Historia del Peronismo*. Buenos Aires: Planeta.

Galasso, Norberto. 1973. *Discépolo y su época*. Buenos Aires: Ediciones Ayacucho.

Halperín Donghi, Tulio. 1993. *The Contemporary History of Latin America*. Durham, N.C., and London: Duke University Press.

Nudler, Julio. 1998. *Tango Judío. Del ghetto a la milonga*. Buenos Aires: Editorial Sudamericana.

Plotkin, Mariano. 1994. *Mañana es San Perón*. Buenos Aires: Ariel.

Pujol, Sergio. 1999. *Historia del baile*. Buenos Aires: Emecé.

Rock, David. 1993. *Nationalist Argentina*. Berkeley and London: University of California Press.

Sasson, Víctor. 1992. Interview by the author, September 7, in Buenos Aires.

Spitalnik, Ismael. 1992. Interview by the author, June 12, in Buenos Aires.

Touraine, Alain. 1998. *¿Qué es la Democracia?* Buenos Aires: Fondo de Cultura Económica.

Ulanovsky, Carlos. 1995. *Días de radio*. Buenos Aires: Espasa Calpe.

Ziegler, Pablo. 1998. Interview by the author, October 2, in Buenos Aires.

3

Socially Conscious Music
Forming the Social Conscience
Nicaraguan Música Testimonial *and* the Creation of a Revolutionary Moment

T. M. SCRUGGS

Songs with decidedly social commentary are commonly recognized to possess a transformative power in society. However, too often this power is ascribed solely to the lyrics of these songs. In fact, song's power lies in *both* the verbal and musical levels of communication, and a crucial aspect of its effectiveness comes from the combination of the two. Song can resonate with peoples' worldview and sense of identity and place as well as offer a view of a different, more favorable world. In this way, music can create a new place, if only sensed and imagined, to identify with. The dramatic events in most of Central America in the 1970s and '80s demonstrate the potent force that music can be. Song—both lyrics and musical material—played a powerful role in the social upheavals in Central America during this time, so much so, in fact, that its importance has inevitably been woven into histories and analyses of these events. Almost every account of this era, across the political spectrum, includes at least a token nod to the use of music to transmit political and social messages and to aid in the process of ideological mobilization of the population.

Considering the salient role that music (and expressive culture generally) has played in the social struggles that engulfed the region, it is somewhat surprising how much has remained undocumented, existing primarily in oral memory. Although the events in Central America spurred an outpouring of publications for roughly a decade and a half, the bulk of scholarship on music has appeared only in short newspaper articles, interviews in newsletters from non-Central American solidarity committees, and other brief writings, which are by nature superficial and in most cases long unavailable. The immense quantity of socioeconomic and political studies about the isthmus, or even the level of careful and sustained attention given to literature and poetry (the latter already established as a preeminent form of expression in Nicaragua), contrasts with the dearth of writings about music. Perhaps a certain passage of time was needed before reflection on and an appreciation for the place of music, as well as other forms of expressive culture, could be given to the violent struggles that took place during these crucial decades. For example, recently, several publications have discussed Salvadoran music of social commitment. There has also been an ambitious reissuing of out-of-print Nicaraguan recordings that include a substantial amount of politically important music from the 1970s and '80s.[1]

This chapter examines popular music in western Nicaragua from the 1960s through the mid-1970s and its contribution toward dramatic social change.[2] The 1960s introduced to Nicaragua new musical directions, which culminated in an extension of a broad-based movement during the last years of the 1970s. With this movement came a mass insurrection that overthrew the existing power structure. Working with such a limited time-frame, and in such a short space, one cannot hope to discuss comprehensively the efflorescence of Nicaraguan music of this period. Thus, I focus instead on three crucial elements involved in the development of the New Song movement in Nicaragua: 1. the successful elaboration of the linguistic and musical vernacular of the popular classes; 2. the use of satire, already laden in vernacular style, to maneuver within certain spaces in the social and political climate; and, more briefly, 3. the music's contribution toward broadening the appeal of radical political ideology through a connection with popular religiosity and a linking of spiritual values to active social responsibility. I concentrate on the key figure of singer-songwriter Carlos Mejía Godoy, who was the principal architect of the new musical movement, and inspired a generation of youth to use music as their means of engaging with the unfolding social struggles of this era.

While studies claim to discuss the social commitment of *music*, a marked tendency has been to examine only the semantic content of the *lyrics*.[3] For example, commentary on musical material—rhythm, tonality, timbre, melodic contour, form, instrumentation, and so forth—in all the articles on Central American political music listed in the bibliography below totals less than a page. This overemphasis on lyrics is understandable, given the training and background of the authors, as well as the fact that defining this category of music commonly revolves around the message contained in the words. The lack of attention to music is not limited to non-Nicaraguan scholars. In Pring-Mill's exemplary analysis of the letter by the Frente Sandinista de Liberación Nacional (FSLN) commandante Núñez Téllez to the Nicaraguan New Song group Pancasán (reproduced on their album, 1980), he notes the leader's "total silence regarding the music" (1987, 186). However, in many instances it is impossible to explain the power of song without considering the synergy of semantic content and the meaning generated from musical content. While propositional meaning, found at the level of language, is distinct from the level at which music transmits meaning, an examination of both types of communicative vehicles is indispensable for the fullest comprehension of their communicative power. To that end, this chapter attempts to integrate an analysis of lyric content with one of musical material to situate the music's social meaning and impact.

Some Preliminary Considerations

Two preliminary points help to provide context for the understanding of Nicaraguan music during this period. First, no one single nomenclature exists for "socially committed music," and the labels that have been employed are revealing for the presupposed meaning behind them. In English-speaking North America the most common term by far has been "protest music," or "protest song." The term *música de protesta* has gained currency in Latin America as well, but many commentators have pointed out the restrictive nature of the word "protest," which describes the music only in terms of denunciation and the limited negativity of opposition, when in fact the music's message proposes equally the positive stance of a world that could and should be brought into being. *Nueva canción*, or New Song, has been a descriptor of the Chilean musical movement since the late 1960s, but it has, in addition, been used in a general sense to label socially committed music throughout Latin America. Another name often found in Hispano-America, *música testimonial*, has also been used in Nicaragua. Adapted from "testimonial literature," the term can specifically imply giving witness to unjust social conditions, much like a limited meaning of *música de protesta*, but it is more often used in the broader sense, that is, to provide a testimony of the world as it is and to describe what is necessary to transform it into a better one.[4] I use these terms interchangeably, along with phrases such as "socially committed" and "political music." After the *triunfo* ("triumph") of the Sandinista Popular Revolution in 1979, an innovative term to describe Central American political music was coined from conflating *volcán* ("volcano") and *canto* ("song") to form *volcanto*. Inspired by the line of impressive volcanoes that distinguishes the topography of western Central America, *volcanto* was offered as a new label to encompass all Central American socially committed music, but in actual practice the term remained essentially limited to Nicaraguan music. As *volcanto* did not come into use until the 1980s, here I refrain from using it to refer to earlier music.

Second, just as El Salvador and Nicaragua received most of the world's attention when Central America became a source for daily news in the late 1970s and '80s, so the political music in those two nations tends to be the reference for New Song on the isthmus. These were not the only countries where New Song emerged; during this same time musicians and groups in Guatemala, Belize, Honduras, Costa Rica, and Panama also strived to find solutions to the region's purportedly intractable social ills. Many were not able to record and the music of others circulated primarily through informal cassette distribution. It was an unfortunate reality that communication between the seven Central American nations was often difficult and that artists frequently remained unaware of socially committed song in neighboring countries. It is fair to say that most Central American musicians had as much, or even more, access to *música testimonial* from outside the region than from their colleagues within the region. This fact makes it difficult to speak effectively of a pan-Central American New Song, but it does not detract from the significance of the music movements within each of the nation-states.

In the Vernacular

Despite the general paucity of historical sources since Nicaragua became an independent nation-state in the 1820s, there is some documentation of topical songs on national politics. An early and relevant, if not prophetic, example is the still-famous "La mama Ramona," sung in the 1850s in the city of Granada during its defense against the North American filibusterer (mercenary) William Walker (for lyrics see Mejía Sánchez 1976, 116–17). The musical precursor to the flurry of activity of the 1970s is the musical proselytization of Augusto César Sandino's movement in the early 1930s. Sandino drew inspiration from the Mexican Revolution in developing a mass movement for reform and defense of national sovereignty. In similar fashion several followers of Sandino turned to the *corrido*, the "musical newspaper" of the Mexican Revolution, to help spread the message of Sandino's fledgling cause. The *corrido* is a strophic song form based on four-line *coplas* ("verses") with simple melody lines and somewhat rudimentary guitar accompaniment. The sometimes expansive sets of *coplas* recount the exploits of leaders and other important figures—in this case overwhelmingly centered on Sandino himself as real-life social actor and emblem of his ideology. Typically the actions in a *corrido* conclude with a moral message—in this instance, championing resistance to foreign control exemplified by the invasion of U.S. Marine Corps troops in 1928.[5]

Aided by the strength of Mexican musical influence in the northern regions where his guerrilla Army in Defense of National Sovereignty (Ejército en Defensa de la Soberanía Nacional) was based, *corrido* broadsheets and oral transmission offered an excellent conduit for Sandino to reach his hoped-for, mostly non-literate audience when the electronic mass mediation of popular music in the country was still in its infancy. These *corridos* were driven underground with the 1934 murder of Sandino and the crushing of his movement by the first member of the Somoza family dynasty and his National Guard (trained by the U.S. Marines). However, just as the post-1960 anti-Somoza movement took on the mantle of Sandino in nomenclature and other regards, so protest music after the 1950s increasingly referenced the man and the myth of Sandino as a touchstone of patriotism and provided a connection with the popular classes from which Sandino came.

While Mexican-style *corridos* were able to encode nationalist messages in the northern rural areas in the 1920s and '30s, the next surge of oppositional activity in Nicaragua involved the southern urban areas and found its musical expression in a popular music that was uniquely Nicaraguan. In the decades following the dispersal and repression of Sandino's movement, the Mexican musical presence, promoted by both recordings and film, remained strong in cities as well as rural areas. For example, the output of Tino López Guerra, the most prominent composer of this era, features several well-known *corridos*. These were non-political *corridos* written in praise of various cities of the country ("Granada de Nicaragua," "Corrido Chinandega," etc.), which were performed by Nicaraguan mariachis in a manner indistinguishable from their northern-Mexican counterparts. Such wholesale borrowings inspired sectors of the middle class to investigate local and traditional expressive culture, in a search for Nicaraguan musical forms that could compete with the continued "sub-imperialism" of Mexican music.

Son Nica

The musical format that became the identifiably national vehicle for the next surge of oppositional music was introduced in the 1940s and became known as the *son nica*. As the title *son* implies, this is a general musical style representative of a region, in this case southern Nicaragua. Unlike other Latin American *sones*, its origin is attributed to one musician, Camilo Zapata. Zapata is acknowledged as the "father of the *son nica*" by the first group of singer-songwriters of socially conscious music who view themselves as following in his stylistic footsteps.[6] Reacting against the dominance of northern-Mexican music in the 1930s, Zapata turned to the *marimba de arco* ("marimba with an arc") trios centered in the Masaya region near Managua. The music of the *marimba de arco*, and the dance it accompanies, is the most widespread musical folk tradition in the southern part of the nation, where the majority population and politico-economic power lie.

The *son nica* contains selected stylistic features from the repertoire of a *marimba de arco* trio, which consists of a marimba with guitar and smaller four-stringed *guitarilla*. The rhythm, a dampened downbeat followed by two fully strummed (and therefore accented beats) is taken from the strumming pattern of the trio's guitar. The tonality of the *son nica* follows that of the main repertoire of the marimba which, due to the diatonic nature of the instrument, is almost entirely in major keys with very little use of minor chords. Such a preponderance of major tonality is unusual in other Latin American music and marks the distinctiveness of the Nicaraguan *son nica*. The melodic contour of *marimba de arco* pieces also corresponds with the melodic shape of many *son nica* compositions, especially those of Camilo Zapata. Combined with lyrics that used some vernacular Nicaraguan Spanish and that referred to distinctively Nicaraguan characters and situations, Zapata's *son nica* was embraced across class lines as a "traditional" style and became cemented as a fundamental marker of popular identity. As recently after its introduction as the mid-1980s, only a few close followers of national music were aware that the *son nica* was not a long-established song form and, in fact, could be traced to the efforts of a still-living individual, a consummate example of the fixing of an "invented tradition" (Hobsbawm and Ranger 1983).

First Steps of Protest

Jorge Isaac Carvallo (sometimes misspelled Carballo) was among the first musicians after the Sandino era to popularize nationally songs openly confrontational to the established order. Although Carvallo composed in various styles early in his career, he became convinced that the *son nica* was the form most appropriate for authentic Nicaraguan expression. This position later led him to criticize the direction of other musicians (see below). His particular musical nationalist stance paralleled his development of a critical social outlook. In 1960, Carvallo returned from studies in Guatemala to see his country with new eyes, viewing it "in a state of tremendous feudalism" (1987). In reaction to his new awareness, he wrote several *son nica* songs with critical social content that became well known on the Pacific Coast, including: "La Juliana," "Pobres los celadores" ("Pity the Security Guards"), and "Campesino" ("Peasant/small farmer"). "La Juliana" narrates the anxiety of a poor *campesino* who fears the *patrón* (a large landowner) will take advantage of Juliana, the object of his love. The lyrics of "Pobres los celadores" and "Campesino" are strikingly direct in their denunciation of injustice and call for rectification of the situation. A security guard is one of the lowest-paying yet most dangerous occupations, and the song calls for appropriate compensation and dignity for these workers.

Even more threatening to the status quo were the verses of Carvallo's "Campesino," which was addressed to the largest part of the labor force. The two-part chorus contains the lines:

Campesino levanta tu frente	Peasant, lift up your head,
también eres gente	you too are somebody,
no te humilles más	don't feel humiliated anymore,
con tus manos izquierda y derecha	with your left and right hands,
hacé[s] la cosecha para los demás.	bring in the harvest for all the rest.
Campesino aprende a leer	Peasant learn to read,
campesino aprende estudiar	peasant learn to study,
campesino si lees y estudias	peasant if you read and study,
será tuyo el suelo donde has de sembrar.	the land you till will be your own.[7]

The lyrics centered on a call for basic literacy, a radical proposition given the abject failure of the national system to provide even minimal education to a great part of the rural working population. One verse denounces the fact that the rural worker toils but "they don't give you even a bit of it [land]," an open appeal for land reform to redress the tremendous imbalance in ownership of productive land. Such pointedly political lyrics were unheard of in the 1960s, and the Somoza government intended them to remain unheard.

The history of this song's eventual diffusion illustrates the contradictory and often chaotic approach of the Somoza apparatus toward music with social content at this time. Carvallo, who had teamed up with another young singer-songwriter, Otto de la Rocha, performed "Campesino" in various public concerts in the late 1960s. By 1970 they were able to release the song on a seven-inch 45 record (see fig. 3.1), and later on an LP (Carballo and de la Rocha ca. 1971), which allowed it a certain level of circulation. The Somoza-controlled media prohibited the song, and independent radio stations understood that they could not dare to broadcast it. Just over a year after the record's release, the director of the main government station, the Radio Difusora Nacional (National Radio), heard the semi-banned song when passing by a union hall (which, at another level of contradiction, was controlled by Somoza). Happening to arrive that day at the studios in an inebriated state, the director announced how catchy and pretty the tune was

Fig. 3.1. Original 45-rpm release of "Campesino."

and promptly instructed the astonished staff to put the record in rotation. Upon hearing one of Somoza's own radio outlets featuring the song, other stations began to air it as well, and "Campesino" achieved a notable level of popularity.

The confusion that could allow a song with such critical content to gain significant air time was a space within which popular song could potentially be used to communicate a social message. This maneuvering room was used to great effect by Carlos Mejía Godoy, the principal composer and performer of music with social content in Nicaragua of his generation. He is commonly referred to as Carlos Mejía in Nicaragua to distinguish him from his younger brother Luis Enrique, a talented musician who also became an important figure in the country's New Song movement. Both are from a musical family from the northern town of Somoto. Carlos Mejía's early career reveals some of the key elements of his artistic formation that later allowed him to play a pivotal role in the nation's music. In 1963, at age twenty, he left the mountainous northern region and began working in radio dramas on various stations in the second largest city, León, and later Managua. As with Carvallo, studying out of the country (in West Germany in 1965) brought about a new appreciation of his homeland. He developed his abilities in verbal art that drew from the country's picaresque storytelling tradition and localized expressions and folk sayings, emphasizing the non-standard parts of Nicaragua's unique vernacular Spanish. He began to compose songs, and one of his earliest efforts (from 1963), "Alforja Campesina" ("Campesino Saddlebag"), achieved national success when it was recorded several years later by the trio Los Madrigales.

In 1967, for a new daily radio show, Carlos Mejía drew from the popular imagination to invent a singular personality, "Corporito," a jesting and ironic elder personality wise in folk wisdom and full of parables expressed in rural-based *campesino* speech (see fig. 3.2). Every day this crusty figure sang a new song or a reworked older tune with some kind of commentary on contemporary events in the lyrics. The popularity of this show featuring Corporito helped advance the fortunes of Radio Corporación, the privately owned radio station that hosted the program. This success in turn allowed Radio Corporación's owners to extend the station's broadcast range to reach nearly all of the nation's Spanish-speaking inhabitants. Eventually the singing figure of Corporito took on a more decidedly political stance, filling a void of sociopolitical criticism otherwise prohibited in the media and public discourse: "Corporito is like the entry room for Nica[raguan] testimonial song" (C Mejía Godoy 1990). This phase of Corporito's career came to an end in 1970 when family members of poor *campesinos* who had been murdered by the National Guard traveled to the capital to ask the now nationally famous radio personality to help them. After Corporito denounced the crimes in one of his songs, the Somoza regime promptly fined Mejía and temporarily shut down the station. Carlos left radio and dedicated himself to public performances and his first major recordings. Through its own actions, the dictatorship unknowingly pushed one of its best-known critics into what would become his most effective role.

It would be difficult to exaggerate the key place of this prodigious creative artist and committed activist in the events that unfolded in Nicaragua in the tumultuous 1970s. In the latter 1980s and '90s I was surprised to hear several Nicaraguans from both sides of the political spectrum evaluate the impact of Carlos Mejía's music as being on par with all other organizing efforts in generating the success of the anti-Somoza struggle. Carlos Mejía Godoy has been a prolific composer and performer, and has amassed an

Fig. 3.2. "Corporito," the alter ego of Carlos Mejía Godoy in the early 1970s.

impressive catalog in an ongoing, active career. Below I analyze selected examples that inspired other musicians involved with the movement for social change that grew exponentially in the 1970s.

Bringing the *Popular* into New Contexts

Carlos Mejía's deepening understanding of and continued research into the vernacular expression of the popular classes are the hallmarks of his songs, as well as a principal reason why a widening circle of the population throughout the 1970s embraced them. As the poet Julio Valle Castillo stated, "Carlos Mejía doesn't sing to the people. The people sing in him and through him and with him" (1980).[8]

In a moment of reflection, Carlos Mejía expressed his unique position: "I feel [pause] legitimized by the people to be their spokesperson" (1990). Many of his lyrics can be read as short poems; together with the writings of Father Ernesto Cardenal, they are generally considered to be the best examples of poetry produced in this decade.[9]

Cardenal's approach of "exteriorism," drawing upon one's own immediate world to create a type of narrative poetry, encouraged Carlos Mejía's development of a vocabulary drawn from popular forms of expression. Many of Mejía's verses are so saturated with localized Nicaraguan phrases and references that I have often found myself struggling to explain and "translate" his songs into standard Spanish for friends from other Spanish-speaking nations, even those from other Central American countries. "Escaliche," Nicaragua's popular street-speech style, combines with a liberal scattering of vocabulary from pre-European indigenous languages (primarily Náhuatl and Chorotega-Mangue) as well as several borrowings from English to produce what Nicaraguans often proudly assert is the most non-standard national Spanish spoken on the continent. As he became more and more popular in Nicaragua, and as events in Nicaragua began to attract the attention of the rest of the world, Mejía's music became increasingly known throughout the Americas. The same factor of strongly localized communication that was a strength within the Spanish-speaking Nicaraguan population then manifested itself as a barrier for perplexed listeners in Spanish-speaking America and Spain, who grappled not only with references to places, flora, and fauna unique to Nicaragua, but also with an entire vocabulary and speech style for which standard Spanish dictionaries offered little aid.

In the early 1970s, Carlos Mejía's Corporito performed together with "Gurmersindo," a character invented and portrayed by Otto de la Rocha (who had earlier sung "Campesino" with Jorge Isaac Carvallo), himself by this time a singer-songwriter of national renown. Though the diffusion of Mejía's music was now limited to the audiences that attended the duo's public performances throughout western Nicaragua, these live appearances led to the gradual exposure of his growing song repertoire. The instrumental accompaniment came from de la Rocha on guitar and Mejía on a large four-octave piano-keyboard accordion. No doubt aided by its strong presence in Mexican *música norteña*, the accordion has had a notable presence in Nicaragua's northern area (Mejía's native region), yet it was rarely used in the populous southern zone. In live performances Mejía began to combine this visual marker of his origin from *las regiones* ("the regions") with the aural marker of northern musical forms, a move that helped to broaden the public's awareness of what constituted the Nicaraguan nation.[10]

Opposition to Somoza, though still limited and sporadic, began to grow steadily. In 1960, a small but prescient group of León university students that rejected subservience to North American cultural models formed the Frente Ventana ("Window Front"). This pioneering group laid the groundwork for a new wave of urban-based, culturally oriented oppositional politics. During demonstrations in Managua, students revived some songs from the Sandino era. In street marches participants emphasized the lyrics and demoted the importance of the melodies, which were not always carried very accurately (Avendaño, Cuadra, and Cedeño 1989, 6). The rural-based, but mainly urban-led, guerrilla-armed opposition took the name Frente Sandinista de Liberación Nacional (Sandinist Front for National Liberation—FSLN), a deliberate move to evoke Sandino's legacy in their creation of an indigenous, leftist movement congruent with national realities.[11] In 1967 Somoza triumphed (again) in fraudulent elections. Carvallo wrote the campaign song for Agüero, the populist candidate from the frustrated business class. As demonstrations erupted in the cities against the dictator's rubber-stamping of another term for himself, the FSLN launched a military attack near the small town of Pancasán. A stinging defeat, it led the still embryonic movement to readjust its strategy and to pursue broader, non-military organizing. This change in orientation included a newfound emphasis on cultural work, which, once the New Song movement began to reveal the mobilizing power of music, would lead Front cadres to contact Carlos Mejía and other musicians.

The Popularization of the Radicalized *Popular*

The tremendous earthquake of December 1972 literally altered the landscape of Managua; it also altered the nation's social and political landscape. The tremors killed thousands and destroyed a major portion of the capital city's, and therefore the nation's, infrastructure. Somoza approached the disaster as an opportunity to extend his monopolistic economic control and diverted much of the international aid into his own pocket as it arrived. The Somoza inner circle's blatant disregard for human suffering and pursuit of personal ambition above national development pushed many more people, including a good portion of the otherwise complacent middle class, into outright opposition. The ineffectiveness of the business sector in confronting the regime's praetorian guards strengthened the still small, but continually growing, FSLN's position as the only serious alternative to the continuance of the Somoza dynasty.

Carlos Mejía captured the feelings of Managuans and other Nicaraguans with a song set in the ruins of the capital, described as "earthquaked Managua." The main character explains that he has received a nickname since the earthquake, one associated with his new employment on a government crew hired to clear the wreckage. Receiving some kind of descriptive name as a child or in adult life is exceptionally common in Nicaragua, and these names are used to such an extent that they often function more as proper names than as occasional nicknames in the English sense of the word. The music is an archetypal *son nica*. Mejía sings the verses solo, and compresses the words together in a syllabic melodic line. This is a common feature of the songs of Camilo Zapata and other *son nica* composers originally inspired by the phraseology of the *marimba de arco* repertoire. Such a rapid delivery of words in this and other songs added to the difficulty of non-Nicaraguans to grasp the meaning of lyrics already permeated with references and vocabulary only intelligible to locals.

"Panchito Escombros"	"Frankie of the Ruins"
Verso 3	Verse 3
En el alboroto de este terremoto	In the tumult of this earthquake,
todo lo perdí	I lost everything,
perdí mi casita que era tan bonita	I lost my house that was so nice,
de La Tenderí.	in the Tenderí neighborhood.
Me puse contento cuando supe el cuento	I was glad when I heard the story
que iban a venir	that many tons of canned meat
muchas toneladas de carne enlatada	were coming
para mi país,	to my country,
pero siempre a la sardina	but the sardine always
se la come el tiburón	gets eaten by the shark,
y el que tiene más galillo	and whoever has the largest throat
siempre traga más pinol.	swallows the most pinol.

(Mejía Godoy 1996 [1973])

The last eight lines of the third (last) verse are a good example of how Carlos Mejía circumvented the reigning restrictive political environment to make a strong social statement. "Canned meat" refers to donations that arrived for earthquake victims, a symbol of the aid that was scandalously syphoned off by Somoza's inner circle and even openly sold to the victims. The last four lines comment on this, but they are actually two common colloquial expressions about the injustice of dominant power relations. "Galillo," literally the uvula, is translated here as "the largest throat" that takes the most "pinol," the toasted corn drink that is especially identified with Nicaraguan *campesinos* (Nicaraguans are nicknamed "pinoleros"). Mejía's denunciation of the corruption of the ruling structure becomes an indirect challenge to those responsible because he quotes popular sayings, deflecting his own authorship. As the FSLN guerrillas used camouflage, so the singer has camouflaged his own attack. At the same time, the use of such colloquial language, so typical of Carlos Mejía's compositions, moves the song (and therefore the message) closer to the popular classes. The locally rooted musical style and the verbal form of expression allow those who recognize these modes as their own to accept more easily such statements as coming from one of their own, even to imagine making the statements themselves.

Contrasting this song with "Juan Terremoto" ("Earthquaked John"), a similar one composed by Carlos's younger brother Luis Enrique, offers insights into the strengths of "Panchito Escombros" that caused it to be embraced by the suffering Managua populace. Both songs treat the devastating consequences of the earthquake and clearly identify with the same humanitarian impulses. The titles of the songs are even designed in similar fashion, around the song's protagonist and his new nickname. Luis Enrique Mejía Godoy dedicated himself exclusively to music, unlike Carlos's apprenticeship in radio dramas, and he has always experimented with a wide variety of musical styles. He moved to Costa Rica in 1967 at age twenty-two, worked in a music company, and played in various commercial popular music groups. The common phenomenon of appreciating one's own homeland when away from it combined with a newfound attitude toward music after he heard New Song used in demonstrations in Costa Rica. He stated, "I realized that song could really be worth something" (1990). From this point on, his creative output addressed Nicaraguan realities from a distinctly political point of view.

"Juan Terremoto" is not a *son nica*, but alternates between a slow 4/4 ballad-like meter with plucked arpeggiated guitar for the verses, and a moderate tempo rhythm imitative of a Chilean *cueca* for the chorus. The lyrics of the chorus are:

Me pusieron Juan Terremoto	They named me Earthquake John,
por el día en que nací,	for the day I was born,
y aunque tanto que se lloraron	and despite all that they cried,
aunque tanto que se pidieron	all their entreaties,

y tanto que se rezaron	and all that they prayed,
la casona para el grande,	the big house is for the rich,
el tuburio para mi.	the hovel for me.

(Luis Enrique Mejía Godoy 1973)

The choice of a *cueca* rhythm reflects the strong influence of Chilean *nueva canción* on Luis Enrique at this early stage in his New Song career. The somber feel of the song is effective in portraying a feeling of loss and isolation, just as the words imply the government and ruling class's abandonment of the victims. Its plaintive description fits what one might conceptualize from a literal meaning of the term *canto testimonial*: song that gives testimony of a situation that cries out for remediation. This approach (along with the *cueca* rhythm), inspired by similar songs by Chilean groups and common to other fledgling protest singers at this time, was appropriate, for example, for the Costa Rican university movement in San José that served as a major outlet for Luis Enrique at the time. He would go on to successfully adapt his musical style to incorporate and synthesize various influences in new and different contexts. But at this juncture, the lively *son nica* "Panchito Escombros" better captured the vitality of Nicaragua's popular classes, who had been traumatized by a cataclysmic event but remained resilient and resourceful. Luis Enrique's song (from his second album, . . . *este es mi pueblo*, 1973) suffered from poor distribution in Nicaragua after its original release in Costa Rica. Nevertheless, one would be hard pressed to find anyone in recent times who can remember "Juan Terremoto," while "Panchito Escombros" lives on in popular memory.

The Politics of Satire

Carlos Mejía's use of vernacular expression naturally led him to include a large amount of satire. Used as a deliberate approach, playful irony and humorous mockery publicly expressed social commentary that other, more direct forms could only communicate out of earshot of the state. Carlos Mejía tapped into "the deep grain of humor that runs through popular culture in Latin America" (Beezley and Curcio-Nagy 2000, xiii), one that includes expressions of sarcastic disdain in the popular classes' critique of dominant power. For example, in Nicaragua's famous colonial play *El Güegüense* (Brinton 1969 [1883]), the complex double entendres that the poor, indigenous main character employs against Spanish authority resonate with contemporary caricaturizations and mockery of symbols and personages of the existing power structure, a verbal discourse exemplary of what Scott has termed "everyday forms of resistance by subaltern groups" (1985).

When embedded in song, a message can enter a realm of public discourse where it is not taken as seriously. However, the message may actually be understood as well as any direct political statement that *would* be repressed. When, in addition, the message is expressed in satirically humorous form, superficially it appears to trivialize the subject. Such comedy forces a figure in authority to risk giving credence to the implied critique by taking it seriously enough to ban the song or punish the artist(s). Someone secure in his position is generally expected to be able to accept a certain amount of "ribbing" or teasing. This trait is especially pronounced in Nicaragua, where friends easily engage in exchanging verbal slights that are not taken at all seriously. In Nicaragua in the early 1970s, one expected this type of "thick social skin" from the Somozas, themselves a seemingly immutable part of the national landscape for almost four decades. Thus, it would have been considered "unmanly" of Somoza to stoop to punishing Carlos Mejía, despite the sharpness of his critical barbs. This social dynamic explains how a radio station was allowed to repeatedly play "Panchito Escombros," while an editorial on the same station that decried the "swallowing of pinol" in less metaphorical terms suffered a swift governmental reprisal.

The presence of satire suffuses Carlos Mejía's song lyrics, but it is also present in other realms: his musical style; the addition of sound effects into live performances and studio recordings; visual aspects of his character Corporito; and the lively antics of his own persona in public performances. For example, Corporito dressed with a worn suit coat and mismatched striped pants. He portrayed a buffoon figure that drew from the immense popularity of circus clowning in a country not yet totally enraptured by television (see fig. 3.2). With this visual "armor," Carlos Mejía was able to make pointed statements in public as part of a comical presentation with nonetheless serious content. As he moved away from using this character, his music became the outlet for his creative sense of irony and play.

The best example of such ironical playfulness from this period is a song that became nationally popular, "Maria de los Guardias" ("Maria of the [National] Guardsmen"). The lyrics follow:

"María de los Guardias"	"Maria of the Guardsmen"
Verso 3	Verse 3
Ajustaba los quince años	I'd just turned fifteen
cuando me mataron al primer marido;	when they killed my first husband;
fue durante un tiroteo	it was during a shoot-out
contra un hombre arrecho llamado Sandino.	with a fierce man named Sandino.
A mi varón lo encontraron	They found my man
de viaje tilinte por El Rapador;	very stiff [from rigor mortis] at El Rapador;[12]

yo lo vide al pobrecito	I saw the poor guy
todo pasconeado como un colador.	full of holes as a colander.

<u>Estribillo</u>	<u>Chorus</u>
Yo soy la María, María es mi gracia	I am Maria, Maria is my name,
pero a mí me dicen María	but they call me Maria of the
de los Guardias.	Guardsmen.
Yo soy la María, María,	I am Maria, Maria,
no ando con razones, razones	I offer neither reasons nor apologies,
ya llevo en mi cuenta, por cuentas	but they say I have five battalions
cinco batallones.	under my belt.

(Mejía Godoy 1997 [1973])

As in "Panchito Escombros," the main character offers her given name and then her common nickname. The lyrics center on a humorous portrayal of the multiple lovers and superficial personal relations inherent in a sex worker's profession. Her main occupation is summed up in the line in the chorus, "They say I have five battalions 'under my belt,'" a phrase whose double-meaning is operative in both Spanish and English (note that she is not even sure how many herself). However, there are other hints of the non-humorous poverty of her position outside of her work. The listener can take for granted the absence of a social life for Maria outside of military circles due to the outcast position of prostitutes and the isolation of the Guard from society in general. At the same time, the lyrics achieve two goals.

First, they puncture the aura of invincibility of the National Guard, and subject to ridicule the soldiers' image as vaunted guardians of the state. The omnipotence of the Guard is challenged in verse three, where the actual name "Sandino" is pronounced out loud, breaking a taboo in public discourse. It is Sandino, meaning one of his troops, who kills her first husband. Sandino is described by the indeterminate adjective "arrecho," which, depending on the context and intent of the speaker, can have a wide set of meanings, from courageous and fearless to just someone who is mad and ready for a fight. The rest of the verse is given over to a detailed description of the dead Guardsman after being killed by a member of Sandino's army. However humorous, the fact remains that the Guardsman lost and died in this instance; the point is made that the Guard can lose and suffer destruction. The listener supposes this transpired in the early 1930s due to the reference to Sandino. However, it obviously had very contemporary ramifications, for at the time of the song the National Guard was engaged in military combat with a new generation of Sandinistas.

Second, the song also highlights the alienation of the Guard from the general public. The soldiers apparently have no families, are incapable of

attracting or maintaining loving relationships with women, or perhaps anyone, and are reduced to having prostitutes be their only contacts with the
opposite sex. On one level the song appealed to a certain virile, macho
imagery many Guardsmen wore as a badge of pride. On another it spoke of
the superficial relationship the Guard had with the rest of society and how
impoverished the soldiers' manhood really was. The Guard nutured a culture within its ranks that placed it apart from and above the civilian population. It drew individuals from society who were attracted to the wielding
of unchallengable power, and it was understood that the job included aug-
menting salaries through extortion of the popular classes. "María de los
Guardias" held this position of supposed superiority up to ridicule at the
same time that it appeared to celebrate, tongue in cheek, part of the Guard's
favored image.

Other aspects of the song heightened the playfulness of the lyrics. Carlos
Mejía sang in a high, pinched voice in imitation of a woman, and also pronounced the lyrics in a manner that presented the main character as rather
unintelligent. "María de los Guardias" was a perfect foil for Carlos Mejía's
clowning performance. He used comical facial expressions and broad gesticulations despite the large accordion strapped to his chest. The music is a typical *son nica*, with solo-sung verses alternating with harmonized chorus, but
the musicians enhance the song with a host of atypical special effects. These
extra-musical additions were brought into the studio recordings. Before the
music begins, one hears a bugle call and a group shout of "¡Viva María de
los Guardias!" (an imitation of the Guard's common cry "¡Viva la Guardia
Nacional!"). Drill-sergeant calls and soldiers' command responses are pep-
pered throughout the song between verses and choruses. The sounds of a
baby crying lead into the second verse's account of Maria's birth and early
childhood. This non-musical addition prepares the listener for the extended
gunfire that precedes and is laid over much of verse three, which recounts
Sandino's victory over Maria's husband. In this way Carlos Mejía, who was
moving closer politically to the Sandinista movement, massively publicized
via the media sounds of battle against the National Guard combined with a
story of the death of a National Guardsman at the hands of followers of
Sandino. All these critical elements appeared in a song that was ambiguous
and open enough to interpretation that it was popular among many
Guardsmen themselves.

Carlos Mejía's songs in the years around the 1972 earthquake were the
fruit of his collaboration with prominent national musicians, some of whom
helped him delve deeper into a Nicaraguan musical aesthetic, and some he
brought into a decidely more nationalized style. An example of the former
were Los Bisturices Harmónicos ("The Harmonious Scalpels," a name

Cantos a flor de Pueblo

carlos
mejía
godoy

CRISTO YA NACIO EN PALACAGÜINA
NAVIDAD EN LIBERTAD
PANCHITO ESCOMBROS
ABUELITA
ALFORJA CAMPESINA
QUE VIVA MANAGUA
UN GAJO DE CHILINCOCOS
TERENCIO ACAHUALINCA
PINOCHO PINOCHET
CHINTO JIÑOCUAGO
MARIA DE LOS GUARDIAS

PRODUCTO CENTROAMERICAN
Ensamblado e impreso en
Costa Rica por Sony
Musica Entretenimiento
(Costa Rica) S. A.

acompañan
Otto de la Rocha
los hermanos Duarte
el Grupo Testimonio
los Bisturices armónicos

Todos los derechos reservados de Carlos Mejía Godoy

Fig. 3.3. Back cover of Carlos Mejía Godoy's first album, *Cantos a flor de pueblo*. As in the photo on the front of the album, he is featured with his accordion.

derived from their primary occupation as doctors), who were part of the growing middle-class interest in folklore studies. This group collected *campesino* songs that they imitated in (sometimes exaggerated) rural performance style as well as reinterpreted into a smoother urban format. Mejía joined the already renowned Enrique Duarte in a series of concerts throughout the country's Pacific Coast area. Duarte, like other professional musicians of similar background who were recruited by Mejía, had previously played in the still very popular Mexican trio style, which features close harmonies with guitar accompaniment. Under Mejía's leadership, his group replaced Mexican forms with the *son nica* and experimented with a variety of other styles. The songs also took on a decidedly political cast. He thus moved many of the musicians who began to work with him on a regular basis in new directions, both musically as well as politically.

In 1973, one year after the earthquake, Carlos Mejía released "Panchito Escombros" and "María de los Guardias" together on a single 45. The 7-inch record's immense success led to his first LP, *Cantos a flor de puelbo* (see fig. 3.3). The album's independent funding alone, which was acquired outside of the usual Somoza-linked channels, made it a milestone in the nation's music industry. The album summarized many years of Mejía's composing and demonstrated his wide range of topics and musical styles. Besides several *son nicas*, the album included "Pinocho Pinochet," which characterizes Pinochet as a U.S. Pinocchio puppet that "speaks in Spanish but thinks in English—'oh yes.'" The farcical lyrics fit the whimsical musical style, a dainty waltz performed with flute and an electric keyboard set to the celeste stop, whose timbre is reminiscent of a child's wind-up toy. Several songs are in the brisk 2/4 meter of *corridos* and polkas. These include "Que viva Managua" ("Long Live Managua"), a *corrido* not unlike those of Tino López Guerra and others of a previous generation. Rather than trumpeting overblown descriptions that are almost interchangeable between any city in Latin America (the most beautiful women, the imposing main cathedral, etc.), the lyrics present local, everyday pleasures that are available to the most humble sectors of the population. The most conspicuous examples are several careful descriptions of street foods unmistakably Nicaraguan. The solo voice of Carlos Mejía and the chorus of children in "Navidad en libertad" ("Christmas with Liberty") are accompanied simply by an organ and drum set without any guitars. The musical effect is one of a universal style—one deliberately not tied to localized forms. This musical universality reinforces the lyrics, which are dedicated to "all the children of the Third World." The song internationalizes the author's social stance and appeals to religious impulses for generosity and fairness foregrounded during the Christmas season.

The success of "Panchito Escombros" and "María de los Guardias" elevated Carlos Mejía to the position of the nation's most popular singer-songwriter and propelled *música de protesta* to national prominence as well. He quickly followed up on his first album and the next year released a second full LP, also independently produced, entitled *En la calle de enmedio* (*On Main Street*, or *In the Street in Between*, as pictured on the album cover; see fig. 3.4). Concerns of national identity in the musical style and form of popular song swirled within the Nicaraguan musical community at this time. Jorge Isaac Carvallo initiated a debate that engaged Carlos Mejía and others over the question of which form of newly composed music should be deemed truly Nicaraguan. Carvallo argued the necessity to distinguish Nicaraguan music from Mexican and other non-national styles and held that the *son nica* was the only appropriate vehicle for national composers. With the *son nica* as his litmus test of true national form, Carvallo further critiqued two principal deviations from this form: tempo and tonality. *Son nicas* with too fast a tempo can be confused with a *huapango* (a *son* from northern Mexico), and a true *son nica* needs to be entirely in a major key and not contain sections of minor tonality. Carvallo cited two of Carlos Mejía's songs as offending

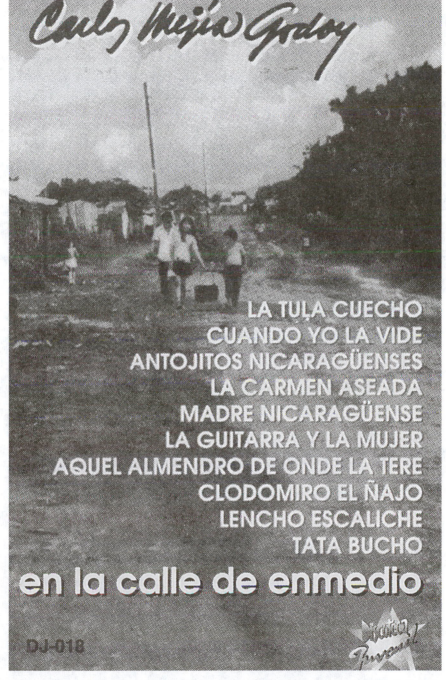

LA TULA CUECHO
CUANDO YO LA VIDE
ANTOJITOS NICARAGÜENSES
LA CARMEN ASEADA
MADRE NICARAGÜENSE
LA GUITARRA Y LA MUJER
AQUEL ALMENDRO DE ONDE LA TERE
CLODOMIRO EL ÑAJO
LENCHO ESCALICHE
TATA BUCHO

en la calle de enmedio

DJ-018

Fig. 3.4. Front cover of cassette version of Carlos Mejía Godoy's second album, *En la calle de enmedio.*

examples: 1. the fast tempo on Mejía's first national success, "Alforja Campesina," which is, in fact, quick enough to move beyond the rhythmic feel of a proper *son nica*; and 2. the alternating minor and major sections of "Cristo ya nació en Palacagüina" ("Christ Was Born in Palacagüina," discussed below), a song that appeared on Carlos Mejía's first album, in 1973, and again on his 1977 album *El son nuestro de cada día* (*Our Daily* Son). Mejía readily conceded that these songs had elements that made them distinct from Camilo Zapata's original *son nica* template, but he defended their appropriateness and their identity as fully Nicaraguan. Most Nicaraguan musicians agreed with Mejía's more ecumenical approach and found Carvallo's position too restrictive and dogmatic. The general population, unmoved by these gate-keeping arguments, wholeheartedly embraced "Cristo ya nació en Palacagüina" to such an extent that it took on the status of being the signature song of Carlos Mejía.[13]

Musicalizing a Theology of Liberation

"Cristo ya nació en Palacagüina" is emblematic of the key role music played in the convergence of religious-based morality with a mobilizing ideology for social change. The growth of the movement against Somoza spread and took root largely due to the successful linkage of the sense of social justice that can be read in the gospels with a sense of responsibility to take whatever action necessary to create such justice in the temporal world. In the 1960s, priests vitalized by the declaration of a "preferential option for the poor" presented at the Medellín Conference of Bishops introduced the social reform message of liberation theology in several popular *barrios* in Managua. The deep root these ideas took among young parishioners became clear when these same neighborhoods later became strongholds of the FSLN in the insurrections against the Somoza regime.

"Cristo ya nació en Palacagüina" (renamed more simply "El Cristo de Palacagüina" for the 1977 version on *El son nuestro de cada día*) was inspired in part from Carlos Mejía's early contact with these socially conscious parishes. The verses, set mostly in a minor key (with a brief move to the relative major), tells the story of a boy born to "someone named Mary" and a carpenter father in the small northern town of Palacagüina. One verse ends with Maria's hope that her son will follow her husband's trade, but—as the tonality changes to major—"the child thinks, 'tomorrow I want to be a guerrilla fighter.'" The chorus, now in a resounding (perhaps even redemptive) major key, proclaims, "Cristo ya nació en Palacagüina." The song transports the central figure of Christianity, Jesus of Nazareth, into the Nicaraguan countryside, in effect making him Jesus of Palacagüina. The liberation-theology concept of Christ being within each human being allows Jesus to take a human form that can be identified with the lived experience of the listener. Within this logic, the song goes on to state that if Jesus were alive amongst us he would take up arms to right the intolerable wrongs the people are suffering.

For obvious reasons (and ones wholly unrelated to Carvallo's musical objections), the conservative church hierarchy did not approve of the song. The government immediately banned it from the radio. Nevertheless, its fame led to an invitation for Carlos Mejía to visit a newly established parish organized around the convictions of liberation theology on the remote archipelago of Solentiname. Here, poet and priest Ernesto Cardenal founded an artistically oriented community that developed poetry workshops and paintings inspired by Latin American primitivism, and brought personal testimony and newly composed songs into services. The Solentiname congregation invited Mejía to compose a Mass that incorporated the beliefs of socially committed Christianity as expressed by the *campesinos* and artisans in Solentiname and elsewhere. He took up the challenge by immediately throwing the invitation out to all Nicaraguan musicians, proposing a collective effort to create a new Mass based on the expressive culture of the popular classes. Even though this national cooperative project did not materialize and Mejía eventually wrote the Mass almost entirely himself, he did enlist contributions from "El Guadalupano" (Pablo Martínez Téllez), a respected *campesino* musician of some renown, and a Miskitu singer (Anselmo Nixon) from the northeastern littoral of the country, who taught Mejía a Moravian hymn in his native Miskitu.

The *Misa campesina nicaragüense*, as it was eventually titled, contained lyrics that drew from the poetry and other testimony of the Solentimane community and music that consisted of original compositions and reinterpretations of familiar folk and popular melodies. The clearly partisan position that favors the poor and laboring classes in the lyrics distinguished it from other Catholic Masses up to this time. Mejía deliberately attempted to include musics from throughout Nicaraguan national territory, for example: a raucous *chichero* brass band found throughout the lower plains to express the feeling of joy in the Gloria; the inclusion of a marimba to represent the Masaya region for the Despedida; a mazurka performed on mandolin and accordion from the northern regions in the Kyrie; and the hymn sung in Miskitu from the Atlantic Coast. The constellation of regional forms in the *Misa campesina nicaragüense* situates it within the history of Nicaraguan music as a unique work that deliberately strove to represent musically the totality of the nation.

In addition to being a move toward regional and ethnic inclusion, the "preferential option" for the popular classes and the valorization of their culture that are so apparent in the *Misa* were part of a process to bring them into a new, reconceptualized Nicaragua. Thus, the *Misa campesina nicaragüense* "nationalized" the Catholic Mass in a double sense: it was actively used in the process of defining the nation "Nicaragua" to include those parts of the population that had been previously ignored or disdained on a class basis as well as a regional and ethnic one.[14] The Mass, finished in 1975, was first celebrated in Solentiname to the acclaim of the parish. Carlos Mejía organized a studio recording in Managua, which became a collective effort involving the many groups of musicians for which his vision called. A highly publicized attempt in 1977 to hold the Mass in the capital was broken up by the National Guard. The celebration of the Mass and distribution of the recordings, now restricted to cassette, went underground. The Mass continued to circulate widely via mimeographed copies, and the recordings were treated as popular song and repeatedly broadcast on the recently established Radio Sandino that reached Managua from neighboring Costa Rica. The *Misa campesina nicaragüense* served as a kind of musical embodiment of the tenets of liberation theology and greatly enhanced the attractiveness of the religious movement to a population that is (at least nominally) almost entirely Catholic.

A Pre-*triunfo* Conclusion

Mejía Godoy's inclusive approach to collaboration on the *Misa campesina nicaragüense* was one of several organizational efforts to extend New Song throughout the western Spanish-speaking part of the nation. The unprecedented impact of Nicaragua's flowering of *música testimonial* confirmed the importance of cultural work to the FSLN. The Front supported the formation in 1972 of the cultural group Gradas ("Steps") by several writers and other artists, and the next year Carlos Mejía founded the Brigada de Salvación del Canto Nicaragüense ("Brigade for the Salvation of Nicaraguan Song"). The loosely organized Brigade helped to valorize rural-based folk forms and aesthetics to urban youth, in this way building a sense of unity between *campesinos* and the urban proletariat. The Brigade, which lasted a few years, overlapped another Carlos Mejía initiative, the Talleres del Sonido Popular ("Popular Sound Workshops"), the first of which, in 1975, was comprised of the various music groups that recorded the *Misa*. The *Talleres* grew to encompass a federation of workshops that became the crucial structure to coordinate and aid the mushrooming number of musicians trying their hand at political song. Most of these new musical groups emerged in Managua and took on names such as: Galpalí ("River Stone," in Náhuatl); Grupo América; Grupo Libertad ("Group for Liberty"); Grupo Pueblo ("Group of the People"); Igni Tawanka ("Light of the People," in Miskitu);

Ocho de Noviembre ("November Eighth," the day FSLN founder Carlos Fonseca Amador fell in combat); Quinteto Wayna ("Quintet of Man," in Miskitu); and probably the most talented, Pancasán (named after the unsuccessful battle of 1967), which was able to clandestinely record a studio album between passing Guard patrols.

At this point, the struggle against the Somoza dictatorship entered a new phase, one beyond the scope of this chapter and that I can only briefly summarize here. A spectacular military action in the heart of Managua by the FSLN in 1974 forced the release of many political prisoners. It also unleashed a state of siege that truly lifted only when Somoza fled the country five years later. The space for the subtlety of critique muted in traditional vernacular and disguised with satire definitively closed. The growing oppositional musical movement embraced openly political content appropriate to the gathering insurrectionary storm. Whereas only a few years earlier Carlos Mejía introduced the name of Sandino into popular song with an ambiguous reference in "María de los Guardias," Pancasán's eponymous song was probably the first to mention the actual FSLN in lyrics and openly referred to the coming of revolution (Pancasán 2000 [1978]). As the political struggle became increasingly militarized, Mejía was forced into exile, where he helped to mobilize international sympathy and support for the opposition. In 1978 most music groups disbanded to take up arms. In that same year, Mejía and his brother Luis Enrique, by this time members of the FSLN, wrote a series of songs that instructed the civilian population in the use of weapons for the approaching general insurrection. These songs are no doubt among the clearest examples of an immediacy of direct communication to achieve a specific goal within Latin American New Song (released on *Guitarra armada* [*Armed Guitar*], 1980 [1978]).[15]

The *triunfo* over Somoza in July 1979 ushered in a new era, flush with new horizons and fraught with unanticipated challenges. The continued flowering of socially committed music in Nicaragua into the 1980s built upon, and was made possible by, the success of previous testimonial music to stimulate the national social conscience and mobilize it into transformative action. This discussion of Nicaraguan New Song illustrates how the power of this music flowed in great part from its linguistic and musical resonance with the expressive style and the spiritual values of the popular classes, a rendering that gave testimony to some of the population's deepest-felt aspirations for a more just and liberated life.

Notes

1. Publications include an insider's account of the role of clandestine media in the form of Radio Venceremos (López Vigil 1994), and an impressionistic description of one of the best-known *campesino* music groups, Los Torogoces de Morazán (González 1994). See also two insightful articles on lyrics from the period (Almeida and Urbizagástegui 1999, and Judson, forthcoming). Earlier publications on Central America include Chilean musician Carrasco (1982) and interviews by Ciechanower (1985a, 1985b, 1988). The series of reissues by Carlos Mántica, Jr. (son of pioneering folklorist and linguist Carlos Mántica) includes practically the entire catalog of Carlos Mejía Godoy (on the Web at www.ibw.com.ni/~cmant/discos). Rounder Records continues to keep in print, if only on cassette for some titles, all their albums of Central American music, as well as titles of Salvadoran and Nicaraguan music purchased by Rounder from Flying Fish Records.

2. Western Nicaragua encompasses the Spanish-speaking part of the country that contains close to 90 percent of the nation's population. Not considered here is music of the eastern zone, known in Nicaragua as the Atlantic Coast, which includes English Creole speakers and Garifuna, Rama, Miskitu and Sumu/Mayanga peoples.

3. Among the many examples of such a "lingocentric" orientation are the most in-depth scholarly studies of protest music in the United States, such as Denisoff (1971, 1972); Greenway (1953); and the excellent study by Lieberman (1989); and sections on the United States in the sociological study by Eyerman and Jamison (1998) and collection of essays and texts in Sakolsky and Ho (1995).

4. Other terms for political music in Hispano-America include *canto nuevo*, particularly for Chilean New Song after the 1973 coup, and *canto revolucionario*.

5. For a transcription of music and lyrics (with English translation) of a version recorded by the northern Nicaraguan group Los Soñadores de Sarawaska of "Los dueles de Sandino," the best known of these *corridos* and still very alive in popular memory, see Scruggs (1998, 758–59).

6. For example, Zapata has consistently been cited as the progenitor of the *son nica* both in public discourse and to me in private by prominent musicians, such as Jorge Isaac Carvallo, Carlos Mejía Godoy, and Otto de la Rocha (e.g., 1988), as well as by Camilo Zapata himself (e.g., 1987). On the other hand, Luis Enrique Mejía Godoy (e.g., 1985) has often voiced the opinion that this sung form must have already existed somewhere in the countryside. This seems a plausible assumption, but no evidence has ever been produced from recordings, folklorist investigations, or extant repertoire. In my own research, it was generally accepted within the communities where the *marimba de arco* is played that the *son nica* dates from its commercial introduction by Zapata.

7. Translations in this and other songs are rather literal, except for the many examples of localized expressions and word play. I have not attempted to produce a rhyme or metric scheme in English that might better offer the reader some of the artistic impact of the verse.

8. Valle Castillo would use the same quote to include Luis Enrique together with Carlos on the liner notes of *Guitarra armada* when released in Nicaragua a year later (1980).

9. As Valle Castillo stated, Carlos Mejía's poems are "perhaps the best libertine poet-

ry—creatively orgiastic—written by the younger generation in the last decade in Nicaragua" (1986) [1979].

10. For further discussion of the role of music in expanding a national consciousness within Nicaragua, see Scruggs (1999).

11. For the intellectual history of radical politics in Nicaragua since 1960, see Ramírez Mercado (1983), and Hodges (1986). Among the many publications on the subject of political and socioeconomic history, see Black (1981); Walker (1982); and Dunkerley (1988).

12. El Rapador was the site of a battle where Sandino's army inflicted significant casualties on U.S. Marines.

13. Carlos Mejía's working quartet after 1975 was known as Carlos Mejía Godoy y los de Palacagüina ("and Those from Palacagüina"), a name not originally related to the song "Cristo ya nació en Palacagüina," but in the public's mind connected with the song after its international success.

14. For more analysis of the *Misa campesina nicaragüense* and its place within folk music–inspired Catholic Masses, see Scruggs (forthcoming).

15. For a brief discussion of later works by Carlos Mejía, see Scruggs (2001).

References

Note: Recordings are from Managua and currently available, unless otherwise stated.

Almeida, Paul, and Rubén Urbizagástegui. 1999. "Popular Music in El Salvador's National Liberation Movement." *Latin American Perspectives* 26/2: 13–42.

Avendaño, Xiomara, Jorge Cuadra, and Francisco Cedeño. 1989. *Cantos de la lucha sandinista*. Mangaua: ENIGRAC—Editorial Vanguardia.

Beezley, William H., and Linda A. Curcio-Nagy. 2000. "Introduction." In *Latin American Popular Culture: An Introduction*. Edited by W. H. Beezley and L. A. Curcio-Nagy. Wilmington, Del.: Scholarly Resources, xi–xxiii.

Black, George. 1981. *Triumph of the People: The Sandinista Revolution in Nicaragua*. London: Zed Press.

Brinton, Daniel G., ed. 1969 [1883]. *The Güegüense: A Comedy Ballet in the Nahuatl-Spanish Dialect of Nicaragua*. New York: AMS Press.

Carrasco, Eduardo. 1982. "Nicaragua, Costa Rica y Puerto Rico." *La nueva canción en América latina*. Santiago, Chile: CENECA, 58–61.

Carvallo, Jorge Isaac. 1987. Interview by the author, August 5, in Managua.

Carballo [*sic*], Jorge Isaac y Otto de a Rocha. 1970. *Campesino/El Peón*. Istmo 07–1720, SISA (seven-inch 45 rpm).

———. ca. 1971. *Nicaragua canta*. Istmo 07–1025, Estereo Náhuatl.

Ciechanower, Mauricio. 1985a. "Carlos Mejía Godoy: Canción en Nicaragua, otra herramienta." *Plural* 14/167: 21–24.

———. 1985b. "Carlos Mejía Godoy: Nicaragua en constante combustión." *Plural* 14/168 (segunda época): 45–51.

———. 1988. "Nicaragua: una cultura de resistencia." *Plural* 18/207: 61–65.

Denisoff, Serge. 1971. *Great Day Coming! Folk Music and the American Left*. Urbana: University of Illinois Press.

———. 1972. *Sing a Song of Social Significance*. Bowling Green, Ohio: Bowling Green University Popular Press.

Dunkerley, James. 1988. *Power in the Isthmus: A Political History of Modern Central America*. London and New York : Verso.

Eyerman, Ron, and Andrew Jamison. 1998. *Music and Social Movements: Mobilizing Traditions in the Twentieth Century.* Cambridge: Cambridge University Press.

González, Iván. 1994. *Las guitarras del fuego de ayer.* San Salvador: Ediciones Arcoiris.

Greenway, John. 1953. *American Folk Songs of Protest.* Philadelphia: University of Pennsylvania Press.

Hobsbawm, Eric, and Terry Ranger, eds. 1983. *The Invention of Tradition.* Cambridge: Cambridge University Press.

Hodges, Donald Clark. 1986. *Intellectual Foundations of the Nicaraguan Revolution.* Austin: University of Texas Press.

Judson, Fred. Forthcoming. "Central American Revolutionary Music Lyrics." In *Marxist Perspectives on Music.* Edited by Regula Burckhardt Qureshi. New York: Routledge/ Garland.

Lieberman, Robbie. 1989. *My Song Is My Weapon: People's Songs, American Communism, and the Politics of Culture, 1930–1950.* Urbana: University of Illinois Press.

López Vigil, José Ignacio. 1994. *Rebel Radio: The Story of El Salvador's Radio Venceremos.* Willimantic, Conn.: Curbstone Press.

Mejía Godoy, Carlos. 1985 [1976]. *La misa campesina nicaragüense.* ENIGRAC NCLP 5012 (1st ed., San José, Costa Rica).

———. 1990. Interview by the author, March 6, in Managua.

———. 1996 [1973]. *Cantos a flor de pueblo.* Mántica-Waid 0396017 (1st ed., San José, Costa Rica).

———. 1999 [1977]. *El son nuestro de cada día.* Mántica-Waid (1st ed., San José, Costa Rica).

———. 2000 [1974]. *En la calle de enmedio.* Mántica-Waid (1st ed., San José, Costa Rica).

Mejía Godoy, Carlos, and Luis Enrique Mejía Godoy. 1980 [1978]. *Guitarra armada.* Managua: Ocarina (1st ed., San José, Costa Rica; also available on Rounder Records 4022).

Mejía Godoy, Luis Enrique. 1971. . . . *este es mi pueblo.* San José: INDICA/CBS 20072, San José, Costa Rica.

———. 1973. *Hilachas del sol.* San José: INDICA/CBS100.048, San José, Costa Rica.

———. 1985. Interview by the author, August 13, in Managua.

———. 1990. Interview by the author, March 5, in Managua.

Mejía Sánchez, Ernesto. 1976. *Romances y corridos nicaragüenses.* Managua: Banco de América.

Pancasán (also, Grupo Pancasán). 2000 [1978]. *Pancasán.* Mántica-Waid (1st ed., San José, Costa Rica).

———. 1980. *Vamos haciendo la historia.* Ocarina MC-001, ENIGRAC.

Pring Mill, Robert. 1987. "The Roles of Revolutionary Song: A Nicaraguan Assessment." *Popular Music* 6/2: 179–90.

Ramírez Mercado, Sergio. 1983. *Balcanes y volcanes y otros ensayos y trabajos.* Managua: Editorial Nueva Nicaragua.

Rocha, Otto de la. 1988. Interview by the author, July 20, in Managua.

Sakolsky, Rob, and Fred Wei-han Ho, eds. 1995. *Sounding Off! Music as Subversion/ Resistance/Revolution.* New York: Autonomedia.

Scott, James C. 1985. *Weapons of the Weak: Everyday Forms of Peasant Resistance.* New Haven, Conn.: Yale University Press.

Scruggs, T.M. 1998. "Nicaragua." In *The Garland Encyclopedia of World Music. Vol 2: South America, Mexico, Central America, and the Caribbean.* Edited by D. Olsen and D. Sheehy. New York: Garland Publishing, 747–69.

———. 1999. "'Let's Enjoy As Nicaraguans': The Use of Music in the Construction of a Nicaraguan National Consciousness." *Ethnomusicology* 43/2: 297–321.

———. 2001. "Mejía Godoy, Carlos." *New Grove Dictionary of Music and Musicians.* 2d ed. Stanley Sadie, ed. London: Macmillan.

———. Forthcoming. "'Folk' Masses and the Musical Re-Indigenization of Catholic Ritual in Latin America." *World of Music.*

Valle Castillo, Julio. 1986 [1979]. Liner notes to *Monimbó* NCLP-5013 (*Vivirás Monimbó* on cassette CE-5013), Carlos Mejía Godoy y los de Palacagüina. Managua: ENIGRAC. Originally released as *Monimbó.* San José, Costa Rica: INDICA.

Walker, Thomas W., ed. 1982. *Nicaragua in Revolution.* New York: Praeger.

Zapata, Camilo. 1987. Interview by the author, August 7, in Chinandega, Nicaragua.

4

Rock Chabón

The Contemporary National Rock of Argentina

PABLO SEMÁN AND PABLO VILA

Many Argentinean middle-class people (including young people who love rock) would regard the kind of rock that is popular among the lower-middle and lower classes (the "popular sectors") as decidedly insufferable. Its nationalism, lack of "depth" and "musical quality," as well as its futile excesses, would surely be among its objectionable qualities, as well as its immersion in a lifestyle that is antipodal to the middle class: it is music of gangs, street corners, guns, knives, and alcohol, of the unemployed and *chorritos* ("petty thieves"). For those who add to their social distance their age, this type of *rock nacional* is totally incomprehensible. Some early chroniclers who observed its development described it as being "from the streets," *chabón* (belonging to the common guy on the street), *futbolero* (linked to the soccer culture), "national and popular," and the like. We define this music as a pro-Argentinean, from-the-outskirts, and neo-oppositional kind of rock, but for reasons of simplicity we will call it *rock chabón*.

On the one hand, *rock chabón* addresses those young people whose social integration is severely hindered by a socioeconomic process that reduces employment and diminishes the culturally consecrated figure of the worker, even as it hallows a consumer culture that frustrates more than satisfies. On the other hand, *rock chabón* is the music of those young people who contest the economic model, and, through this response, affirm and transform a positive nucleus of the preexistent popular culture. We believe that popular culture's expressions are not merely reflections of the hegemonic culture, or manifestations of resistance (i.e., symbolic maneuvers in the reduced space available in the political project of the "Other"). It is actually via such expressions that popular culture becomes the product of the creative processes that characterize any symbolic activity through which people demonstrate their capacity to construct meaning.

However, this capacity is not ahistorical; on the contrary, it is historically anchored. Thus, *rock chabón* ties the aesthetics of rock to a post-populist reading of Argentinean society. This post-populism is not "post" in the sense of something "after," something distinct from the past and without contact with it. It is "post" in the sense of a relief from and, simultaneously, a new articulation of the past. This replacement is culturally novel within the history of *rock nacional*, because it does not express the political disenchantment of the middle class (a thematic issue that was and still is very important to many adherents of the genre). Rather, it gives expression to the more polyvalent voice through which popular-sectors youth relate to democracy, to the dismantling of the last (but still important) vestiges of the welfare state, and to the historical imaginaries[1] generated by the Peronist experience, which fueled the dreams of integration (more or less egalitarian) that characterized the Argentina already dying in the late 1980s and early '90s.[2]

Rock Chabón Defined

A trip through Buenos Aires and its surroundings in the late 1990s would offer us, like a postcard, testimony to the results of an enormous and traumatic (both in its dimensions and its inequity) process of social and economic transformation. The groups of young people who gather daily on corners to chat, "do nothing," and listen to music share hopes and rancors that, from the point of view of the market, are unimportant.[3]

The street-corner group or gang seems to be a key locale for the socialization of these young people, and the music they listen to is *rock nacional*, but a very peculiar version of the genre. Like many other youth subcultures in Latin America (the *cholos* on the U.S.-Mexico border form a very interesting comparison), these young people enjoy "oldies." But Argentinean musical tradition provides its own oldies, not the American oldies the *cholos* rely on to help in the construction of their identities. Many Argentinean gangs listen to the original *rock nacional*, the first tunes sung back in the 1960s and '70s, for example, those melodies made popular by Tanguito, Moris, Manal, Vox Dei, El Reloj, and Almendra (Kuasñosky and Szulik 1994, 277). It is as if people without a future had to rely on the past to construct a valued identity in a country where they have no place.

But these young people not only like oldies, but also the *rocanrol* ("rock and roll") of Viejas Locas, a band from Piedrabuena, a neighborhood very similar to their own. Viejas Locas's song "Botella" ("Bottle") states: "You are my only love, my bottle of alcohol." Another group, of similar socioeconomic profile, neighborhood, and social habits, proclaims that they belong to Patricio Rey y sus Redonditos de Ricota's tribe. During a train trip that they took to see "their" band 250 miles away from Buenos Aires,[4] they continuously sang one of their preferred leitmotifs: "To be a Redondos fan, you have to have two things: a bottle of wine and a woman in your bed."[5] Trying to explain the explosion of popular-sectors bands that sprang up in the early 1990s, D'Addario argues that some *rock nacional* musicians used to address the lower-class audience, while they assisted in its actualization:

> Many of the rockers of the 1980s (from Luca Prodan to Juanse) began to relate what the common people below the stage were experiencing. In the 1990s, common people jumped up and occupied the stage. There are no visible differences between the members of La Renga, Viejas Locas, Dos Minutos, Attaque 77, Flema, Gardelitos, etc., and the fans that buy tickets to see their shows.[6]

However, the confluence of bands and the public does not point to the existence of a specific musical subgenre. The unity we attribute to the phenomenon is the product of a common thematic in *rock chabón*'s lyrics, a particular way of reading social reality, and the more or less homogeneous way in which the public receives and categorizes its messages. In this sense *rock chabón* not only exists because there is a definable corpus of lyrics and some easily identifiable groups that perform them but also, and perhaps more importantly, because this *rock nacional* subgenre has introduced to Argentine culture a particular kind of musical perception.[7] Of course, from time to time, analytical categories coincide with real happenings, and the most important *rock chabón* groups or their allies appear together in a particular event. One such occurrence took place in October 1997, when the *Madres de la Plaza de Mayo* commemorated the twentieth anniversary of their first march around the Plaza demanding to learn the fate of the *desaparecidos*, their children who "disappeared" (i.e., were abducted and murdered by government thugs) during the right-wing military dictatorship of the 1970s and '80s.

What we want to emphasize here is that there is a very similar way of composing songs and of "reading" social reality among these groups, though they are different in many other respects. In this intersectional space we find, among others: Divididos (which performs a *rock nacional* variant that mixes punk music, blues, Argentinean folk music, and the kind of rock popularized by the Rolling Stones); La Renga (a band that performs a blues-based type of rock); Almafuerte (which adheres to a version of rock characterized as "electric," "heavy," or "metallic"); Attaque 77 (with a basically punk aesthetic); Dos Minutos (a group that considers itself Attaque 77's heirs and performs punk music as well); Los Fabulosos Cadillacs (a combo that cultivates a rock influenced by Latin rhythms); Los Piojos (a band that mixes rock with Argentinean and Uruguayan carnival music—*murga* and *candombe*, respectively); and Flema and Superuva (both punk groups). Two other groups are also very important members of the subgenre, Patricio Rey y sus Redonditos de Ricota and Sumo, but they constitute very special cases within it. This is because they are at once an integral part of the *rock chabón* movement and its historical antecedents as well.

The members of Almafuerte, Attaque 77, and Dos Minutos belong to the same social class as the people who follow them, the broadly defined "popular sectors," while the members of the other groups come from middle- and upper-middle-class environments.[8] In a similar fashion, *rock chabón*'s public is heterogeneous, but mostly composed of young people belonging to the popular sectors.[9] We will occasionally refer to other groups that are less systematically linked to the cultural climate that characterizes *rock chabón*, either because of their important position in the field of *rock nacional* in general, or because they are formations that antecede current *rock chabón* groups. It is important to point out the massive appeal of these groups. All of them have sold large numbers of recordings, and between 1987 and 1995 they were awarded "group of the year" honors in polls conducted among the most important rock musicians of the country.[10] All of them influence the production of other groups and regularly perform in front of very large audiences (140,000 people attended the performance of Patricio Rey in April 2000, for example). Having a massive audience, the emergence of this type of rock speaks to a particular way of knitting change and continuity in certain central dimensions of Buenos Aires's urban culture.

Rock Chabón and Populism

Rock chabón is the music of the sons and daughters of those who identified themselves as "Peronists," but also of those others who, after the apogee of Peronism, became workers aspiring to social mobility, equal legal protection, and consumerism (expectations that Peronism itself had helped to create). *Rock chabón* is the rock of those youths who, longing for the world of their elders, find an alternative to their exclusion from the neoliberal socio-economic model in this form of musical expression, the street-corner gang, or by soliciting money to buy beer or tickets to a rock concert. They think, with good reason, that they could not find such an alternative in any of the traditional political venues in contemporary Argentina: that is, in the major political parties that support, in doctrinaire fashion, the very economic model that marginalizes these young people.

Thus, *rock chabón* becomes the expression of a popular identity/difference within *rock nacional*, a genre that hitherto did not allow the production of any such thing. While in the past *rock nacional* won listeners, record buyers, and fans in this group, it never before authorized them as the movement's "intellectuals." Therefore, *rock chabón* is a musical practice that helps in the construction of an identity of "marginalized young people belonging to the popular sectors" through the different alliances those youngsters establish between their diverse imagined narrative identities and the identities that *rock chabón* sets forth.

As we have noted above, *rock chabón* could be characterized as pro-Argentinean, from-the-outskirts, and neo-oppositional. Those characteristics acquire their full meaning if *rock chabón* is understood in its interdependence and interaction with the populist cultural matrix to which these three characteristics belong. Of course, this is not the only way to read *rock chabón*'s place in contemporary Argentina, but we emphasize this reading for two reasons. First, the populist inheritance is a crucial component in the "oppositional" and "pro-Argentinean" plots of this kind of rock. Second, the elaboration of the populist inheritance is one of the processes that makes intelligible a current social dynamic in which very diverse and multiple identities prosper and appear unconnected to one another. In other words, our hypothesis is that the social subject historically constituted by populism in Argentina occupies an important place in the interpellations[11] and narratives that make possible this type of rock.

When we discuss populist interpellations and narratives, we are not only referring to those produced by the Peronist regime itself; we are also alluding to the social imaginary that guided expectations of social integration held by subaltern groups from the beginning of the first Peronist government (1945) through a long period of disintegration of the populist model that has ended in our own time. This populist imaginary, far from being destroyed after the Peronist experience of 1945 to 1995 (and the very brief interregnum of 1973 to 1975), has undergone a long process of degradation that exhibits, to a surprising degree, the resilience of its most important constituent elements. According to Tulio Halperín Donghi (1994), populist mechanisms and expectations of integration lasted (in some respects they are still present today) much longer than their underlying economic rationale.

Stressing the importance of this long period in which populist images and subjects were in crisis but still present, Nun and Portantiero affirm that:

> the current emergence of a new political regime coincides with the prolonged decomposition and decadence of the accumulation social regime, that is, with the crisis of a capitalist stage and the structures, institutions, images, and the kind of actors that characterized that particular stage. (1987, 48)

Thus, the mutations in the sociodemographic profile that have changed the popular sectors' world,[12] being mediated by the persistence of such an imaginary, "do not tend to be reflected immediately at the level of the new political and ideological struggles" (Nun and Portantiero 1987, 113).

This process manifests itself, for instance, in the fact that the idea of poverty as a transitional stage (i.e., the hope of moving up the socioeconomic ladder) only recently ceded its predominance in the representations of the popular sectors among which the *rock chabón* dynamic emerged (Minujín and Kessler 1995). This populist imaginary successfully offered— along with the interpellation *pueblo* ("common people," as millions of Argentineans identify themselves) and a series of very structured narratives—not only identities and rights that referred to egalitarian perspectives but also the legitimacy of protest to support those perspectives. In this way, a set of expectations not only implicated a conciliatory ideology, but also contained elements of extreme social contestation, something that differentiates Peronism from other Latin American populisms.

Beyond a model of economic development based on domestic manufacture and restriction of imports, Peronism was characterized by a very particular political dynamic. Within the context of the organic association between the trade unions and the political system, and the consecration of labor rights, popular identities were inscribed in an antagonistic dichotomy: the *pueblo* of Peronist discourse was the basis of nationality, of patriotism against the "not-really-Argentineans" of Argentina—*oligarcas* ("oligarchies"), imperialists, communists, traitors, and the like. That was also the *pueblo* to which rights were owed and that the people considered the source of national sovereignty. The functioning of this scheme encompassed several levels of Argentinean society, but in relation to the popular sectors, Peronism created a political language that was "able to give public expression to the[ir] private experiences" (Martuccelli and Svampa 1997, 29).

In this sense, Peronism was not only a political regime that articulated social relations at a macro level; it also organized a particular culture that informed everyday life and culture. The reading of Peronism as a "structure of feeling," a formation at the level of culture as actually lived, is crucial to our argument, which presupposes a displacement from resources usually linked to politics toward others linked to culture. Different studies identify the various levels and forces that this phenomenon acquires. Daniel James (1990, 40) describes how within the Peronist culture a vision developed that went well beyond the imbrication between trade unions and state, to encompass more subtle aspects of personal experience. The effects of Peronist social and political interventions impacted everyday life, creating social identities, expectations, habits, and cultural resources that, as Elizabeth

Jelín shows (1996a, 1996b), crystallized in a notion of personal dignity. This fact, which was previously observed from a macrosociological and historical perspective by J. Torre (1983, 285), is analyzed by Jelín from the point of view of an "everyday-life cultural perspective" that involves notions of "pride and self respect" (1996a, 40).

Thus, the effectiveness of populist interpellations and narratives persists beyond the disappearance of the socioeconomic conditions that originally sustained that political regime. At the same time, due to their historical content in Argentina, those interpellations and narratives can generate discourses of social opposition. To summarize the relation between populist discourse and *rock chabón*, Pollack underscores this aspect of imaginaries in general:

> Its memory . . . can survive its disappearance, assuming the form of a myth that, because it cannot anchor itself in the political reality of the moment, nourishes itself on cultural, religious or literary references. Then, the faraway past can become the promise of a future and, sometimes, a challenge thrown toward the status quo. (1989, 11)

Populism has to be viewed as a subtext that is simultaneously mediated by other texts (in our case the texts developed by tango, the discourses about the neighborhood, and the like). However, we are not dealing with a kind of impact that works by inertia, in the sense that populist interpellations and narratives are activated simply because they are present in the mediations of those other texts. On the contrary (and this is crucial for our argument), those populist interpellations and narratives are activated by current, actual subjects also exposed to other kinds of discourses (the very broad rock discourse, for instance).

It is precisely through this process that the populist interpellations and narratives are transformed into something different from what they were, that is, they become our pro-Argentinean, from-the-outskirts, and neo-oppositional kind of rock. Those other discourses are also the product of a collective memory, and they go beyond being merely informative. For many young people (fans and musicians alike), those interpellations and narratives are a vital reference for defining their presence in the rock world and Argentinean society as well, a society that has changed in relation to what their parents had envisioned. For these young people, moving up the social ladder by means of education and employment is neither a possibility nor a dream. It is, instead, a facet of a past that is often characterized as "glorious." For many of popular-sectors youngsters of the 1990s, such dreams and goals became merely symbols of their disillusionment.

Rock Chabón in the History of *Rock Nacional*

In its over thirty years of history, *rock nacional* has become increasingly mass-mediated. It started with the consolidation of the recording market and concert circuits between 1970 and the beginning of the military dictatorship in 1976. In the early 1980s, due to the convergence of a series of factors that gave impetus to its expansion, *rock nacional* became still more popular. The delegitimation of English and American rock because of the Malvinas war, coupled with the new political openness resulting from a weakened dictatorship, made the mass media more accessible to Argentinean rockers, who took advantage of the situation to consolidate their popularity and leadership within a conflictive relationship with the military. This conflictive relationship not only existed because *rock nacional* symbolized opposition to the dictatorship, but also because the rockers were demonized by the military. In the minds of many young people, *rock nacional* became one of the few movements that resisted the dictatorship by sustaining a youth identity that was fiercely repressed (symbolically and factually) by the military (Vila 1985, 1987a, 1987c, 1989, 1992, 1995, and forthcoming). In the process of achieving mass mediation, *rock nacional* was progressively identified as the music that represented urban youngsters, and this rock of the early 1980s unified around a set of themes sustaining the association between rock and rebellion.

These narrative plots revolved around the definition of rock as a resistant "attitude" toward something that was generically defined as "the system," understood alternatively as an oppressive bureaucratic apparatus, capitalism, and the cultural industry. At the same time, the narrative plots discursively opposed rock to a music considered "commercial," opposition that implicitly questioned art commercialization in particular and cultural industries in general. One curious symptom of this cultural climate was the quasi-proscription within *rock nacional* of anything that signified dance. Dancing was considered synonymous with frivolity, and the social actor who was deemed the antipode of a rocker was the *bolichero* (a young dance-hall *habitué*). This "other" kind of youngster made dancing the most important activity of his/her leisure time. If in this general sense *rock nacional* consituted a "classic" agenda of social contestation, it is important to point out that within the movement itself there were specific musical variants that were the origin of what is usually known (for lack of a better term) as "protest songs."

In tandem with this general development of the genre, *rock nacional* produced stylistic variants that addressed specific aspects of different young people's cultural and social milieu. Those variants represented and helped create a very heterogeneous constituency. Throughout this process, some of these variants either came from or (more commonly) responded to the public of the poorest sectors of society. These musical traits relate to what is known as "heavy rock" (or Spanish blues), which for many years established itself as the industrial workers' rock, or "outskirts rock" (*rock suburbano* in the original Spanish formulation, referring to Buenos Aires's industrial suburbs or "industrial corridor" as the habitat of both rural immigrants and industrial workers).

With the return of democracy, *rock nacional* lost the monolithic image it possessed during the dictatorship, exemplified, for instance, by the constituency of the most important combo of the period, Serú Girán, whose members represented a kind of synthesis of the entire rock past with its different styles and ideologies (Vila 1989). If there were musical/political debates during the dictatorship, they were relegated to a secondary place to defend *in toto* a social actor symbolically homogenized by the demonizing attitude of the military dictatorship (Vila 1995). But the stylistic/political debate within *rock nacional* itself is something essential in analyzing the appearance and consolidation of *rock chabón* ten years later. To the *metálicos,* "punks," and "rockers" that exited during the last part of the 1976 to 1983 dictatorship, other denominations were added over time, variants of the *rock nacional* movement that did not feel represented by those labels. Thus we witnessed the appearance of: 1. the *divertidos* ("happy ones," e.g., Los Abuelos de la Nada, Los Twist, Las Viudas e Hijas de Roque Enroll, etc., many of them produced by Charly García, one of the major figures in the history of *rock nacional*), rock groups that generally belonged to the middle classes and utilized irony in contesting the establishment; 2. the *underground* (Patricio Rey y sus Redonditos de Ricota, Sumo, etc.), combos that also belonged to the middle classes but that rapidly developed a popular-sectors constituency lured by the underground's proposal of independent production and small concerts to confront the commercialized machinery of mainstream rock; and 3. the "modern" or "pop" variety (Virus, Soda Stéreo, Zas, etc.), which revindicated dancing and the corporeal dimension of rock, something traditionally overlooked by the *rock nacional* mainstream.

Of course, at this time, as had already happened before the dictatorship (Vila 1995), different struggles over the rock label as well as rock ideology and its social representations rapidly appeared, in a renewed (and always fruitless) attempt to separate the wheat from the chaff within *rock nacional*, to establish which one would be the "appropriate" interpellation and main narrative to address the urban youngsters of the period:

> Asked about the state of rock today, Solari answered that rock is nothing but "the official music of the system." How can you change the situation? [His

answer] First, with a rocker life as an initial attitude and not a bourgeois model of aspiration. (Solari 1985)

What we, the musicians, can do is to contribute to the level of individual change. For instance, if somebody understands through our music that to accept the body is a very intelligent way to face life, we will have fulfilled our mission. (Virus 1985)

[Since the Radical Party came to power], musical groups have had success with a theme of false festivity: conchetitos[13] of Martínez or San Isidro [two of the most upscale Buenos Aires neighborhoods] who can perform because they have money, like Los Helicópteros or Soda Stéreo, people who didn't go into the streets and have nothing to do with true rock and roll, which really comes from below. (Prodan 1986)

In the mid-1980s, for the first time in its history, the *rock nacional* move-ment developed one of the most important features of the international rock movement: the emphasis on the body, pleasure, and leisure as important symbolic markers that construct youth identity. In Grossberg's words, "rock and roll's relation to desire and pleasure serves to mark a difference, to inscribe on the surface of social reality a boundary between 'them' and 'us'" (1984, 234).[14] Now, the Argentine rock movement can agree with Simon Frith that rock is at once music that disturbs and relaxes, and Virus, Soda Stéreo, and other groups can claim, for the first time, their legitimate partic-ipation in the movement.[15]

This emergence, however, was not without turmoil. Part of the rock public felt that the rise and success of the new proposals linked with the body and pleasure were symptoms of crisis. What for some people was a revindication of pleasure was for others mere frivolity:

Soda Stéreo makes only sonorous shit. Let me explain: you can hear all their records and they don't give you any message, and don't say anything to you. *Rock nacional* was always "to shout truths claiming justice."[16]

The crisis appeared particularly serious because, unlike the polemics of the past (a kind of internal debate), this one intersected for the first time with the economic interests of the big record companies. Since 1982, these had transformed the traditional circuit of *rock nacional* dynamics (concert/ ratification of the songwriter's proposal/issue of the record) (Vila 1987b) into one that had its origin in the record and payola. These changes made the "natural" or "internal" resolution of the ongoing debate (that is, by the youths themselves in relation to their necessities) more difficult. Thus, a young rocker tried to explain to another rocker through letters to the editor of the most important rock magazine of the 1980s how, since the return of democracy in 1983, commercial interests had determined more than ever the success of *rock nacional* musicians:

> In your letter you said that you don't understand those people who say that the new musicians [Zas, Soda Stéreo, Virus, and so on] are plastic, and you said that, if they are famous, it is because we [the young] make them famous. You are wrong. There are many "top musicians" who really are *caretas* ["maskers"], who were invented by the record companies and journalism, and if anybody made them famous, it was all the *caretas* that you find among the youth. How can you explain that Zas has so many followers [its album *Rockas vivas* sold 300,000 copies] and a musician like Spinetta, who for twenty years has been making poems and music at the best international level, has fewer fans than Zas?[17]

We can also analyze the feeling of crisis that was prominent among rockers in the mid-1980s in another way, that is, as a fear of losing the idea of *rock nacional* as a "movement." *Rock nacional* began to lose its place as the only support of youth identity during the dictatorship when other interpellators appeared on the public scene: political parties, the human-rights movement, and trade unions on the one hand, and all the consumption-and-pleasure trends that could be described as "post-political," on the other. These proved more influential than *rock nacional* in the new social and political climate and were very effective in the construction of a youth identity. Thus, at this time of democratic openness, the *rock nacional* movement no longer needed to accept all its stylistic-ideological variants, the imperative to perceive the underlying unity in each of its different musical initiatives. During the dictatorship, the interplay between the social situation of many young people and *rock nacional*'s interpellations and narratives helped build a valued youth identity, at a time when other valorizing social interpellations and narratives were either absent or directly denied youth as subjects.[18] In the second part of the 1980s, however, we have a fragmentation of youth identity, not only among political or trade-union youth, rockers, and student militants, but also within the rock movement itself. It is no accident that the prominent place music occupied in the construction of youth identity (and in the idea of "movement" itself as representing such a collective identity) during the dictatorship was, step by step, being lost.

We can even propose some kind of axiom: the greater the diversity in the reception of musical styles, the lesser the cohesion of the movement to which they correspond. This is something that was apparently in Charly García's mind at the time:

For some time now [*rock nacional*] has been losing some of its key characteristics: buying records, exploring, being conscious of the movement, and so on. In this stage the music is more consumed than understood or comprehended. [We are witnessing a] switch from a demanding, interesting public, or one that in some way shares an idea with the musician, to another without position. . . . It's like consuming without questioning. (1986)

However, the debate over *rock nacional* by the mid-to-late 1980s shared much in common with previous polemics about the proper narratives and interpellations for addressing contemporary Argentinean urban youth. These advocated either the maintenance at all costs of the initial libertarian proposal, or its accommodation (in different ways) to the new times and the new adolescent cohorts, but always (at least among the most important *rock nacional* musicians) revindicating its role: "Walking always on the borders of the system, composing songs that, with luck, help to change somewhat the collective unconscious, the *coco* [head] of the people" (García 1986).

All of these changes occurred within the framework of a sociopolitical process that did not radically modify the social situation (either symbolically or in reality) of the popular sectors' young people. However, that would change, six or seven years later, under the auspices of the neoliberal agenda advanced by President Carlos Menem. In this sense, the *rock nacional* variant we are analyzing constitutes a polemical reaction to the entire history of the *rock nacional* movement.

But it was actually García himself who first constructed and described the new epoch in his songs of the early 1980s, questioning the old rocker credo. In relation to the anti-commercial stand that had historically characterized *rock nacional* (and much of his own career as well), Charly's lyrical alter ego sang that:

El se cansó de hacer canciones de protesta	He was tired of writing protest songs
y se vendió a Fiorucci;	and sold himself to Fiorucci [a famous Italian clothes maker];
él se cansó de andar haciendo apuestas	he was tired of making bets
y se puso a estudiar.	and started to study.
No creo que pueda dejar de protestar.	I don't think he can stop protesting.

("Transas," *Clics modernos*, 1984)

Regarding the emergence of dancing as something "legitimate" within *rock nacional*, he claimed:

Yo tenía tres libros y una foto del Ché.	I used to have three books and a photo of Ché [Guevara].

Ahora tengo mil años	Now I am a thousand years old,
y muy poco que hacer;	and I have very little to do;
vamo'a bailar.	let's dance.

("Rap del exilio," *Piano Bar*, 1985)

As if it were necessary to add something else, he pointed out the following about the resistance to the system that once characterized *rock nacional*:[19]

No voy en tren, voy en avión,	I don't travel by train, I travel by plane,
no necesito nadie alrededor.	I don't need anybody around me.

("No voy en tren," *Parte de la religión*, 1987)

or

Yo no quiero vestirme de rojo,	I don't want to dress myself in red clothes,
yo no quiero volverme tan loco,	I don't want to become so crazy,
yo no quiero esta pena en mi corazón.	I don't want this pain in my heart.

("Yo no quiero volverme tan loco," *Charly García*, 1983)

This positioning, and that of the *rock nacional* variants that appeared at the time, defines the point of contrast and departure from which *rock chabón* constructed its own musical style. There were, of course, other tributaries, but these variants played a key role for at least two reasons. First, they were an integral part of the *rock nacional* historical-cultural field. Second, they succeeded in shattering what then appeared to be a unanimous consensus about the fundamental characteristics and meanings of the genre. At the same time, Charly García posed some of the issues that most influenced the character of *rock chabón*'s own response to traditional *rock nacional* content. In this way, our analysis reveals rock as a mixture of modernity and militancy, and that some rockers responded with a modern style that poses a minimal response to a (real or supposed) grand narrative crisis. Synthesizing the spirit of the 1980s, Charly García wrote:

Si me gustan las canciones de amor y	If I like love songs and
me gustan esos raros peinados nuevos,	those weird new hair styles,
ya no quiero criticar,	I don't want to criticize any longer,
sólo quiero ser un enfermero. . . .	I only want to be a nurse. . . .
Si luchaste por un mundo mejor	If you struggled for a better world
y te gustan esos raros peinados nuevos,	and like those weird new hair styles,
no quiero ver al doctor,	I don't want to see the doctor,
solo quiero ver al enfermero.	I only want to see the nurse.

("Raros peinados nuevos," *Piano Bar*, 1985)

In time, a different proposal emerged as a counterpoise to this "modern" rock version expressed by García, one with its own rereading of both Argentinean social reality and *rock nacional*'s history and position regarding it. This new proposal was different and more traditional than García's and, in a very specific way, also contested the status quo: *rock chabón*.

Rock Chabón as the Rock of the Outskirts

One of the main characteristics of this new type of rock is its *suburbial* or outskirts character. This statement by La Pandilla del Punto Muerto underscores the relationship:

> We are the sad unemployed who use music as a medium to transmit our ideas. In songs like "Requiem porteño" we denounce the "disguised *conchetos*" or "the kids sleeping under the bridges" . . . *our idea of struggle has nothing to do with the confrontational ways of La Torre, speaking about* Madres de la Plaza de Mayo. . . . , *We prefer to hear Discépolo* [one of the most important tango songwriters of the 1930s and '40s], *who speaks about little cafés and Pompeya* [a working class neighborhood], *instead of the great bourgeois rock bands*. (1987) [Emphasis added]

With this declaration of principle, the band pointed out two things simultaneously: first, a very specific definition of its music and lyric tastes; second, a particular critical stance regarding "the system." We will consider only the first issue in this article, because it deals with the assumption and rereading of the familiar popular neighborhood as a site of social belonging.[20]

Rock chabón lyrics make continuous references to the *barrio* ("neighborhood") as the privileged locale of the social actor. These references are expressed in different ways. First, at an obvious level of signification, we encounter repeated geographical references in the songs. Secondly, those allusions are directed to at least two interrelated themes, that is, the appraisal of the neighborhood in itself, and the presentation of a valued social existence anchored in the neighborhood.

Therefore, the "tool box" of expressive resources utilized by *rock chabón* includes particular forms of language that have their origin in the popular neighborhood. The most significant of these are frequent references to tango and the use of Lunfardo (the Argentinean argot associated with the inhabitants of the poor neighborhoods).[21] Moreover, song lyrics refer to the traditions or practices of the popular sectors, anchored in the neighborhood, to account for a very specific ambience. These practices include socializing in the streets or among a group of peers (*una barra de amigos*), street fighting, and alcohol consumption (cheap wine and, lately, beer), all typical neighborhood group rites. These kinds of traditions end up signifying the neighborhood itself. However, those practices have, simultaneously, relations of continuity and discontinuity with the neighborhood tradition to which they appeal as their source. All this redefines the neighborhood itself.

Most of these songs not only talk about the everyday lives of many young people in the poor suburbs of the big Argentinean cities, above all Buenos Aires, but also about the *rock chabón* circuit itself, a circuit that at once represents and symbolically constructs its constituency. The lifeworld of the young people who follow *rock chabón* is constantly mentioned in the genre's lyrics, connoting the neighborhood as both a place that differs from, but also belongs to, the city. In the spontaneous sociology of many of *rock chabón*'s lyrics, the neighborhood is a contradictory product of the city's life cycle.

On the one hand, the poor neighborhood is the locale that includes those affected by the redefinition of the city in contemporary Argentina.[22] The popular neighborhood becomes the collective entity that encompasses, imaginarily, diverse actors who inhabit it in the present or the past, like those actors who lived there before the process of industrialization. These include *guapos* ("tough guys") of the original tango, the "survivors" of the industrialization process of the 1930s, and the more contemporary social actors who underwent the deindustrialization process of the 1970s and the major urban changes of the last fifteen years. This all-encompassing popular neighborhood of the songs is what gives refuge to those who, in the middle of all those processes (identity-construction processes included, of which *rock chabón* is one), identify themselves with, or articulate a lineage of, wretchedness. *Rock chabón* is neither the rock of the winners nor of the city's owners, but rather the rock of the young victims of a violent, abrupt, and traumatic societal restructuring.

On the other hand, in *rock chabón*'s lyrics (and in the everyday experience that those songs reflect and constitute) the popular neighborhood is the site of a type of life that has its own values, emotions, and specific rules. It is precisely here where one can feel the presence of a tango matrix that, although *rock chabón* does not usually reflect a tango influence, has a prominent place in the construction of the descriptions/prescriptions we will clarify below. *Rock chabón* employs a quasi-*tanguero* approach to the neighborhood thematic, not because the musical envelope follows tango's "meter," but because it thematizes the neighborhood in a *tanguero* "key."

In this manner, the neighborhood and *lo barrial* ("life in the popular neighborhood") constantly appear in *rock chabón*'s lyrics, which idealize, criticize, or simply reveal the lifeworld that makes them possible. Both the neighborhood and its everyday life are represented in those songs by a series of recurrent themes that, moving constantly between the proclamation, the chronicle, and the identity narrative, evidence a sociocultural anchoring and social commentary.

For instance, drinking alcohol with the *grupo de la barra* ("peer group") is the object of unanimous approbation among the *rock chabón* bands that we analyze here. In fact, one author associates beer with his most profound feelings, as if he were dealing with a capricious woman:

Yo estoy enamorado de vos	I have been in love with you,
desde hace mucho tiempo.	for a very long time.
Me gusta tu cuerpo esbelto,	I love your elegant body,
pero más me gusta lo de adentro.	but I love much more the inside.
Muchas veces me di vuelta por vos	Many times *me di vuelta por vos* [literally "I turned around because of you," but in this context meaning "I got drunk because of you"],
y muchas más dadas vueltas yo tendré.	and many more *dadas vueltas* I will have.
Siempre te he sido fiel,	I've always been faithful to you,
pero vos conmigo no lo sos.	but you are not faithful to me.
Cerveza yo te quiero,	Beer, I love you,
Cerveza yo te adoro.	Beer, I adore you.

(Dos Minutos, "Canción de amor," *Valentín Alsina*, 1994)

Making alcohol consumption a positive experience refers to a rite of passage: to drink alcohol is to abandon childhood, and it symbolizes opposition to the regulated spaces and times of school and work. Simultaneously, because the bottle circulates from hand to hand, it seals a common bond inspired by the lifeworld of the *varones* (another expression for "tough guys") of tango. Another song by Iorio makes this quite apparent:

Cervezas en la esquina	Beer on the street corner
del barrio varón,	of the tough-guy neighborhood,
rutina sin malicia,	routine without malice,
que guarda la razón.	which preserves reason.
Quien olvidó las horas de juventud,	The one who forgot the time of his youth,
murmurando se queja	mumbles complaints
ante esa actitud.	about this attitude.
Allí me esperan,	There they wait for me,
mis amigos en reunión,	my friends in a gathering;
mucho me alegra sentirme parte de vos.	I really like feeling I am a part of you.
Conversando la rueda ya se formó,	While talking, the clique was already formed,
y las flores se queman buscando un sentido,	and the flowers are burned looking for a meaning,
mientras la noche muestra	while the night shows

la calle en quietud,	the quiet street,
la intuición esquinera	the street-corner intuition
encendió mi luz,	kindled my light,
tu risa alejó mi soledad,	your smile moved away my solitude,
esos momentos que viví,	those moments I've lived,
no los he de olvidar.	I am not going to forget.
se que muchos cavilan,	I know that many people ruminate,
buscando el por qué	trying to understand why
preferimos la esquina	we prefer the street corner
y no mirar la tele.	and not watching television.
Yo la creo vacía de realidad,	I believe TV is empty of reality,
la verdad en la esquina está latiendo;	the truth is throbbing in the street corner;
aunque me corran hoy,	if they move me away by force today,
mañana volveré,	tomorrow I will come back,
y con cerveza festejaré	and I will celebrate with beer.
Tu risa alejó mi soledad,	Your smile moved away my solitude,
esos momentos que viví,	those moments that I've lived,
no los he de olvidar.	I am not going to forget.

("En la esquina," *Hermética*, 1990)

In a direct line of filiation with the most traditional tango poetics (present in the recurrent use of phrases like "the tough-guy neighborhood" and "street-corner intuition"), these lyrics portray a key institution in the everyday sociality of the popular sectors' young people: *la barra*. In this way, the peer group, the street-corner gang, the group of friends is one of the privileged subjects of *rock chabón* narratives. Consisting mostly of young males, it is the site for conversation, alcohol rites, and any type of physical confrontation. The street gang is a nomadic group that disputes territorial dominance with other such gangs, as well as with the police. This results in one of the most important subjects of the sociological narratives of many of the popular sectors' young people: theirs is a world of street gangs that oppose power institutions. Alongside the gang, the street has a privileged place in this song (and in the social imaginary that the song reflects and constitutes). Much more than a territory, the street is a symbol of truth, because in the song it is displayed as the opposite of the cold and untruthful world represented by television.

The overlapping of gang, beer, and street is present in another song that also anticipates an associated issue: the symbolic register of violence:

Estás en el kiosco,	You are in the *kiosko*, [small neighborhood store],
tomás una cerveza.	you drink a beer.
Corre el tiempo, seguís con	Time goes by, [and] you continue with

la cerveza.	the beer.
A lo lejos se ve una patrulla,	Far away you can see a police car, [and]
alguien grita: "Allá viene la yuta [policía].	somebody shouts: "There they come, the cops.
Descarten los tubos [botellas];	Throw away the bottles;
empiecen a correr."	start running."
La yuta está muy cerca;	The cops are very close;
no da para correr.	there is no time to run.

(Dos Minutos, "Demasiado tarde," *Valentín Alsina*, 1994)

These lyrics describe and idealize a world of guns, theft, police, and violence. Let us consider some examples. The first relates to the street-fight scenario. The occupation of the street, the antagonism between groups of young people, entails the capacity both to mete out and become the object of violence. This flows naturally from the dispute between gangs over "turf." The various gangs are distinguished from one another by their neighborhood of residence, musical preferences (to which they attach a string of different attributes), and even their soccer affiliation. Many times the fights, as shown in the song "Pelea callejera" ("Street Fight"), start for "no reason," perhaps because two gangs entered the same physical space at the same time:

Una banda venía por la calle	A gang came across the street,
y la otra por la vereda.	and the other one walked along the sidewalk.
Uno de ellos boqueó	One of them said something to the others,
y la pelea se armó.	and the fight started.
Relucían las cadenas,	Chains glittered, [chains are a common gang weapon in Argentina]
relucían las navajas,	knives shone,
un disparo de una .22	a shot from a .22
en el lugar se escuchó.	was heard there.

(Dos Minutos, "Pelea callejera," *Valentín Alsina*, 1994)

Guns and other weapons occupy a prominent place here. However, they do not refer to dangerous men or rejected objects (as happened with the hippie culture), but to the basic survival equipment of the man on the fringes. Either in marginal or central places, weapons of different kinds are a constant and naturalized presence in the everyday lifeworld of *rock chabón*'s constituency. With the advent of *rock chabón*, weapons (their exhibition, thematization, and use), a constant in other cultural products of this

Argentinean social sector, have been incorporated into rock, a genre that used to marginalize them.

Another important issue that points to the presence of the popular neighborhood and its sociocultural ambience in *rock chabón*'s thematic is the police and the opposition to their presence. Much more than the figures of the "state" or "capitalism," or any other entity derived from them, to *rock chabón*'s public and performers the "police" evoke all of their enemies *en masse*: the social system and its money imperatives; the constant surveillance of their everyday life; limited access to objects of desire; and the archenemy that threatens their lives.[23] The police presence is evoked not only in the lyrics, but also in the customs of the young people who attend rock concerts. Thus, very often rock concerts start, almost ritually, with chants sung by the public dedicated to the police. At the same time, most concerts close, again almost ritually, with displays of police force that usually produce dozens of detainees. The three elements we have discussed so far in this section—street fights, weapons, and despising the police—appear paradigmatically together in a Dos Minutos song. (The name of the band itself is an allusion to the common police expression "*dos minutos de advertencia*"—"you have two minutes to move or to stop what you were doing"):

Carlos se vendió al barrio de Lanús,	Carlos sold out to the Lanús neighborhood,
el barrio que lo vió crecer;	to the neighborhood where he was born;
ya no vino nunca más	he never returned
por el bar de Fabián	to Fabián's bar,
y se olvidó de pelearse	and he forgot to fight,
los domingos en la cancha.	Sunday afternoons, in the soccer stadium.
Por las noches patrulla la ciudad	During the nights he patrols the city,
molestando y levantando a los demás.	molesting and incarcerating other people.
Ya no sos igual,	You are not the same,
ya no sos igual.	you are not the same.
Sos un vigilante de la Federal [Policía Federal]	You are a federal cop,
sos buchón [alcahuete],	you are a whistle-blower,
sos buchón.	you are a whistle-blower.
Carlos se dejó crecer el bigote	Carlos grew a moustache,
y tiene una nueve para él.	and has a 9mm on him.
Ya no vino nunca más	He never returned here,
por el bar de Fabián	to Fabián's bar,
y se olvidó de pelearse	and he forgot to fight,

los domingos en la cancha.	Sunday afternoons, in the soccer stadium.
El sabe muy bien que una bala,	He knows pretty well that a bullet,
en la noche, en la calle, espera	during the night, in the street, is waiting
por él.	for him.

("Ya no sos igual," *Valentín Alsina*, 1994)

In this song, the neighborhood affiliation also appears as the positive identity the protagonist abandons, earning him the negative identity of "being a cop." Regarding *rock chabón*'s continuous reference to weapons, the lyrics state: "and he has a 9mm pistol for himself." Why is it so important to point out that now Carlos, the cop, has a 9mm pistol for his personal use? Because with this phrase the author of the song stresses an obvious aspect of the suburban young people's culture, where "we" implies the collective ownership of weapons. Moreover, the sharing of weapons is opposed to two other possible relationships, that is, guns as private property on the one hand, and guns as state monopoly on the other: "Carlos has a gun and he doesn't lend it."[24] This reference to the collective ownership of guns, instead of responding to a kind of revolutionary logic, refers to a very peculiar presence of guns in the everyday life of certain Argentinean social groups nowadays. Guns appear naturalized, at the same level of any other implement in the everyday toolbox of these young people, like the hammer, trowel, or facing tool used by their proletarian bricklayer fathers.

A fourth image that appears prominently in *rock chabón*'s lyrics is theft. In most cases, the reference is either naturalizing, justificatory, or both. This is exemplified by one of Patricio Rey y sus Redonditos de Ricota's songs:

Si esta cárcel sigue así,	If this jail continues like this,
todo preso es político.	every inmate is a political prisoner.
. . . obligados a escapar,	. . . forced to escape,
somos presos políticos.	we are political prisoners.
Reos de la propiedad, los esclavos políticos.	Prisoners of property, the political slaves.
Si esta cárcel sigue así,	If this jail continues like this,
todo preso es político.	every inmate is a political prisoner.

("Todo preso es político," *Un baión para el ojo idiota*, 1985)

Another song, this time by Divididos, appears less involved with "anti-private property" connotations and attempts to show how robbing (as the legitimate use for a .38-caliber revolver) can be a "normal" alternative to a Saturday-night get-together.

No eran más de seis	There were no more than six,
y uno dijo "ya."	and someone said "right now."

Bailaron ropa, ropa,	They dance *ropa, ropa,*
	[referring to the gang's burglarizing a
	clothing store and stealing clothes],
salieron a saquear.	they went out to rob.
Acariciando lo áspero el sábado pide	Fondling roughness, Saturday asks
por un precio.	for a price.

("Sábado," *Acariciando lo áspero*, 1991)

These lyrics are only few examples of a vast array of songs whose thematic is very similar. That is, they describe, reflect, make sense, and help in the construction of the meaning that thousands of young people who consider *rock chabón* "their" music attach to their everyday-life practices. At the turn of the century, this is an everyday life that, as a result of the unmerciful economic adjustment that Argentina has undergone in the last fifteen years, has a component of violence novel in the history of Argentinean popular sectors.

Rock Chabón and Rereading History

On the basis of this analysis, we believe that *rock chabón* is a musical practice that aids in the construction of an identity one could label "an excluded/marginalized young person of the popular sectors." *Rock chabón* accomplishes this through the different alliances those young people establish between their diverse imagined narrative identities (that have much to do with their re-reading of post-populist Argentina) and the imaginary essential identities *rock chabón* manifests in its musical practices (that also relate to an important rereading of both Peronism and the history of young people's music in Argentina).

In this sense, the musical meanings and significations *rock chabón* treats (through its lyrics—the only object of analysis here—its music and performances) produce in the popular sectors' young people the conviction that "in the real world out there" some essential identity exists of a "young person of the popular sectors who does not have a place in the neoliberal, post-populist Argentinean political project." (They consider this their "essential" identity, something that, by definition, is always a fiction.) This imaginary effect is a result of the fact that these youth experience *rock chabón* as something that acts materially upon their bodies through specific mechanisms of identification and recognition. This in turn results from the intimate interaction between musicians and public, and among the public itself, through the identifying mechanisms that construct those who are *del palo* (of the same group, band, or subgenre, as the case may be).

Musical performativity in general, and *rock chabón* performativity in particular, is a type of discourse that, through a process of repetition and its inscription on the body, has the capacity to produce what it signifies. It is precisely for this reason that *rock chabón* does not "reflect" a previously constituted social actor, but, on the contrary, offers one of the most important discourses in helping to constitute this actor. Anchoring a supposedly essential identity in the physical body, it gives to this cultural construction some sense of reality that other types of discourse cannot offer.

Notes

1. According to Jacques Lacan, the "imaginary" (as a noun) is a dimension of our relationship with the world by which we apprehend the real, a dimension that is lost forever because it is always framed by the symbolic, i.e., by the codes of a culture that names and orders it. Moreover, the three dimensions of imaginary, real, and symbolic are always articulated and present simultaneously.

2. Pablo Alabarces, talking about a very similar actor, defines these types of young people as an interpretive community that "defies the disciplinary spaces" and would constitute itself as the neoliberal agenda's alternative (1995, 20).

3. A report from the *Encuesta Permanente de Hogares* made by the Instituto Nacional de Estadísticas y Censos gives a succinct illustration of the situation faced by these young people. Between October 1990 and October 1999, the unemployment rate increased from 6 percent to 16 percent. If we combine the unemployment rate with the underemployment one, the number jumps to 30 percent, and of course, that number is still higher for poor people. The concentration of wealth (the transfer of income from the poorer sectors of society to those more powerful) shows very eloquent variations. In 1980, 30 percent of the poorest families who lived in the Greater Buenos Aires shared 11.4 percent of the total income, while 10 percent of the richest ones appropriated 29.1 percent of that income. In 1997, those figures were 7.7 percent and 36.7 percent, respectively. According to a recent study by UNICEF, there are 205,000 lower-class adolescents in Argentina who neither study nor work, of whom 90,000 live in the Greater Buenos Aires (*Página 12*, February 8, 1999).

4. It is quite common for these young people to follow their bands wherever they perform, no matter how far the concert is from Buenos Aires.

5. Quoted by Fernando D'Addario, *Página 12*, October 4, 1998.

6. Ibid.

7. This particular scheme of musical perception allows, for instance, "acceptance" as a part of the subgenre of groups that only marginally cultivate the key elements of the genre, like Las Pelotas and Los Pericos.

8. Groups like Dos Minutos, Attaque 77, Flema, or Superuva (to name only some of the most important ones) are formed by young people who, due to their social origins, break with a constant that (with some exceptions such as Pappo and Vox Dei) has characterized *rock nacional* from its beginnings: middle-class musicians were the performers of the popular sectors' music. During the movement's beginnings, this role was played by Manal, Pescado Rabioso, and the different incarnations of Riff (taking into account, however, that Riff's leader was Pappo, himself a member of the popular sectors, but not the other members of the band). In the 1980s, the same role was played by Sumo and Patricio Rey y sus Redonditos de Ricota. Nowadays, Divididos, Los Caballeros de la Quema, and Los Fabulosos

Cadillacs continue the tradition. It is precisely because of this tradition that *rock chabón* inaugurates, in a more or less mass-mediated way, the presence of popular-sectors musicians making songs for a public very similar to themselves in socioeconomic terms.

9. This description does not apply to Sumo. The group does not exist any longer, and the class bias we are referring to is manifested in the type of public that continues to buy and listen to its records.

10. According to the annual polls conducted by *Página 12* and *Clarín* between 1987 and 1995.

11. The notion of "interpellation" was introduced by Althusser in his "Ideological State Apparatuses" essay (1971). According to Althusser, "ideology 'acts' or 'functions' in such a way that it 'recruits' subjects among the individuals (it recruits them all), or 'transforms' the individuals into subjects (it transforms them all) by that very precise operation which I have called interpellation or hailing, and which can be imagined along the lines of the most commonplace everyday police (or other) hailing: 'Hey, you there!'" (162–63).

12. Some of the most important mutations that occurred in the last fifteen years or so are the heterogenization and fragmentation of Argentinean society (Nun and Portantiero 1987). By this we mean all the phenomena related to the decrease in the numbers of salaried industrial workers and the increase in the numbers of unskilled workers, as well as the increase in non-manual salaried work in general. This is the mutation that defines the implosion of the capitalist accumulation regime that privileges the internal market. This implosion occurred prominently during the 1980s. What also characterizes this economic change is the extension of work-salaried relations to the interior of the middle classes, while the entrepreneurial sectors of those classes reduced their participation in the economy. At the same time, the popular sectors diminished their participation in the labor force due to the passage of many workers from the industrial sector to the salaried service sector. Moreover, within the popular sectors the number of salaried workers decreased and the number of self-employed increased. Among the middle classes the precariousness of employment increased as well. Upon this base of a weak-salaried condition and generalized self-employment appears what we can term the "new poor" and the general pauperization of the 1990s. This is characterized by an incredible increase in unemployment, moving from the historical figure of 5 percent to an astonishing 20 percent.

13. The term *conchetito* is sarcastically used in *rock nacional* to identify upper-middle-class young people.

14. The author's key idea is the concept of affective investments: "The rock and roll apparatus affectively organizes the everyday life of its fans by differentially cathecting the various fragments it 'excorporates' along . . . three axes (youth as difference; pleasure of the body; post-modernity). The result is that it locates, for its fans, the possibilities of intervention and pleasure. It involves the investment of desire in the material world according to vectors which are removed from the hegemonic affective formation. . . . The affective investments of the rock and roll apparatus empower its audiences with strategies which . . . define a level of potential opposition and often, survival" (Grossberg 1984, 240).

15. "The point I am making is that the central tension of rock—it is a source of pleasure that is both disturbing and relaxing—is not just the effect of the struggle

between record companies and artists or audiences. The tension is also contained within the industry, within the audience, within the musicians, within the music itself" (Frith 1981, 268).

16. "Daniel," *Cantarock*'s letters to the editor, 1987.
17. "Esteban," *Cantarock*'s letters to the editor, 1987.
18. When we refer to the "social situation of youth," we are not referring to some kind of "objective" or "pre-discursive" social position, but to the perception that young people themselves have about their social position at any given time, as summarized by the hegemonic common sense of a particular epoch. That common sense, of course, is the result of a previous discursive struggle over meaning in which one version of reality has provisionally crystallized itself as "natural" or "given." It is precisely in relation to such a provisional crystallization of meaning that the counter-hegemonic interpellations and narratives direct their contesting action.
19. From a classic rocker perspective, the "system" means the existing social order. It can have (cumulatively or alternatively, depending on the context) the following connotations: capitalism, dictatorship, bureaucracy, cultural industry, war, etc.
20. Argentina in general (and Buenos Aires in particular) was characterized for many years by the existence of a very intense and complex neighborhood social life, especially in the case of popular-sectors neighborhoods. In that regard, most of the social relationships people were engaged in beyond their working activities were organized on a neighborhood basis. Therefore, the sport club, local bar, street-corner group, neighborhood theater, library, and *sociedades de fomento* (pro-neighborhood, grass-roots organizations and social clubs) were some of the many institutions that organized everyday life in the different popular-sectors neighborhoods of the city.
21. Tango was the epitome of neighborhood music for many years.
22. Regarding this issue we follow and summarize the most important conclusions pointed out by some of the principal analysts of Argentina's social structure. Among the valuable books written on the issue, we have found two particularly helpful texts, Minujín and Kessler (1995) and Nun and Portantiero (1987).
23. Much more than in the past, Argentina's society has witnessed in recent years a very important increase in police violence, in which young people are shot or even kidnapped and directly executed by the police. (Centro de Estudios Legales y Sociales, "Informe sobre la actuación de fuerzas de seguridad en la Argentina," February 1996).
24. In Argentina, as in most Latin American countries, the ownership of non-sportive weapons is a state monopoly.

References

Alabarces, Pablo. 1995. "Fútbol, droga y rock & roll." *Boletín de la Facultad de Ciencias Sociales de la Universidad de Buenos Aires* (November): 15.

Althusser, Louis. 1971. *Lenin and Philosophy and Other Essays*. New York: Monthly Review Press.

Frith, Simon. 1981. *Sound effects*. New York: Pantheon Books.

García, Charly. 1986. Clipping from *Clarín* (?).

Grossberg, Lawrence. 1984. "Rock and Roll and the Empowerment of Everyday Life." *Popular Music* 4: 225–58.

Halperín Donghi, Tulio. 1994. *La larga agonía de la Argentina peronista*. Buenos Aires: Ariel.

James, Daniel. 1990. *Resistencia e integración: el peronismo y la clase trabajadora Argentina, 1946–1976*. Buenos Aires: Editorial Sudamericana.

Jelín, Elizabeth. 1996a. "La matriz cultural Argentina, el Peronismo y la cotidianidad." In *Vida cotidiana y control institucional en la Argentina de los 90*. Edited by Elizabeth Jelín. Buenos Aires: Grupo Editor Latinoamericano, 25–40.

———. 1996b. "Imágenes sociales de la Justicia: algunas evidencias." In *Vida cotidiana y control institucional en la Argentina de los 90*. Edited by Elizabeth Jelín. Buenos Aires: Grupo Editor Latinoamericano, 117–36.

Kuasñosky, Silvina, and Dalia Szulik. 1994. "Los extraños de pelo largo. Vida cotidiana y consumos culturales." In *La cultura de la noche. La vida nocturna de los jóvenes en Buenos Aires*. Edited by Mario Margulis. Buenos Aires: Compañía Editora Espasa Calpe Argentina, 263–91.

La Pandilla del Punto Muerto. 1987. Clipping from *Cantarock* (?).

Martuccelli, Danilo, and Maristella Svampa. 1997. *La plaza vacía: las transformaciones del peronismo*. Buenos Aires: Losada.

Minujín, Alberto and Gabriel Kessler. 1995. *La nueva pobreza en la Argentina*. Buenos Aires: Ariel.

Nun, José, and Juan Carlos Portantiero. 1987. *Ensayos sobre la transición democrática en la Argentina*. Buenos Aires: Punto Sur.

Pollak, Michael. 1989. "Memoria, Esquecimento, Silencio." *Estudos Históricos* 2/3: 3–15.

Prodan, Luca (leader of Sumo). 1986. Clipping from *Clarín* or *Cantarock* (?).

Solari, Indio (leader of Patricio Rey y sus Redonditos de Ricota). 1985. Clipping from *Clarín* or *Cantarock* (?).

Torre, J. 1983. "La ciudad y los Obreros." In *Buenos Aires. Historia de cuatro siglos*. Vol. 2. Edited by José Luis Romero and Luis Alberto Romero. Buenos Aires: Editorial Abril.

Vila, Pablo. 1985. "Rock Nacional. Crónicas de la resistencia juvenil." In *Los nuevos movimientos sociales/1. Mujeres. Rock Nacional*. Edited by Elizabeth Jelín. Buenos Aires: Centro Editor de América Latina. Colección Biblioteca Política Argentina No. 124: 83–148.

———. 1987a. "*Rock nacional* and dictatorship in Argentina." *Popular Music* 6/2: 129–48.

———. 1987b. "Tango, folklore y rock: apuntes sobre música, política y sociedad en Argentina." *Cahiers du monde Hispanique et Luso-Brésilien (Caravelle)* 48: 81–93.

———. 1987c. "El rock, música contemporánea argentina." *Punto de Vista* 30: 23–29.

———. 1989. "Argentina's *Rock Nacional*: The Struggle for Meaning." *Latin American Music Review* 10/1: 1–28.

———. 1992. "*Rock nacional* and dictatorship in Argentina." In *Rockin' the Boat: Mass Music and Mass Movements*. Edited by Reebee Garofalo. Boston: South End Press, 209–29.

———. 1995. "El rock nacional: género musical y construcción de la identidad juvenil en Argentina." In *Cultura y pospolítica: El debate sobre la modernidad en América Latina*. Edited by Néstor García Canclini. México: Consejo Nacional para la Cultura y las Artes, 231–71.

———. Forthcoming. "A Social History of Thirty Years of Rock Nacional (1965–1995)." In *The Universe of Music: A History*. Edited by Malena Kuss. New York: Schirmer/Macmillan.

Virus. 1985. Clipping from *Clarín* or *Cantarock* (?).

Part II

Locality and Interlocality

North America and Cuba

5

Crossing Borders

Mexicana, Tejana, and Chicana Musicians in the United States and Mexico

John Koegel

Since 1848 and the Treaty of Guadalupe Hidalgo (which ended the Mexican-American War of 1846–1848) and the establishment of the boundary between the United States and Mexico, Spanish-speaking musicians have continuously crossed back and forth across the international border. They have also carried back and forth across the border folk-, popular-, and art-music styles and repertories that have enriched musical life in both the U.S. Southwest and Mexico. So, too, have they crossed the boundaries between the many manifestations of popular culture in the twentieth century: film, radio, television, recordings, concerts, musical theater, and print media. They have also moved between a "mainstream" English-speaking context and local Spanish-speaking culture in the Southwest (the area with the greatest concentration of Mexicans and Mexican Americans). While most of these musicians have been male, a number of women have made significant contributions to musical life on both sides of the border, especially in the realm of popular music. This article examines the careers of some of the most important mexicana (Mexican), tejana (Texas-Mexican), and chicana (Mexican-American) musicians of the twentieth century. It also examines the ways in which these women performers and their repertories have crossed both boundaries and borders.

The emphasis here on women's musical activities is meant to enrich the existing scholarly narrative and interpretation of Mexican and Mexican-

American musical life and to signal the important contributions of Mexican-American and Mexican women to popular song over the past century. While the contributions of a number of women musicians active in the public sphere on both sides of the border are examined here, two tejana musicians are especially featured: Lydia Mendoza and Selena Quintanilla. Their lives and careers demonstrate many of the issues and circumstances faced by other women musicians in Mexico and the United States. Therefore, they serve as both historical models and examples for the future.

Mexicana, Tejana, and Chicana Musicians

Mexico experienced great turbulence at the end of the *Porfiriato* (the government of Porfirio Díaz) in the early 1900s and during the Mexican Revolution (1910–1920). The anti-Catholic reforms under the presidency of Plutarco Elías Calles and the resulting Cristero revolt (1926–1929) also affected national life. This turmoil was directly reflected on the musical stage in overt and covert representations or insinuations of social and political injustices, upheavals, and events. A parade of Mexican presidents, generals, and other military, political, and social figures appeared on the musical stage in one guise or another: Porfirio Díaz, Venustiano Carranza, Francisco ("Pancho") Villa, Álvaro Obregón, and Plutarco Elías Calles. Interestingly, some of the most potentially subversive political and social commentary was inserted into song lyrics sung by the female leads, secondary female characters, and the chorus girls. This may have helped to diffuse the incendiary nature of the satire; it might also have served to intensify the explosive nature of the commentary. These subversive representations sporadically attracted the attention and ire of the changing governments during the 1910s and '20s, and sometimes resulted in fines, theater closures, arrests, jail sentences, and exile for musicians, actors, playwrights, librettists, and composers. Like the Broadway musical of the 1910s and '20s, the Mexican *revista* ("musical review") stressed the immediacy of the humor and songs, as well as the pulchritude and minimal clothing of the chorus girls and female principals. Like the Broadway review (especially the Ziegfeld Follies), the Mexican *revista* also sold sex. Unlike the Broadway review, however, the social and political commentary was often of a strong nature in the Mexican musical theater, and working-class sensibilities and concerns were addressed to a much greater extent.[1] The Mexican musical stage flourished during this time of relative freedom, and theatrical producers were willing to accept the risks involved in order to meet the audience's expectations. Thus musical theater helped serve as a form of social and political commentary and as an escape mechanism for pent-up resentment against social and political conditions and injustices. It also encouraged audiences to laugh at the foibles of human nature. Women musicians and actresses had a primary and crucial role to play in this theatrical environment.

Since the early twentieth century, mexicana, tejana, and chicana musicians have made recordings as vocal soloists and in vocal duets and trios, and as instrumentalists (guitarists, pianists, accordionists, violinists). They have performed the theatrical and popular songs current in Mexico, as well as local and regional Mexican-American musical forms, and various types of mainstream American popular music. They have also recorded opera arias, as well as zarzuela, operetta, and musical-theater songs. Almost all of the musical styles known in Mexico in the past century have also been known in the Southwest. They all appeared in one form or another on the Mexican musical stage. Various instrumental (male) styles popular along or near the U.S.-Mexico border are quite important today in the regional music scene in the United States: *conjunto* and *música norteña* (accordion-led ensembles) in Texas, and *banda* ("wind band") music from the northwestern state of Sinaloa and in California, for example. However, women's participation in these instrumental ensembles has been limited. Nevertheless, women have gained entry into this male-dominated musical world in recent years. A notable example is the all-female Mariachi Reyna de los Angeles, from Los Angeles.

Commercial recordings of popular music strongly reflect contemporary trends and fashions in musical repertories and genres, as well as singing and instrumental performance styles. This is especially true of the Mexican and Mexican-American musical scenes. Because the recording industry was first established in the United States and Europe and later spread to Latin America, commercial recordings of Mexican popular and classical music were first made in the United States. Firms such as Berliner, Zonophone, Bettini, and Edison released recordings of Latin American and Mexican music in the United States as early as the 1890s for the local and Latin American export markets. However, Mexican musicians apparently did not begin to record in Mexico until 1904, when the American Victor Company visited Mexico City on a recording expedition. Male vocal duets (with guitar accompaniment), such as Ábrego y Picazo and Rosales y Robinsón,[2] recording for the Victor Company in 1904,[3] were among the very first Mexican musicians to make recordings in Mexico. Though the history of the first commercial recordings made in Mexico is still generally undocumented, it is probable that male musicians were the first to make commercial recordings there.[4] Women made commercial recordings at a later date; however, noncommercial recordings of Mexican folk and popular songs were made in Los Angeles as early as 1904 by local chicana singers (Koegel 1998, 1999).

Ábrego and Picazo's recordings of 1904 and following years—as well as the later commercial recordings by mexicana musicians starting in the

1910s—are characterized by an easy shift between rural and urban singing styles. These recordings reflect the musical repertories performed by male and female musicians for working- and middle-class audiences in the *carpas* ("tent shows"), *tandas* (short variety shows), civic and church halls, and *teatros* ("theaters") throughout rural and urban areas in Mexico and the Hispanic Southwest during the first decades of the twentieth century. Since the duet repertory was immensely popular at the time, comic and theatrical songs, love songs, and song parodies were often performed and recorded in the popular duet style—with *primera* ("first") and *segunda* ("second") voices in parallel thirds and sixths—a hallmark of Mexican popular music.

A number of Mexican and Latin American women active in the overlapping fields of concert music, opera, zarzuela, operetta, musical theater, and popular music recorded for American companies in New York, in other centers of early recording activity in the United States, and in Mexico and Latin America after the turn of the century. For example, Cuban operatic soprano Rosalía Gertrudis de la Concepción Díaz de Herrera y Fonseca (1864–1948), whose stage name was Rosalía Chalía, was probably the first Cuban and one of the very first Latin American musicians to make recordings (Díaz Ayala 1994, 49–51, 297–303). She recorded more than 165 operatic arias as well as Spanish zarzuela songs and Latin American popular songs in New York, circa 1898/1899–1903, and again in 1912, for the Bettini, Zonophone, Victor, and Columbia labels (Spottswood 1990, 1759–63). Rosalía Chalía moved from Havana to New York in 1893, where she made her professional debut in 1894. She later embarked for Italy and returned to Cuba in 1896. Though she appeared elsewhere in opera, Chalía inexplicably appeared only once with the regular company at the Metropolitan Opera, as Santuzza in Mascagni's *Cavalleria rusticana*, on December 17, 1898. After the Spanish-American War, she was honored in 1900 for her efforts on behalf of Cuban independence. Chalía also performed in opera and operetta in Mexico, Italy, Spain, and Latin America (Olavarría y Ferrari 1961, vols. 3–5),[5] and was known for promoting Cuban compositions in her performances. Díaz Ayala asserts that she also made radio broadcasts with the Metropolitan Opera in 1925 (1994). She lived for many years in the United States, only returning permanently to Cuba to stay a few years before her death. As the first recorded Cuban musician, Rosalía Chalía was recently inducted into the Latin Music Hall of Fame.[6]

The very first Mexican-American musician—who was born and resided in the United States—to make commercial recordings was probably singer Eugenia Ferrer. Ferrer (also a pianist) recorded eighteen songs in New York for Emil Berliner (the inventor of the flat disc) in 1898 and 1899 (Koegel 1999, 2000). She was the daughter of the important San Francisco guitarist-composer Manuel Ferrer,[7] some of whose musical repertory she recorded, including the songs "Los lindos ojos" and "El jaleo de Jérez" (Spottswood 1990, 1869–70; Charosh 1995). These songs and instrumental pieces formed part of the large salon repertory of the late nineteenth century, which falls in between the art-music, musical-theater, and popular repertories. As with other "ethnic" recordings, Eugenia Ferrer's eighteen Berliner discs were recorded for the local Hispanic market as well as for Latin American record buyers. Proof of their success in Latin America is the interesting fact that in 1999, a century after their first release, a number of Ferrer's recordings turned up for sale in Uruguay on the Internet on eBay. They were sold to a collector in Argentina.[8]

Two of the most famous mexicana singers and actresses active during the first half of the twentieth century were known on both sides of the U.S.-Mexico border and throughout Latin America and Spain. Soprano Esperanza Iris (ca. 1881–1962; see fig. 5.1), in her day called the *Emperatriz de la opereta* ("Empress of Operetta"), was famous for her roles in European operetta (especially Viennese works) and Mexican zarzuela (notably Carlos Curti's *La cuarta plana* [1899]). She was also known for her pioneering status as one of Mexico's few major theatrical impresarias after whom theaters were named (actresses María Guerrero and Virginia Fábregas [1870–1950] were two others). The Teatro Esperanza Iris in Mexico City was built in her honor and inaugurated in 1918, with President Venustiano Carranza in attendance (Rico 1999; Zedillo Castillo 1989). Besides serving as a venue for Iris's own theatrical company, the Teatro Esperanza Iris hosted the most important Mexican and foreign musicians and performers, who appeared there in a variety of genres: opera, zarzuela, operetta, musical comedy, *revistas*, plays, concerts, musical acts, and other events. (It was later converted into a cinema; it presently operates as the Teatro de la Ciudad de México.) Iris also toured throughout Mexico, the United States, Spain, and Latin America with her operetta company. While in New York, Iris made ten recordings for Columbia Records, including excerpts from Curti's *La cuarta plana* and Leo Fall's 1907 operetta *La princesa del dólar* (*Die Dollarprinzessen*) (Spottswood 1990, 1984). She may have also made recordings of songs from zarzuelas and operettas in Mexico. Iris made a few films in Mexico during the 1930s, including *Mater Nostra* (1936) and *Noches de gloria* (1937). However, her greatest contribution to Mexican cultural life was the role she played as a major theater star and promoter.

Spanish-born singer, actress, and dancer María Conesa (1880s?–1978; see fig. 5.2), an important presence in Mexican and Hispanic-American popular culture for many decades, was known as *La gatita blanca* ("The White Kitty") after her first appearance in Mexico City in the popular zarzuela (by

Fig. 5.1. Esperanza Iris.

Vives and Giménez) of the same name in November 1907. Celebrated for her abilities as a dancer, comedienne, and singer of light music in musical reviews and zarzuela, La Conesa was also notorious for her risqué manner of acting and singing. Censorious critics such as Luis G. Urbina sniffed that she could read the *Our Father* and make it sound salacious.[9] Indeed, she was censured for obscenity on stage by government authorities on several occasions, including for her performances in *La gatita blanca*. She also periodically attracted the attention of governmental officials in the 1910s and '20s because of the political nature of some of the musical reviews in which she appeared. However, such attention only served to heighten public interest in her stage appearances and increase box-office revenue. While in New York sometime between 1907 and 1909, Conesa recorded songs from her smash hit *La gatita blanca*, as well as couplets from theatrical pieces and Mexican zarzuela songs (Spottswood 1990, 1785–86). In this way her most popular songs were made available to city dwellers as well as to those in the provinces who could not travel to the capital or other cities to see and hear her in person. While in New York in 1917, María Conesa took part in an early and strange attempt at a musical film. George R. Webb, for his Webb Singing Pictures, directed a number of actors and singers, including Conesa and opera singer Giuseppe Campanari, who agreed to be filmed. Other musicians and singers, performing behind a screen, pretended to represent those appearing on the screen. Enrico Caruso reportedly sang behind the screen but did not appear on film.[10] Conesa's amazing longevity as a major participant in Mexican popular culture over at least five decades (stage, screen, recordings, personal appearances) was matched by few other performers (Alonso 1987; María y Campos 1996; Dallal 1995; *El país de las tandas* 1984; Olavarría y Ferrari 1961, vol. 5; *Del rancho al Bataclán* 1984).

Another mexicana to make recordings in New York early in the century was soprano Carmen García Cornejo, who performed in opera and concerts on both sides of the border.[11] García Cornejo recorded a series of Mexican songs by composers such as Manuel M. Ponce and Miguel Lerdo de Tejada in New York in 1917. These songs, while part of the popular repertory, also cross the boundaries separating art song, popular song, and folk music. The celebrated composer, pianist, and conductor Miguel Lerdo de Tejada (1869–1941) accompanied García Cornejo on the piano on her 1917 recordings. During these sessions, they recorded his songs "Sin tí," "Asómate a la ventana," and "Perjura" (perhaps his best-known song), as well as Ponce's "A la orilla de un palmar" and "Estrellita," an evergreen standard (Spottswood 1990, 1896–97). Both "Perjura" and "Estrellita" were well known in Mexico, the United States, Europe, and Latin America, and achieved a canonic status in the popular "light classical" repertory. They

Fig. 5.2. María Conesa.

were also part of a core group of Spanish-language songs well known to English-speaking audiences from the 1920s through the '50s in concert, film, and radio performances, and on recordings. They are performed and recorded today by Spanish and Latin American opera singers for their cross-over albums (e.g., Plácido Domingo and José Carreras).

The *canciones románticas* ("romantic songs") García Cornejo performed in public and recorded with Lerdo de Tejada in 1917 are similar in musical style and poetic sentiment to those published in New York in 1919 in the collection *Canciones mexicanas*.[12] This collection was an attempt by García Cornejo and her musical arranger Guillermo A. Posadas to enter the rough-and-tumble music-publishing world of Tin Pan Alley.[13] While its primary intended audience was probably the Spanish-speaking community in the United States, García Cornejo and Posadas may have hoped that *Canciones mexicanas* would also reach the English-language sheet-music buyer. Unfortunately, García Cornejo's later musical activities are somewhat obscure.

Female duet singing has long been an important aspect of Mexican popular music, and many female duets were professionally active in Mexico and the U.S. Southwest from the 1920s through the '70s. Las Hermanas Padilla are considered to have been the first really to popularize the form on both sides of the border (though other groups such as Las Hermanas Águila sang in this style at an earlier date). Known as the Mexican Andrew Sisters, Las Hermanas Padilla—Margarita and María, born in Tanhuato, Michoacán—got their start by singing on Spanish-language radio in Los Angeles in the mid-1930s, appearing alongside such performers as Los Madrugadores (led by Pedro J. González, 1896–1995), comic singers Chicho y Chenco (Narciso Farfán and Crescencio Cuevas), and baritone Rodolfo de Hoyos (1896–1980). They began a recording career in 1937 that would last several decades, recording many Mexican songs in Los Angeles and New York between 1937 and 1942 for the Vocalion, Okeh, and Columbia labels, and later for RCA Victor, Discos Azteca, and Discos Imperial. They were often accompanied on their 1930s recordings by the orchestra of Manuel S. Acuña, a prominent musician active in the Mexican music scene in Los Angeles (Spottswood 1990, 1769–80).

Las Hermanas Padilla performed their extensive repertory, encompassing *corridos*—then somewhat rare for women singers—and almost all the other popular song types of their day, on the radio, in theaters and night-clubs, and in other venues in the United States, Mexico, and Latin America. They were quite successful in all of their musical endeavors, and over a period of time learned to assert themselves in dealing with managers, booking agents, and record-company officials in order to best represent their financial and personal interests. Their performing activities decreased with their marriages in the mid-1940s, Margarita to Mexican songwriter Victor Cordero in 1945 (the author of the famous *corrido* "Juan Charrasqueado"), and María to mariachi musician Memo Quintero. Margarita eventually moved to Mexico City, while her sister María stayed in Southern California. Their recordings are still appreciated in Mexico and the United States, and several compilation compact discs have been released in recent years. Las Hermanas Padilla were followed by many other female duets, including Las Hermanas Mendoza and Carmen y Laura (see below).[14]

The style made popular by these and other female duets on both sides of the border before and after World War II was mirrored in the 1970s by the well-known Mexican duet Las Jilguerillas. This duo exemplifies the standard Mexican and Mexican-American duet style and repertory: equal *primera* and *segunda* voices, blended vocal sonorities, melodies sung in parallel thirds and sixths, and an emphasis on comic and romantic repertory (from both the male and female perspectives). The continued popularity of groups such as Las Jilguerillas (their recordings are frequently played on Mexican radio today) and Las Hermanas Padilla demonstrates the continued viability of this sound ideal in Mexican and Mexican-American popular music.

The activities of the (male) record producers and promoters of the early Spanish-language record labels in the United States were very important in the development of the Mexican-American popular music scene. The mainstream American record labels (RCA Victor, Columbia) stopped recording Mexican-American music during the early 1940s, because of World War II and the union-led ban on commercial recording. However, at the end of the war, and after the lifting of the recording ban in the mid-1940s, these companies did not resume recording Mexican-American popular music for some time.

As a result, entrepreneurs such as Armando Marroquín (1912–1990), frustrated by the lack of interest shown by the major record labels, took matters in their own hands and established record companies to supply recordings for the juke-box business. Marroquín literally started making recordings in the family kitchen, later moving his activities to more suitable quarters. The recording success of the duet of Carmen y Laura (Marroquín's wife and sister-in-law) attracted the interest of record distributor Paco Betancourt. Together Marroquín and Betancourt founded Discos Ideal, in Alice, Texas. Discos Ideal issued a series of recordings, circa 1946–1958, by such important Texas-Mexican performers as Paulino Bernal, Narciso Martínez, Chelo Silva, Valerio Longoria, Carmen y Laura, and others.

The sisters Carmen (b. 1921) and Laura Hernández (b. 1926), the duo of Carmen y Laura, recorded with some of the most important Texas musicians, including accordionists Narciso Martínez and Paulino Bernal, and orchestra leader Beto Villa, exponents of both the *conjunto* and the *orquesta* ("dance band") styles. Marroquín backed Carmen y Laura as well as other female singers with various *conjuntos, orquestas,* and mariachis in order to reach out to both working- and middle-class record buyers. Marroquín knew that middle-class tejanos favored the *orquesta,* partly because of their social aspirations, while the working class generally preferred the indigenous *conjunto* in a reaction against the perception of the *orquesta* as *jaitón* ("high-tone") (Peña 1985a, 1985b, 1999a, 1999b).

During the 1950s, one of the most popular singers in the U.S. Southwest and northern Mexico was Chelo Silva (Consuelo Silva, 1922–1988), whose deep and sultry renditions of Mexican boleros were highly appreciated. Along with Lydia Mendoza—and later Selena—Chelo Silva was one of the most important of all tejana solo singers. She got her start in the music business performing in her hometown of Brownsville, Texas, and later in other areas of South Texas and along the U.S.-Mexico border. Her fame gradually spread through radio performances, some with singer and guitarist Américo Paredes (for a time her husband). After a hiatus from singing in the late 1940s, she resumed her career in the 1950s, rising to the top of the profession within a few years. The record contract she signed with Columbia Records in 1955 assured a greater distribution for her recordings, and increased her personal fame and popularity, as her recordings were sold throughout the Southwest, Mexico, and in Latin America. She also recorded for Discos Falcón and Discos Ideal in Texas. Appearing on both sides of the border well into the 1970s, she performed with such popular luminaries as singers Javier Solís, Lola Beltrán, José Alfredo Jiménez (also famous as a songwriter), and orchestra leader Xavier Cugat.[15] In 1994, Chelo Silva's son Leslie Pérez summed up the public's identification with his mother: "The public could feel what she was going through with my dad [Leopoldo Pérez Morales] . . . the problems, and in reality what all the other Mexicans were going through and the people could relate to that."[16] Unlike many of the other women musicians of her generation, Chelo Silva frequently sang songs, including boleros, from a female perspective—a rare practice until at least the 1960s—though most of the authors of her songs were male.

Tejano, or *música tejana,* the general term for contemporary Texas-Mexican popular music, encompasses many earlier and present-day musical styles to create a hybrid mix: polka, *ranchera,* blues, rock, jazz, *cumbia,* and so forth. The hybrid status of contemporary tejano music is reflected in the various awards given during the annual Tejano Music Awards ceremony, sponsored by the Texas Talent Musicians Association since 1980, and held in the Alamodome in San Antonio. For example, some of the categories include awards for Tejano Norteño, Tejano Crossover, and Tejano

Country.[17] Tejana/o musicians active in the 1980s and '90s sang retrospective styles such as *rancheras* and boleros, with the backup of varied instrumental groups, as well as contemporary styles popular in Mexico, the Caribbean, and Latin America (*cumbias*). The singers Selena and Laura Canales are good examples of this trend. Canales (b. 1954), dubbed *La reina de la onda chicano* ("The Queen of the Tejano Wave"), performed in a flourishing tejano music scene during the 1970s and '80s as part of Laura Canales and Encanto (Burr 1999, 71–72). Before Selena arrived in the tejano music world in a strong way in the late 1980s, Laura Canales was one of the most important tejana singers. Her success was validated by four consecutive Tejano Music Awards for Best Female Performer (1982–1985).

Tejana musician Eva Araiza Ybarra (b. ca. 1958; see fig.5.3) has had a successful career as a solo accordionist and leader of her own ensemble, Eva Ybarra y Su Conjunto. Relatively few Mexican-American or Mexican women play the accordion professionally because of popular prejudice against women accordionists in the male-dominated world of *conjunto* music and the dance hall (Tejeda and Valdez 2001). However, because of Ybarra's example, their number is growing. One way Ybarra fostered interest in her instrument was through her recent residency as a visiting artist in the ethnomusicology program at the University of Washington School of Music. (By contrast, many Euroamerican girls and women played accordion from at least the 1950s, especially in the Midwest, and specialized in favorite pieces such as "Nola" and "Lady of Spain.") Through her recordings on the Rounder label and her live performances, Eva Ybarra has shown herself the equal of the best male accordionists (Flaco Jiménez, Mingo Saldívar) and has demonstrated her ability to compete on the same turf as men. She is also an accomplished songwriter. Her second recording on the Rounder label, *Romance inolvidable* (1996), is notable for having all but one of the songs written by women.[18] Ybarra also includes the *corrido* by her friend Gloria García Abadia (with brassy Mexican banda-style accompaniment), which narrates García Abadia's difficult and dangerous trek from her home in Tuxtla Gutiérrez, Chiapas, to San Antonio, Texas.

A significant group of musicians of Mexican-American and Hispanic-American background have been active as performers in various mainstream American popular and folk music traditions since the 1950s. Folksinger Tish Hinojosa (Leticia Hinojosa, b. 1955; see fig. 5.4), a native of San Antonio, Texas, started her career singing English-language songs, including her own compositions. In recent years she has alternated performing and recording in Spanish and English, and has sought out a mixed audience (Hudson 2001). One of her best efforts with Spanish-language material is her 1995 album *Frontejas* (Rounder CD 3132). This album contains an eclectic mix of

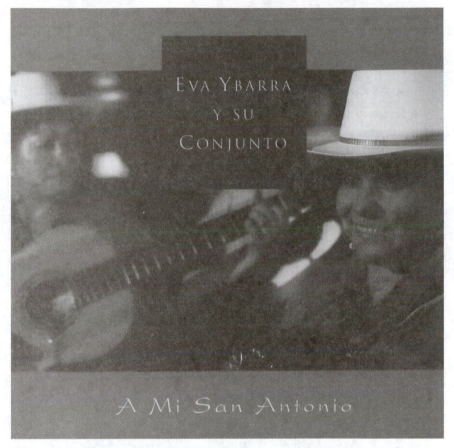

Fig. 5.3. Eva Ybarra. Rounder CD 60560. Courtesy of Rounder Records.

songs: the traditional "Pajarillo barranqueño," Yucatecan composer Ricardo Palmerín's "Las golondrinas," Alfonso Esparza Oteo's "Déjame llorar," as well as several songs by Hinojosa herself—"Otro vasito," "Las Marías," and a *corrido* in honor of tejano folklorist and singer Américo Paredes, "Con su pluma en su mano" ("With a Pen in His Hand"), a humorous reference to Paredes's important book *With a Pistol in His Hand* (1958). Accompanying Hinojosa on this recording are four famous Texas-Mexican accordionists: Eva Ybarra, the brothers Flaco Jiménez and Santiago Jiménez, Jr., and Mingo Saldívar. Though Tish Hinojosa has released several albums on major labels (Warner Brothers, A&M Records), a number of her recordings have been released by Rounder Records, a smaller company specializing in regional U.S. and world-music traditions underrepresented by larger recording conglomerates. Like many other performers today, Hinojosa markets her own recordings at

Fig. 5.4.   Tish Hinojosa. Rounder CD 3132. Courtesy of Rounder Records.

her live concerts and through her website on the Internet.[19] Thus, she reaches her audience in ways that are not as commonly used by large multinational recording companies.

Popular singer Linda Ronstadt (b. 1946) is a member of the musical Ronstadt family of Tucson, Arizona. Her grandfather, Federico José María ("Fred") Ronstadt (1868–1954), born in Sonora, Mexico, was a musician and a Tucson businessman (Ronstadt 1993). Linda's aunt, Luisa Espinel Kassler (b. 1892, d. ?), Fred's daughter, was a professional singer in Europe and the United States who specialized in Spanish and Latin American folk and art music (Sheridan 1984).[20] Linda's father, Gilbert Ronstadt, Fred's son, was also a musician. Though she has long had a love for Mexican music, Linda Ronstadt did not begin her musical career in that field. Rather, she entered the rock-and-roll scene in 1964 with the folk-rock trio The Stone Poneys. She subsequently had an important career in mainstream popular music, and later ventured far afield into opera (Puccini's *La bohème*) and operetta (Gilbert and Sullivan's *Pirates of Penzance*). In 1987 she released the very successful album *Canciones de mi padre*, a collection of Mexican popular songs and mariachi music, accompanied by Mexico's most famous mariachi ensemble, Mariachi Vargas de Tecalitlán (with arrangements by Rubén Fuentes, the dean of Mexican arrangers). She also appeared in live performances with Mariachi Vargas de Tecalitlán, singing songs from this album. The album title honors her grandfather, father, and aunt, Luisa Espinel, who compiled a songbook of the same name, published by the University of Arizona in 1946 (Espinel 1946). A videotape of the live *Canciones de mi padre* performances was also released. *Canciones de mi padre* was followed by the album *Mas canciones*.[21] Ronstadt further celebrated her cultural heritage by appearing in Luis Valdez's television production of *La pastorela*, a modern version of the traditional Mexican Christmas shepherd's play with music performed by members of El Teatro Campesino (based in San Juan Bautista, California). Ronstadt appeared alongside such prominent musicians as Lalo Guerrero and Flaco Jiménez.

Lydia Mendoza

Tejana singer and guitarist Lydia Mendoza, born in Houston, Texas, in 1916, is one of the most important Mexican-American musicians of the twentieth century (see fig. 5.5). Few musicians in the Mexican or Mexican-American traditions approach her in the diversity of her musical repertory (she recorded more than 1,000 songs in many different genres), the longevity of her career (spanning six decades), and continued public esteem (inside and outside the Spanish-speaking community) (Strachwitz 1993; Mendoza 2001). Happily, the Texas–Mexican border community and musical tradition she represents, once marginalized by "mainstream" English-speaking society in the Southwest, is now celebrated as an important regional American cultural expression.

While Lydia's father, Francisco Mendoza, as family patriarch, was undoubtedly the dominating figure in the Mendoza family, it was her mother, Leonora, who had the most lasting influence, musical and formative, on Lydia and her siblings. Forced by her husband's incapacity to assume the role of breadwinner when her children were still young, Leonora Mendoza developed (with the intermittent assistance of Francisco) a professional musical group made up of her daughters (and later also her sons). The Familia Mendoza performed regularly in San Antonio's Plaza de Zacate

Fig. 5.5. Lydia Mendoza, "the poor people's songbird," plays guitar as she sits in front of a microphone (perhaps in her home), San Antonio, Texas. Published August 2, 1938. Courtesy of the UT Institute of Texan Cultures at San Antonio.

alongside and in competition with duos, trios, and quartets of male Mexican singers, guitarists, accordionists, and fiddlers. While the Mendoza family sang in many different places in the 1920s and '30s—in cotton fields for Mexican migrant workers, in restaurants, stores, and other locations—it was at the Plaza de Zacate in San Antonio that they garnered their first real notice. Their success in San Antonio (and elsewhere) was assured by many factors: the excellence of the female Mendoza's voices (especially Lydia's), their wide-ranging repertory of popular songs (some composed by Leonora) and more traditional songs and instrumental music, mother Leonora's developing financial astuteness, and the novelty of a youthful female group performing in competition with the more usual male groups.

The Mendoza Family traveled from Kingsville, Texas, where they were then living, to San Antonio in March 1928 in order to make recordings for the Okeh Phonograph Corporation. Francisco Mendoza had seen an advertisement placed in San Antonio's Spanish-language newspaper *La Prensa* on February 28, 1928, soliciting the services of Mexican musicians to make "ethnic" recordings. The family was paid $140 for recording eleven songs on March 8 and 10, 1928, as the Cuarteto Carta Blanca. This was the name given to the group by Francisco Mendoza when asked by the record producer for a name to put on the record label; thinking quickly, he named the group after the famous Mexican beer of the same name (he had earlier worked in the Carta Blanca bottling plant in Monterrey, Nuevo León). Of these eleven recordings, ten were released on the Okeh label and by associated companies. Some have been rereleased on compact disc by Chris Strachwitz on the Arhoolie label.

Despite this first recording venture, the family's economic status only temporarily improved, and the Mendozas were forced by necessity to travel to Michigan on an *enganche* ("labor contract") to work in the sugar-beet harvest. Not finding this sort of labor agreeable, the family once again took up the role of entertainers and performed for the many Mexican seasonal workers in the area. This alternation between working as performers and at any other jobs available to them would continue well into the 1930s, after Lydia Mendoza had established her reputation in the Hispanic music world in the Southwest.

As the Mendoza children grew up, they were given increasingly important roles in the family musical group. However, it was ultimately Lydia who attracted the most interest and who had the most important role as a solo singer. What helped Lydia most in establishing and retaining the attention of a faithful audience in Texas, the Southwest, and in Mexico (and later in South America) was the large number of solo recordings she made, beginning in 1934. Part of the demand for recordings by Lydia Mendoza and other Mexican-American musicians was stimulated by the need for records to play in jukeboxes in Mexican-run *cantinas*, nightclubs, and restaurants.

Lydia had an exceptional ear and a magpie-like ability to acquire songs from all kinds of sources; many of the songs in her repertory were acquired from her mother, Leonora. However, she was essentially a self-taught musician. At different times in her career she played the six- and twelve-string guitar, violin, and mandolin. However, it was on the twelve-string guitar that she developed her own fine and distinctive accompaniment style. Whereas other members of her family exhibited their acting and dancing skills during the family shows with which they toured throughout the Southwest until mother Leonora's death in 1952, Lydia often limited her participation to singing and playing in her solo act. Even after the advent of Lydia's fame, the Mendozas performed frequently throughout Texas and the Southwest in *carpas, cantinas*, restaurants, village and church halls, at private parties and events, on the radio, and in city auditoriums and theaters.

During World War II, when Lydia Mendoza had temporarily retired from public performance, her sisters María (1922–1990) and Juanita (b. 1927) formed Las Hermanas Mendoza, and performed regularly in nightclubs, theaters, and on tour, always under the ever-vigilant eye of mother Leonora. After the war, they continued their musical career—sometimes accompanied by sister Lydia—and made an extensive series of recordings, principally for Discos Azteca in Los Angeles and Discos Ideal in Alice, Texas. They ultimately became one of the most important female duets, and were known throughout the Hispanic Southwest and Mexico, rivaling for a time the popularity of Las Hermanas Padilla.[22] After the death of mother Leonora in 1952, and the subsequent marriage of María, Las Hermanas Mendoza disbanded. Such a thing was a common occurrence at the time. Marriage, childbirth and child-rearing, male interference, and the expectations of husbands or family members often made it difficult for Mexican and Mexican-American women musicians to realize their full potential as performers.

A comparison can be made between the Mendozas and other touring Mexican family theatrical and musical groups active in the Southwest at about the same time. The theatrical family troupe led by Spanish-born composer, singer, and theatrical manager Manuel Areu (1845–1942) performed throughout Spain, Mexico, Cuba, and the Southwest for many years before and after the turn of the century (Montano 1976; Bissell 1987; Sturman 2000). Like the Mendoza family, some members of the Areu family and their relations achieved lasting fame or notoriety. For example, the famous *tejana* singer and comic Beatriz Escalona (1903–1979), known as "La Chata Noloesca," was married for a time to Manuel's son, bass José Areu. Escalona, a native of San Antonio, Texas, adopted the stage name of "La Chata" (snub-nosed) Noloesca—an approximate anagram for Escalona. She was one of the most important figures on the Spanish-language stage in the United States and was well known for her comic songs and sketches, in which she usually presented herself in the role of a *peladita* (a wise-cracking working-class Mexican woman). She appeared to great acclaim throughout the

United States and in Mexico and Cuba in musical reviews, *tandas*, on television, radio, and in other theatrical contexts (Ybarra-Frausto 1989; Arrizón 1999). She also recorded comic skits and songs in Los Angeles during 1925 to 1928.

Strachwitz compares the Mendozas to another musical family, the Carter Family (the American folk icons)—Mother Maybelle, Sara, and A. P. There are indeed similarities between the life stories of these two families. Both came to recording almost by chance at about the same time; both groups sang popular and traditional music, broadcast on the radio, and were headed by men, but featured the women of the family in the main singing roles.

It has been said of Lydia Mendoza that she "represents our [Texas-Mexican] history, she is important, she is the first star of tejano music specifically and of Mexican-American music in general" (Strachwitz 1993, vii). Undoubtedly, Lydia's songs appealed to all classes of Mexican-American society. However, the image she most consistently promoted throughout her long musical career was that of a singer for the working classes. The text to a *huapango* composed for her by a tejano songwriter sums up this attitude.

Cancionera de los pobres,	I am a singer of the poor,
cancionera y nada más;	a singer, nothing more;
mi guitarra es mi compañera	My guitar is the companion
de mis cantos de arrabal.	of my songs from the poor part of town.

(Strachwitz 1993, 135)

Some enthusiasts of Mexican and Mexican-American popular music formulate a definite and distinctive split into "rural" and "city" voices. Some seem to place a higher value on rural voice types than on singing styles cultivated in urban areas, possibly because they may see the former as more "authentic" (Strachwitz 1993, ix–x). However, this privileging of one type over the other does not take into account several factors. First, the dissemination of a multitude of musical repertories and preferred singing styles (nasal, bel canto, crooning, harsh-sounding, full-voiced, loud, etc.) is widespread throughout Mexico and the Hispanic Southwest in both rural and urban areas. Second, formally trained and untrained popular singers from both rural and urban backgrounds often have possessed prodigious vocal abilities, for example, José Mojica, Lydia Mendoza, Lucha Reyes, Linda Ronstadt, Tito Guizar, Pedro Infante, Jorge Negrete, and Guty Cárdenas. Personal choice, individual vocal abilities, popular fashion, and other factors are often more important in determining vocal style than an urban or rural origin.

Lydia Mendoza is a good example of a singer with a cross between so-called "city" and "country" voices. Though she sang in the *estilo popular*

("popular style"), the style of vocal production she used on her early recordings from the 1930s exhibits certain touches derived from salon music of turn-of-the-century Mexico and Italian opera. It is important to remember that an Italianate vocal style (especially the use of portamento, or sliding between pitches) has had a definite influence on Mexican popular singing styles since the nineteenth century. It seems natural that Lydia was influenced to some extent by an operatic vocal style: her father was a great fan of Italian operatic tenor Enrico Caruso, and he owned quite a number of Caruso's recordings. Touring Mexican and Spanish musical theater performers with their repertory of zarzuela songs and lighter couplets—some showing the influence of Italian-style singing—also had a definite influence on musicians in the Hispanic Southwest, among them Lydia Mendoza.

According to Chris Strachwitz, Lydia Mendoza and members of her family made separately and together more than 1,200 recordings between 1928 and 1987. This enormous recording activity is documented in Strachwitz's valuable discography of Lydia Mendoza's recordings. Both Chris Strachwitz's discography and Richard Spottswood's monumental discography of ethnic recordings in the United States before 1942 attest to Lydia's wide-ranging repertory and her immense productivity as a recording artist. A short list of some of the types of popular songs she recorded over many years—from Mexico, the Caribbean, Latin America, Spain, Europe, and the United States—includes the bolero, polka, tango, *corrido, canción, serenata, danzón, danza, pasodoble, son*, fox [trot], rumba, and *ranchera*.

How she encountered all these different song and dance types is not revealed to any great extent in her autobiography. However, one can well imagine that Lydia, ever in search of new repertory, picked up songs and dances in many different ways and in many different locations. She heard radio, film, and later television broadcasts of Spanish-language material; she also encountered new repertory during her direct encounters with other musicians, in the Southwest, Mexico, and in South America. She might also have purchased some of the many *cancioneros* ("songbooks") with the texts to current popular and traditional songs (however, these usually did not contain the music to the songs). San Antonio, her hometown for several years, had a number of Spanish-language publishers and newspapers. Some of these printers, as well as Spanish-language bookstores and music stores, issued songbooks for popular consumption.[23] An often repeated anecdote reveals that Lydia learned her signature tune "Mal hombre" ("Wicked Man") from a gum wrapper—gum manufacturers printed the words to popular songs as an enticement to potential buyers. Indeed, she learned the words to many songs in that manner.

A startling thing about the songs that Lydia sang throughout her long career is that most were sung from the male point of view. It is still puzzling why Lydia and almost all other Mexican and Mexican-American women singers active before about 1960 sang so many male-oriented songs, many of which were highly misogynistic in content. One possible explanation is that few women were active as songwriters in the popular-music world in Mexico or the United States before World War II. The very active Mexican composer María Grever (María Joaquina de la Portilla Torres, 1884–1951), long resident in the United States, is a notable exception. The other side of this coin is that almost all Mexican songwriters were male, and, though they probably did not despise or mistrust women as a rule, they operated within a certain set of societal expectations as to the favorite themes of popular songs. Mexican popular song often presents women as unfaithful, fickle, and vainglorious creatures. However, the obvious truth is that most Mexican and Mexican-American women were and are faithful and steadfast companions, lovers, and wives; indeed, more men than women were probably unfaithful to their loved ones.

Manuel Peña (1999b) offers another possible explanation for this common theme of the treacherous woman. In the United States, Mexican-American men and women were often relegated to second-class citizenship by the dominant Euroamerican society. Perhaps Mexican-American men, belonging to an oppressed group, passed on this attitude to another oppressed group, one that was under their own control—Mexican-American women. However, this explanation does not account for Mexican songs with misogynistic content sung in Mexico by Mexican male and female singers for Mexican audiences. Certainly the concept and practice of machismo and the fact that Mexico has always been a patriarchal and male-dominated society helped foster the image of the treacherous woman in Mexican popular song. The treacherous-woman stereotype may also have served to ensure the continuation of male hegemony and to put women in their place. One wonders, though, how much Mexican men have really adopted this attitude in their own lives. Lydia Mendoza and her sisters María and Juanita discuss this practice in their family autobiography (Strachwitz 1993). When singing these male-oriented themes, they replaced the male voice or narrator in their minds with a female one. Thus, the treacherous woman became a treacherous man.

While never forgotten by Hispanic Americans in the Southwest, Lydia Mendoza was discovered beginning in the 1970s and '80s by non-Spanish-speaking audiences. Since that time, she has received many honors and much acclaim for her long and important musical career. She appeared at the American Folklife Festival in Montreal in 1971 and in the film *Chulas fronteras* in 1976.[24] She later performed for President Carter at the Kennedy Center in Washington, D. C., and in 1982 she received the National Heritage Fellowship Award. James Griffiths's biographical sketch of her in *Ethnic Music in America* sparked renewed interest in her career (Spottswood 1982). The rerelease in the 1980s and '90s by Chris Strachwitz on the Arhoolie and Folklyric labels (on LP and CD) of many of her recordings brought her voice and music to a new generation.[25] Lydia Mendoza was inducted into the Texas Women's Hall of Fame in 1985, and in 1991 she was the first woman to be inducted into the Conjunto Hall of Fame. Most recently, she was among the 1999 National Medal of Art recipients honored by President Clinton (other musicians honored that year included singers Aretha Franklin and Odetta); also in 1999, she received the National Association for Chicana and Chicano Studies Lifetime Achievement Community Award. Another sign of her importance is that her second autobiography has been published, by Oxford University Press, as *My Life in Music / Mi Vida en la Música* (Mendoza 2001).

Selena Quintanilla

Besides Lydia Mendoza, the other female Mexican-American singer who has attracted great interest among both Spanish- and English-speakers is Selena Quintanilla Pérez (1971–1995; see fig. 5.6). Though her career was much shorter than Lydia Mendoza's because of her tragic and early death, she accomplished a great deal in a relatively short period of time. Unlike earlier women singers who had to sing a male-oriented song repertory, Selena was able to assume a female identity in her music. She also had a wide-ranging repertory of Spanish- and English-language songs and sang in a number of musical styles (e.g., *cumbia*, *norteña*, mariachi, mainstream pop).

Selena's father, Abraham Quintanilla, was a professional musician, and between 1957 and 1971 he performed with the band Los Dinos in South Texas. Because of his own professional experience, he recognized very early that his daughter had musical talent. He encouraged Selena to sing and allowed her to perform in public as early as age eight. Selena and the Quintanilla family musical group became a professional band in 1981, when Selena was ten. Selena moved from Lake Jackson, Texas, to Corpus Christi, Texas, in 1982, where she lived until her death. They also adopted the name of Los Dinos, and later Selena y Los Dinos.

While English was her first language, she was taught to sing in Spanish by her father. Later in life she became more proficient in Spanish, though she always spoke with something of an American accent. This accent vanished when she sang, however. By the time of her greatest fame in the 1990s, she

Fig. 5.6. Studio photograph of Selena Quintanilla, taken by Rick Vasquez, San Antonio, Texas. Courtesy of the UT Institute of Texan Cultures at San Antonio.

was able to converse freely in Spanish, and gave interviews for Spanish-language television and radio in Spanish. Whatever her proficiency in Spanish, she always remained firmly rooted in Texas-Mexican border culture, and even at the highpoint of her career, when she was earning a substantial amount of money, she still lived in her home area of Corpus Christi. Though she immersed herself in Mexican-American society, she also moved easily between English- and Spanish-language contexts and situations.

Early in her career Selena received significant recognition and validation of her musical talents. She first won the Tejano Music Award for Female Entertainer of the Year in 1987, and eight other Tejano Music Awards followed.[26] Also early on she began what would become a major recording career. Selena and Los Dinos recorded on a number of local Texas labels before 1989. In 1989 she signed a contract with the multinational Capitol/ EMI Latin label, which greatly improved her financial position, as well as the sophistication, distribution, and market share of her recordings. Whereas before her Capitol/EMI Latin contract her recordings mainly circulated in Texas and northern Mexico, afterward they were distributed in many parts of Mexico and Latin America as well as throughout the United States.

The hit song "Como la flor" became Selena's signature tune, and *Amor prohibido* (1994) her best-selling album. Before her death, she had reached new English-language audiences and was entering the popular-music mainstream. She did this with no intention of giving up her tejano and Hispanic audiences. Her posthumous album *Dreaming of You*, a crossover work, was released four months after her death in the summer 1995 and was a decided success. Had she lived, her career would undoubtedly have ascended to even greater heights.

Selena's tragic death was mourned by millions of her Spanish-speaking fans, who viewed her as an important representative of Hispanic culture within the mainstream of modern American life. The tragedy of Selena's murder (by a member of her personal entourage) also touched people outside the Hispanic community. Her memory was honored in the film biography *Selena* (directed by Gregory Nava), released in 1997 by Warner Brothers two years after her death, and by the documentary film *Selena Remembered* (directed by Cecilia Miniucchi), released in 1997 by EMI Latin with the cooperation of her father Abraham Quintanilla and the Quintanilla family.

An outpouring of grief occurred immediately after her death. Personal shrines were constructed in people's homes in veneration of Selena's memory. The new medium of the Internet was also used to express public grief about her murder. A number of Selena websites were set up, which recorded people's feelings about Selena and her music (Peeters 1998). On a related note, I found a used copy of one of the many books oriented toward the popular market published soon after Selena's death. An anonymous fan wrote appropriately on the title page of this book: "Enjoy life because you don't know when you are going to go. Just like Selena Quintanilla Pérez."

A number of writers and journalists jumped on the Selena bandwagon soon after her death (Arrarás 1997; Cantu and Ávila 1996; Limón 1994;

Martínez 1998; Novas 1995; Patoski 1995; Richmond 1995; Ruiz 1995; Villalobos 1995). Some exploited her memory with poorly researched and sensationalistic reportage. Others provided more sensitive and accurate accounts of Selena's life, career, and tragic end. Selena continues to be of interest to a large public and is interpreted in intriguing ways. She has been connected with the Virgin of Guadalupe, and viewed almost as a saintly personage (Pellarolo 1998). Others see her as a cult figure, and compare her to other Latin American women who died at a young age (e.g., Eva Perón). Selena was also compared to Madonna in terms of her stylized presentation of female sexuality, though she was never viewed as a "bad" girl in the same way that Madonna has been. Though Selena did often dress for public performances in a somewhat provocative manner, she apparently did not intend to project an image of sexual promiscuity.

At this time it is not possible to determine with certainty if Selena's music will live on in a significant way in the future. While she made a big impact on the local, national, and international popular music scenes during her lifetime, she may in the future be remembered more for the tragic details of her death than for her music. Only time will tell. It seems most probable, however, that the accomplishments and recordings of a number of these mexicana, tejana, and chicana musicians will be remembered and esteemed in the future. Additional opportunities will no doubt continue to be available to women musicians in the future as fewer restrictions are placed on women's progress now than they were in the past.

Notes

1. *Del rancho al Bataclán* (1984); *El país del las tandas* (1984); *El País de las tandas: Mexican Rataplán* (LP MNCP-0011, Discos del Museo Nacional de Culturas Populares, 1983); *El país de las tandas: Cachitos de México* (LP AAM 0012, Asociación de Amigos del Museo Nacional de Culturas Populares, 1987).
2. Rafael Herrera Robinsón's 1904 cylinder recording of the "Corrido de Jesús Leal" is included in *The Mexican Revolution: Corridos* (Arhoolie CD 7041–44).
3. Jesús Ábrego and Picazo (Picazo's first name is unknown to me) version of "La rancherita" (recorded in 1905) is included on the compact disc *Duetos mexicanos* (Asociación Mexicana de Estudios Fonográficos, AMEF T-44–04).
4. The recording activity of Mexican musicians in the United States from the turn of the century is well documented in Spottswood (1990).
5. Jesús Blanco Aguilar, ed. *Homenaje a la soprano Rosalía "Chalía" Díaz de Herrera* (Havana: Museo Nacional de la Música, 1984), cited by Díaz Ayala (1994).
6. A CD anthology of twenty-five of Rosalía Chalía's early recordings (1898–1912), with operatic arias and Spanish-language songs, is available as Truesound Transfers, TT-2025; Truesound Transfers Website: http://www. truesoundtransfers.de.
7. Koegel (1999, 2000). Mexican-born composer, guitarist, and music teacher Manuel Y. Ferrer (1832–1904) was an active and important figure on the musical scene in San Francisco from his arrival circa 1850 until his death. He was the

founder of a musical dynasty, and many of his children followed him into musical careers, including his daughter Eugenia. His *Compositions and Arrangements for
Guitar* (San Francisco: Matthias Gray, 1882, later reprint issues) is one of the most
important nineteenth-century anthologies of guitar music. The International
Guitar Research Archives (Ronald Purcell, Director) at California State University,
Northridge, is the major repository for Manuel Y. Ferrer's music. IGRA website:
http://www.csun.edu/~igra/igra/igra.html.

8. The Library of Congress owns eight Berliner recordings by Eugenia (Eugenie M.)
Ferrer: "La calesera," "Si tú quisieras," "El zorzico de Bilbao," "El jaleo de Jérez,"
"El café de Puerto Rico," "Triste," "La naranjera," and her father's song "Los lin-
dos ojos."

9. *El imparcial* (Mexico City), Nov. 11, 1907.

10. "Webb Singing Pictures," Internet Movie Database: http://www.imdb.com.

11. Carmen García Cornejo performed in the United States and Mexico with Mexican
operatic tenor José Mojica (1896–1974). The struggles they experienced in New
York in the 1910s are humorously recounted in Mojica's autobiography, *Yo,
pecador* (Mexico City: Editorial Jus, 1956); translated as *I, A Sinner* (Chicago:
Franciscan Herald Press, 1963). They are also portrayed in the film biography of
Mojica, *Yo, pecador.*

12. Guillermo A. Posadas, arr., *Canciones mexicanas: Colección Carmen García Cornejo*
(New York: Mexican Song Publishing Company, 1919), copy at the University of
California, Berkeley.

13. Posadas was an orchestra conductor, radio music director, arranger, and composer. His waltzes *Abandonado* and *Sufrimiento de amor* were well known in Mexico
and the United States. He also composed the film scores to the 1933 Mexican
films *El tigre de Yautepec* and *El prisionero trece*. In the 1930s, Posadas directed the
musical program Calendario Artístico, broadcast on XEW, the important Mexico
City radio station.

14. *Tejano Roots: The Women (1946–1970)* (Arhoolie CD 343).

15. Chelo Silva, *La reina tejana del bolero* (Arhoolie CD 423).

16. Ibid.

17. Tejano Music Awards Website: http://www.tejanomusicawards.com.

18. Eva Ybarra y su Conjunto. *A mi San Antonio* (Rounder CD 6056); *Romance inolvidable* (Rounder CD 6062).

19. Tish Hinojosa website: http://www.mundotish.com.

20. Luisa Espinel was married to the important one-armed artist Charles Kassler (they
later divorced). Sometime during the 1930s, Kassler included Espinel as a musical figure from early California in the WPA-sponsored mural he painted at
Fullerton High School (Fullerton, California). This mural has recently been
restored.

21. Linda Ronstadt, *Canciones de mi padre* (Asylum CD 60765–2); *Mas canciones*
(Elektra CD 9 61239–2).

22. Juanita and María Mendoza, *Las Hermanas Mendoza: The Mendoza Sisters—Juanita
and María* (Arhoolie CD 430).

23. Examples of these types of songbooks published in San Antonio, Texas include:
Canciones populares mexicanas (F. Aguirre & Co, 1919); *Ruiseñor mexicano: colección de
canciones populares* (Casa Editorial Lozano, 3rd ed., 1924; 4th ed., 1925; 5th
ed.with supplement, 1928; 6th ed., 1936).

24. *Chulas fronteras & Del mero corazón: Soundtrack Recordings from Two Tex-Mex Classics* (Arhoolie CD 425). Video versions of *Chulas fronteras* and *Del mero corazón* (BF 104) released by Brazos Films, are available through Arhoolie Records.
25. Lydia Mendoza, *"Mal hombre"* (Arhoolie CD 7002); *First Queen of Tejano Music* (Arhoolie CD 392); *La gloria de Texas* (Arhoolie CD 3012); *Vida mía* (Arhoolie CD 7008); *La alondra de la frontera—Live!* (Arhoolie CD 490).
26. Tejano Music Awards website: http://www.tejanomusicawards.com.

References

Alonso, Enrique. 1987. *María Conesa.* Mexico City: Océano.

Arrarás, María Celeste. 1997. *Selena's Secret: The Revealing Story Behind Her Tragic Death.* New York: Simon and Schuster.

Arrizón, Alicia. 1999. *Latina Performance: Traversing the Stage.* Bloomington: Indiana University Press, 1999.

Bissell, Sally Joan. 1987. *Manuel Areu and the Nineteenth-Century Zarzuela in Mexico and Cuba.* Ph.D. diss., University of Iowa.

Burr, Ramiro. 1999. *The Billboard Guide to Tejano and Regional Mexican Music.* New York: Billboard Books.

Cantu, Tony, and Alex Ávila. 1996. "Cashing in on Selena: How the Tejano Queen's Murder Caused an Economic Phenomenon." *Hispanic* (June 1996): 18–23.

Charosh, Paul. 1995. *Berliner Gramophone Records: American Issues, 1892–1900.* Westport, Conn.: Greenwood Press.

Dallal, Alberto. 1995. *La danza en México: Tercera parte: La danza escénica popular, 1877–1930.* Mexico City: Universidad Nacional Autónoma de México, Instituto de Investigaciones Estéticas.

Díaz Ayala, Cristóbal. 1994. *Cuba canta y baila: Discografía de la música cubana. Vol. 1: 1898 a 1925.* San Juan, Puerto Rico: Fundación Musicalia.

Espinel, Luisa. 1946. *Canciones de Mi Padre: Spanish Folksongs from Southern Arizona.* Tucson: University of Arizona Press.

Hudson, Kathleen. 2001. "On Dreaming: Tish Hinojosa." In *Telling Stories, Writing Songs: An Album of Texas Songwriters.* Austin: University of Texas Press, 158–61.

Koegel, John. 1998. "Preserving the Sounds of the 'Old' Southwest: Charles Lummis and His Cylinder Collection of Mexican-American and Indian Music." *ARSC Journal* 29/1: 1–29.

———. 1999. "*Canciones del país*: Mexican Musical Life in California after the Gold Rush." *California History* 78/3: 160–87, 215–19.

———. 2000. "Manuel Y. Ferrer and Miguel S. Arévalo: Premier Guitarist-Composers in Nineteenth-Century California." *Inter-American Music Review* 16/2: 45–66.

Limón, José. 1994. "Selena: Sexuality, Performance, and the Problematic of Hegemony." *Reflexiones 1997.* Neil Foley, ed. Austin: University of Texas Press, 1–27.

María y Campos, Armando. 1996. *El teatro de género chico en la revolución mexicana.* Mexico City: Consejo Nacional para la Cultura y las Artes, Dirección General de Publicaciones (reprint of 1956 ed.).

Martínez, Sarah Guzmán. 1998. *Selena: Celluoid Representation of a Mexican American Female.* M.A. thesis, University of Texas at Austin.

Mendoza, Lydia. 2001. *My Life in Music / Mi Vida en la Música: Lydia Mendoza: Norteño Tejano Legacies*. Yolanda Broyles-González, ed. New York: Oxford University Press.

Montaño, Mary Caroline. 1976. *The Manuel Areu Collection of Nineteenth-Century Zarzuelas*. M.A. thesis, University of New Mexico.

N.A. 1984. *Del rancho al Bataclán: Cancionero del Teatro de Revista*. Coyoacán: Museo Nacional de Culturas Populares.

N.A. 1984. *El país de las tandas: Teatro de Revista, 1900–1940*. Coyoacán: Museo Nacional de Culturas Populares.

Novas, Himilce, and Rosemary Silva. 1995. *Remembering Selena: A Tribute in Pictures and Words*. New York: St. Martin's Griffin.

Olavarría y Ferrari, Enrique. 1961. *Reseña histórica del teatro en México, 1538–1911*. 5 vols. Mexico City: Porrúa. *Índices a la Reseña histórica del teatro en México*. Mexico City: Porrúa, 1968.

Paredes, Américo. 1958. *With His Pistol in His Hand: A Border Ballad and Its Hero*. Austin: University of Texas Press.

Patoski, Joe Nick. 1995. *Selena: Como la Flor*. New York: Boulevard Books.

Peeters, Hans J. 1998. *Selena on the World Wide Web: A Speech Community in Cyberspace*. M.A. thesis, California State University, Hayward.

Pellarolo, Silvia. 1998. "Reviv/s/ing Selena." *Latin American Issues* 14: 51–75.

Peña, Manuel H. 1985a. "From Ranchero to Jaitón: Ethnicity and Class in Texas-Mexican Music (Two Styles in the Form of a Pair)." *Ethnomusicology* 29/1: 29–55.

———. 1985b. *The Texas-Mexican Conjunto: A History of a Working-Class Music*. Austin: University of Texas Press.

———. 1999a. *The Mexican American Orquesta: Music, Culture, and the Dialectic of Conflict*. Austin: University of Texas Press.

———. 1999b. *Música Tejana: The Cultural Economy of Artistic Transformation*. College Station: Texas A & M University Press.

Richmond, Clint. 1995. *Selena! The Phenomenal Life and Tragic Death of the Tejano Music Queen*. New York: Pocket Books.

Rico, Araceli. 1999. *El Teatro Esperanza Iris: La pasión por las tablas. Medio Siglo de Arte Teatral en México*. Mexico City: Plaza y Valdés.

Ronstadt, Federico José Maria. 1993. In *Borderman: Memoirs of Federico José María Ronstadt*. Edited by Edward F. Ronstadt. Albuquerque: University of New Mexico Press.

Ruiz, Geraldo. 1995. *Selena: The Last Song. The Life, Passion, and Death of the Queen of Tejano Music/Selena: La Última Canción. Vida, Pasión y Muerte de la Reina de la Música Tejana*. New York: El Diario Books.

Sheridan, Thomas. 1984. "From Luisa Espinel to Lalo Guerrero: Tucson's Mexican Musicians before World War II." *Journal of Arizona History* 25: 285–300.

Spottswood, Richard, ed. 1982. *Ethnic Recordings in America: A Neglected Heritage*. Washington D.C.: Library of Congress, American Folklife Center.

———. 1990. *Ethnic Music on Records: A Discography of Ethnic Recordings Produced in the United States, 1893–1942. Vol. 4: Spanish, Portuguese, Philippine, Basque*. Urbana: University of Illinois Press.

Strachwitz, Chris, and James Nicolopulos, eds. 1993. *Lydia Mendoza: A Family Autobiography*. Houston: Arte Público Press.

Sturman, Janet. 2000. *Zarzuela: Spanish Operetta, American Stage*. Urbana: University of Illinois Press.

Tejeda, Juan, and Arelardo Valdez, eds. 2001. *Puro Conjunto: An Album in Words and Pictures*. Austin: University of Texas Press.

Villalobos, Alfredo. 1995. *Selena: The Murder Trial/El juicio contra Yolanda Saldívar, la asesina de Selena*. N.p.: United Publishing Co.

Ybarra-Frausto, Tomás. 1989. "La Chata Noloesca: Figura del Donaire." In *Mexican-American Theatre: Then and Now*. Edited by Nicolás Kanellos. Houston: Arte Público Press, 41–51.

Zedillo Castillo, Antonio. 1989. *El teatro de la Ciudad de México: Lustros, lustres, experiencia y esperanzas*. Mexico City: Sociocultur DDF.

6

A Chicano in a Cuban Band

Okan Ise and Songo in Los Angeles

JAVIER BARRALES PACHECO

I played in an Afro-Cuban music ensemble in Los Angeles during the years 1985 to 1987, called Okan Ise. It was the first group to introduce the music of the popular Cuban ensemble Los Van Van ("The Go Go's") to Los Angeles. A central part of the band's repertoire was *songo*, a contemporary urban popular style derived from the *son*, a staple of Afro-Cuban music. The performance of this music and the musical choices made by Okan Ise in California comprise an interesting case study in music marginalization, internally and externally. Internally, there are factors of competency, that is, one's preparation, training, technique, maturity, psychology, and conditioning. Externally, a number of political questions are forced upon the Latin musician who encounters, in addition to artistic and economic obstacles, racial and ethnic struggles in the daily game of survival (Blum 1978, 144). While the two latter factors are commonly linked to the former (artistic and economic obstacles), it is quite a different story to uncover the dynamics of primary group prejudice and internal censorship. A main point in this chapter will be cultural competence under the impact of static and changing social forces affecting aesthetic development.

I will examine the phenomenon of music that is reflective of social change, new social networks, and sociocultural alignments. I offer my personal experience as a case study of one process of transculturation (cultural reconfiguration or recentering), a term coined by anthropologist Fernando Ortiz.[1] The Ortiz theory features a two-way cultural interchange that can take place anytime, in a myriad of situations, when two distinct cultures come into contact with one another. Ortiz developed his theory as a response to North American anthropologists of the 1940s who used "acculturation" as a way of explaining the process of interaction and mutual influence between cultures. Looking at the word from a Latin American perspective, Ortiz saw great ambiguity in the term, which seemed more like a soft theory for the one-way imposition of the colonizers' culture. He sought to undermine the homogenization implicit in the word "acculturation." I would agree with Silvia Spitta (1997, 166) that Ortiz's "transculturation" should be understood as two-way, multilevel cultural interchanges, borrowings, displacements, and recreations. Key to transculturation is reciprocity. My experiences with Latin Americans of distinct races and nationalities have involved equal "give-and-take," a sense of sharing and borrowing ideas, a displacement of my own unchallenged and previously held smug or incorrect beliefs, resulting in the creation of a new identity shaped in part by useful or positive interactions. I will explore the affective character and consequences of *songo* as I experienced this music. *Songo* formed part of a progressive Afro-Cuban movement in Los Angeles among a select group of energetic veteran musicians in 1985. But before entering into the discussion of this collective formation, it is important to provide briefly some cultural context and historic background for my own experiences.

My Musical Background

I was born in Palo Alto, California, on April 22, 1949, a couple of years after my parents migrated to this country from Mexico. Although I was exposed to tropical music at home (through radio and records), I was never especially fond of it. Nonetheless, I eventually came to appreciate the impact of the conga drums, and this focused my attention on the music. One of the first Cuban musical influences on me was the recordings of Mongo Santamaria. This music was appealing because of the incorporation of jazz and Latin idioms. In 1973 an African-American friend and drummer, Michael Lea, exposed me to the music of Puerto Rican pianist/composer Eddie Palmieri. Again, I was attracted to the mixture of jazz and Latin idioms. I began to appreciate the intricate polyrhythms inherent in Latin percussion. Thereafter, the challenges offered by rhythmic complexities contributed to my growing interest in this music. At the same time I came into contact with people of Puerto Rican origin and learned more about their culture firsthand. During the early '70s, Puerto Ricans from around the Bay Area (from Morgan Hill to San Francisco) would converge for a day at Blackberry Park in Cupertino for the annual celebration of Día de San Juan. This was my first experience of hearing Latin music performed communally in the open air.

My own first direct exposure to Afro-Cuban music came when I met percussion master Francisco Aguabella (of Matanzas, Cuba).[2] Among his many recording credits, Aguabella had performed for choreographer Katheline Dunham, jazz trumpeter Dizzy Gillespie, salsa star Eddie Palmieri, and the Latin rock group Malo. In 1974 I was privileged to be invited to record on his album *Aguabella Hitting Hard!*, playing acoustic piano. This record attempted a crossover between the American and Latino markets. The material was diverse, ranging from funk and pop to merengue and Brazilian jazz. Regrettably, the recording company did very little to promote the record, and within a couple of years of its release, the album appeared in the 99–cent bins of small retailers. However, my brief association with Aguabella proved a very fruitful learning experience. By 1976, I was composing Latin jazz and salsa pieces as coleader and musical director of my own ensemble, Salsa Alacrán. All this prepared me for the next step in my career, *songo*.

Songo

Songo is a fairly recent (1970s) Cuban dance craze. It did not become known in the United States until after the mid-1980s. The chief promoter of this style is the group Los Van Van, whose leader and composer is Juan Formell. Their instrumentation consists of three violins, three trombones, piano, bass, flute, drums, congas, and a pair of singers. This combination gives them great breadth of sound, as light as a chamber *charanga* (with violins and flute) and as brassy as a *conjunto* (with trombones). Its uniqueness is based upon the instrumentation and adoption of some new musical influences. One of the greatest innovations of *songo* features a trap drum set instead of the traditional timbales. Gerard and Sheller describe the style this way:

> The songo drum-set style is based on the figures played on the timbales, which, in turn, were adapted from the segunda patterns and palitos patterns used in rumba. In essence, then, the new Cuban drummers are playing rumba on the trap set. (1998, 99)

Bongos are also absent from the rhythm section, and the clave beat is reversed. Instead of a 3+2 pattern, *songo* is played in 2+3. Also, rather than playing a straight *tumbao* rhythm, the conga player creates more spirited, freer patterns and variants. Gerard and Sheller state that the *conguero* is playing more "open tones" than are used in routine *tumbao* patterns. Polyrhythmic exchanges between the drum set and the *conguero* as well as the rest of the ensemble are more frequent. The texture of polyrhythms is dense and, depending on the number of the players in the ensemble, spacious. The harmonic patterns are taken from a number of new sources, not necessarily Cuban. The non-musician cannot help but notice the uniqueness of this style, which Nina Linart dubbed an "original and progressive blend of Cuban musical forms."[3] Because I grew up with the beat of the trap drum set, and the bass drum lending its thick sound, I was attracted to the sound of Los Van Van's mixture of drum set with congas. I believe Western audiences also gravitate more toward the snare- and bass-drum timbre.

I had first moved to Los Angeles in the fall of 1982 to begin graduate studies in ethnomusicology at UCLA. As a curious musicologist and musician working his way through graduate school, I had the opportunity to perform a wide variety of Latin music with a number of Latino groups in Los Angeles.[4] There are numerous opportunities and venues for musicians, both traditional and non-traditional. During my time there (1982–1990), I performed with Dominicans, Puerto Ricans, Nuyoricans, Cubans, Colombians, Hondurans, Mexicans, African-Americans, and Brazilians.

Okan Ise

It was a great coincidence that my first real exposure to *songo* and Los Van Van came in 1984 while working as a production assistant with Howard Dratch and Eugene Rosow at Lion's Gate Studios in Santa Monica for the film *Routes of Rhythm* (hosted by Harry Belafonte).[5] I was translating the lyrics of "Sandunguera," a song by Juan Formell, and remember being instantly mesmerized by its sensuality. The singer, Pedro Calvo, wore a big white hat and exuded a unique blend of sensual machismo and charm. Watching the band's performance, I was attracted to the sensuousness of this catchy dance music. The following year, I began to play *songo*, not just listen to it. In fact, from 1985 to 1987, I was the lone Chicano musician in a predominantly Afro-Cuban group in Los Angeles. The band was christened Okan Ise, which, according to its leader, Juan Oliva, is Lucumí for *buen corazón*, or "good heart." This group introduced the music of Juan Formell to Los Angeles. For two intensive years, I was involved in a group performing a progressive music different from the prevailing tide of club commercialism and "Top 10" conformity. We presented music not previously heard in local nightclubs. For me, this was a great learning experience in inter-ethnic/inter-racial relations, multiculturalism, cross-cultural aesthetic contrasts, and the exciting challenge of arranging music in the style of Cuban *songo* (see figs. 6.1–6.3).

I met Juan "Long John" Oliva through my friend Frank "Cuco" Martínez, Jr., from a Puerto Rican salsa band in which we had both worked. Frank was born in Chicago, the son of a respected musician and steeped in the tradition of *santería*.[6] Cuco referred me to Juan, and I was asked to come meet the other members and audition for the pianist position. After the audition, I was chosen because the majority felt my playing "fit in" better

Fig. 6.1. Okan Ise. From left to right: Ricardo Jiménez, Nengue Hernández, Frank "Cuco" Martínez, Jr., Nengue Hernández, Jr., author, and Juan "Long John" Oliva.

Fig. 6.2. Okan Ise. From left to right: Author, Cuco, Nengue, Ricard, Lil Nengue, Alberto Blanco, Dan Weinstein, and Tom Ross.

than a younger, local pianist, also Afro-Cuban, who had originally been rehearsing with the group. Actually, I was more experienced than my Afro-Cuban counterpart. My technique (stronger *montuno* patterns) and prior experiences with Cuban music had prepared me for the challenge. Moreover, my enthusiasm for the music was genuine, and they sensed that; we seemed to blend together quite naturally.

Juan Oliva was a committed and talented percussionist with the energy and conviction to bring progressive Cuban music to the United States. Before arriving here, Juan lived in Puerto Rico. While there he befriended some of that island's most creative musicians. Juan performed as lead percussionist and recorded with two of the most progressive groups in Puerto Rico, Batacumbele and Zaperoko.[7] These groups created music that combined the Puerto Rican *plena* with Cuban *batá* drumming, the rumba, and *songo*. However, this experience was short-lived. He recalled that the Puerto Ricans were very proud and nationalistic, and he soon felt outnumbered and manipulated. Therefore, he decided to try Los Angeles. Juan encountered good fortune almost immediately. He met bandleader Willie Bobo and toured around California with his group. (Only later did it become clear to me why Juan would have chosen to live in Los Angeles instead of the majority-Cuban metropolis of Miami.[8]) After his work with Bobo lessened, Juan became obsessed with forming his own group. He soon thought of forming an original band with a sound based on the style and material of Los Van Van, the highly acclaimed contemporary ensemble from Havana.

At that time, the growing popularity of Los Van Van aroused a great deal of curiosity. Their very name hints at the influence of American pop music. By adopting some of the music of this group, we would be preparing the way for success while the demand for this music grew. The Van Van material was catchy, diverse, sophisticated, and allowed plenty of room for musicians to move technically. Cuban musicologist Victoria Elí Rodríguez (1989, 293) cited the innovations of leader/bassist/arranger/composer Juan Formell as: 1. rhythmic function of the violins (in addition to their previous melodic function); 2. bass accompaniment with greater harmonic and rhythmic latitude; and 3. increased use of three-part harmonies. She adds that while Formell has designated some of the Van Van songs as pertaining to the new style, *songo*, she places this under the typological complex of the *son*. Thus, *songo* is a hybrid, not a rhythm. It is a style with influences from rock, jazz, and classical to Brazilian music. Sue Steward (1999, 84) also credits the "quick, inventive percussion" of Chanquito (José Luis Quintana) as having contributed to the rhythmic creation of *songo*.

Beginnings

Rehearsing out of a small room in a rented house in Inglewood, the initial nucleus of the group included (in addition to myself):

Name, Musical Instrument	Origins
Juan "Long John" Oliva, drums	Belén, Havana (immigrated 1982)
Nengue Hernández, vocals/perc.	Havana (immigrated at age ten)
Frank "Cuco" Martínez, bass	Chicago (moved to L.A. in 1956)
Alberto Blanco, violin	Camaguey, Cuba (immigrated 1979)
Ricardo Jiménez, congas	Havana (immigrated 1981)

We all knew other members would soon be joining us, but since we six were the main ones who had struggled to establish this organization, we considered ourselves the basic core of the group. Ethnically, Oliva, Hernández, Martínez, and Jiménez are Afro-Cuban, while Blanco and I are *mestizo*. But there were never any rivalries or divisions caused by our separate backgrounds. There was a marvelous degree of cooperation among all members, and we were like a family. It was as if we were a part of a new social experiment, united by a mutual desire to succeed collectively. The payoff came during actual performance. Everything seemed to work together naturally. We realized how easily we could fit parts together, and there was a good intuitive communication among us. Alberto was a showman on violin, Nengue had the vocal muscles of an Olympic runner, Frank was fluid, tasteful, and very harmonic in his bass patterns, and Jesús González was as steady as a clock and tuned to the ebb and flow of the ensemble's strength. There were also instances when we used Nengue's phenomenal twelve-year-old son on congas.

Juan was new to the trap drums but knew how to cull the sounds he wanted. He would also control the climax and dynamics of the band by his cymbal crashes, recovering into a softer pattern, and then raising the percussive level again. I felt an easy syncronicity with everyone. It took us very little time to learn new material and blend together. The music was a lot of fun to play, and we practiced song parts over and over again until they were second nature. Rehearsals were long and strenuous, yet exhilarating. One could walk away from practice feeling much had been accomplished. Indeed, we were capable of acquiring a sizeable repertoire within a couple of months. There were no immediate contracts pending, but everyone kept faith in the group's eventual triumph.

After rehearsing rigorously for about six months, the core of the group was consolidated. We had not yet performed at large venues, only at occasional private parties at the homes of Los Angeles *santeros* (practioners of *san-*

Fig. 6.3. Okan Ise. From left to right: Nengue, Ricardo, Lil Nengue, Juan, Cuco, author, and Alberto.

tería). Now it was time to think about adding a horn section. This would be indispensible. The beauty of Juan Formell's sound is in that very contrast between the light flute and strings and the more powerful trombones. I started writing additional parts for the two trombones and flute player we hoped to find. We were fortunate in meeting Arte Webb, an African-American master of the flute who hailed from Philadelphia and was newly arrived on the West Coast. He had jazz experience as well as experience playing on great recordings with some of the top *salseros*.[9] Though he spoke very little Spanish, Arte seemed to understand most of what transpired in the group. Arte committed to working exclusively with the band and became another inner-core member. Unfortunately, we could not secure such loyalty from any of the brass players. The trombonists, who performed with us in varied combinations of pairs, were Duane Benjamin, Michael John Daigeau, Tom Ross, Dick Rinde, and Dan Weinstein. The first two are African-American, and the latter three, white. They all balanced rigorous schedules performing with numerous other ensembles. Benjamin and Daigeau often toured nationally with top African-American entertainers.

Juan Oliva set the tone for the group with the name of the ensemble, Okan Ise. He was courteous, considerate, humorous, and playful. From the outset of my integration into the group, I realized immediately that I was a minority. However, since I had never experienced being in a predominant-ly Afro-Latino ensemble, I felt compelled to join. It had been a propitious time for me to make a great change, as I was recently separated from my *boriqua* ("Puerto Rican") wife and living hundreds of miles from my extended Mexican family. Cubans are generally very hospitable, so I felt very much a part of everything. It was a challenge I welcomed, a laboratory in interethnic and multicultural relations.

One thing in particular prepared me technically (as well as ethnically) for this undertaking. From 1984 to 1985, I worked weekends near downtown with a Honduran group, Los Costeños.[10] The club, Rick's Place (at Washington and Vermont), had once been a Mexican nightspot and was now frequented almost exclusively by a Honduran clientele. In the other salsa groups with which I had been associated, there was usually a fair mix of diverse nationals. In the repertoire, no single culture was dominant, though the emphasis was on Puerto Rican or Nuyorican salsa arrangements. But I generally did not have to adjust to the foreign speech patterns of the other members. However, in Los Costeños, as in Okan Ise, I was not accustomed to the types of idiosyncrasies inherent in regional accents, speaking dynamics, nonverbal codes, volume, or intensity. I was often unable to grasp the direction of a conversation or to "catch" acknowledgement or nuances of humor. It was also hard to express my views when the tempo of the conversation grew faster than the pace at which I had been accostumed to speaking.

The Cuban Connection

Juan Oliva and Alberto Blanco had grown up in Cuba and come to the United States during the Mariel boatlift of 1980. Unlike the largely white, middle- and upper-class professionals and scions who abandoned the island from 1959 onward, the *marielitos* were mostly male, averaging thirty years of age, ten years younger than the earlier exiles. Among this new group were more blacks and mulattoes. María Cristina García (1996, 68) noted that they represented 15 to 40 percent, compared to 3 percent of the 1959 to 1973 migrations. Media coverage was extensive, and soon America realized the new refugees were no longer from the island's elite. Between April and October of 1980, a total of 124,776 Cubans arrived in the United States. In sharp contrast to the earlier migrations, the Mariel exiles were not even considered legitimate refugees by the federal government or the larger society. As a group, the *marielitos* did not receive the open-armed welcome that their countrymen had enjoyed upon their arrival in the 1960s. Roberto Suro (1999, 164) quoted Monsignor Malsh: "Never in the history of the United States did any immigrant or refugee population receive the kind of help that was made available to the Cubans during their early years here."[11]

While we eventually (over the period of two years) enlarged our repertoire to include a number of current works from Cuba, we were also obliged to learn a number of older standards for the purpose of maintaining good relations among the established community. What we were doing was adjusting our musical offerings to appeal to conservative Cubans. Musical decisions were made to conform to Cuban-exile politics. Personally, I could not see why we had to reach such cultural compromises. As a person who had always enjoyed the freedom to choose whatever musical directions I wished to follow, I bristled at suggestions that we had to tread carefully in the selection of material. This was anathematic to me. I failed to understand early on that Juan and Alberto were under a lot of pressure to maintain a certain political posture in their respective neighborhoods.

Because the Cuban-American community comprised a large population with the potential for a lot of performance contracts, it was very important not to be perceived as pro-Castro in any way. I knew that we had to adopt some early (1940s–'50s) material to "balance" the current repertoire. It was important not to rely completely on the Van Van material because to do so would be considered an affront to the conservative Cubans; it would be seen as a sign of "haughtiness." Juan tried numerous times to explain this. But it was hard for me to fathom making musical decisions in order not to "antagonize" a certain social segment. For Cuban society in Los Angeles between 1984 and 1986, the songs "Guantanamera," "Tres lindas cubanas," "Pare cochero," "Sublime ilusión," "La vida es un sueño," and "Son de la loma" were pieces pertaining to the "safe" pre-Castro Cuba, so they were considered very important in the repertoire. We could not be perceived as openly promoting modern Cuban culture. We were supposed to be discreet, and this meant we had to sandwich the standards into the performance hour. But we were also allowed some latitude, and I was pleased to contribute some of my own pieces. Therefore, our material began to develop along original as well as commercial lines.

Originals (*) and Various Standards
"Pare cochero," *son montuno*
"Sublime ilusión," *bolero danzón son*
"Echame a mi la culpa" (P. Alonso), *guaracha*
"La vida es un sueño" (A. Rodríguez), bolero
"Yerba buena" (E. Oliva), *nueva canción*
"No hay distancia" (Leonor P. De Brea), bolero
"Salmo VIII," samba*
"Amor nuevo," rumba*
"En tránsito," *son**
"Con paciencia," *guaracha**
"Tres lindas cubanas," *son*

Concert Debut

Our first major public performance took place at the Los Angeles Theater Center on September 29, 1985. I had been called by a music director at the Center who wanted to discuss organizing a Latino musical program that would also include poetry. I agreed to accompany the poetry recitalist and also to perform some of my own music as soloist. Therefore, on the program, my name appeared above the band's. I did not realize for months afterward that this situation stirred up resentment among some members in the group, who interpreted it as a subtle but crude attempt on my part to assume the leadership. For Juan Oliva, this was a direct challenge to his authority. However, at the time he said nothing about it. The last thing I wanted was to usurp control of the band; therefore, I never thought he would be very concerned about this small detail.

Juan Oliva had prepared a lengthy and eloquent introduction. In it, he revealed his admiration for Afro-Cuban legendary figures such as Rita Montaner, Celia Cruz, Chano Pozo, Beny Moré, and Juan Formell, all of whom had inspired the group's formation. I then proceeded to make a few comments about the *batá* drums. Jesús, Nengue, and Juan were poised together on one side of the stage, each with a different-sized concave *batá* drum at the ready to begin the evening's set by performing a short *santero toque* dedicated to San Lázaro (St. Lazarus). After that opening, we proceeded through a carefully rehearsed sequence of pieces. Of the eight musical works performed that evening, five were my own original songs. Among them, the tune "Nuevas realidades" ("New Realities") referred to changing one's orientation in the world. It was perhaps a premonition of the kind of experience I was living everyday with my Cuban peers. It was a time of new orientations and alignments for me. My "new realities" comprised the adoption of Cuban music and the peripheral cultural influences of my fellow band members. I directly experienced what Victoria Elí Rodríguez had declared, that "Cuban music is a form of cultural behavior of the Cuban people" (1994, 91). At least among all the members of Okan Ise, music was our primary *raison d'etre*. When we were not practicing music, we were analyzing new recordings, watching recently imported Cuban music videos, or commenting upon the strengths or weaknesses of particular artists. Speculation about the music world was the most important topic of conversation, followed by an interest (mainly among Juan, Nengue, and Alberto) in baseball and other sports.

The Music of Juan Formell

The two Juan Formell numbers that we presented that evening were "Montuno sin complicaciones" ("Montuno without Complications") and

Ex. 6.1. Juan Formell, "Montuno sin complicaciones," piano interlude.

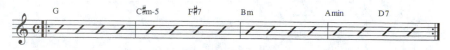

Ex. 6.2. Juan Formell, "Montuno sin complicaciones," chorus.

"La rumba no está completa" ("The Rumba Is Not Complete"). Both were well received. In the latter work, there is a long pause with only the pulsation of the clave and the *conguero* playing a *guaguancó* pattern. Then, the following interlude appears twice in the piano (see ex. 6.1).

"Montuno sin complicaciones" begins with a jazz-inspired melody that follows a shifting tonal center and later features this recurring harmony throughout the chorus (see ex. 6.2).

This pattern was often stretched to great lengths by adding new chorus lines. Another break sequence, where the ensemble drops out, leaves only the driving piano pattern. Then the singer improvises lightly and introduces the next chorus, whereupon the entire group re-enters, building to another dynamic crescendo. The combination of trombones, flutes, and violins, added to a rich harmonic and percussive palette, gives this piece its unique character. Ex. 6.3 shows the opening of the number.

Okan Ise was not limited by the exigencies of nightclub commerciality. This would later work against us. The Van Van material was simply the foundation over which our original material was being added. There was an idealism about creative music-making in Okan Ise that was absent from the Hondurans or any of the other music groups that I had played with before. Los Costeños was merely a house band organized and maintained by the club owners and subject to their capricious whims. However, in Okan Ise we experienced the freedom to embellish the new songs with our inspirations. Most of our numbers grew in duration once we started adding dynamic sections and diverse choruses. By dynamic sections, I mean parts where the other instruments fall out, leaving only the keyboards to do a *montuno* pattern while the singer returns with a new chorus. This builds for a few bars,

Ex. 6.3. Juan Formell, "Montuno sin complicaciones," opening.

then the drummer signals another entrance and the whole group re-enters, gathering new momentum. The problem with this was that it made all our songs longer. When we went into nightclubs (featuring *salsa romántica* formats), our over-extended material tended to tire out the dancers, who were unused to spending long periods on the dance floor. Certainly we must have exasperated the club owners, too. We were too "progressive" for the kinds of commercial limitations placed on all Latin dance bands in clubs. By lowering and raising the dynamics of a piece, Nengue could extend his *pregones* (vocal improvisiations), and the result was a longer tune. Another technique that was common was doubling the time, or switching to a fast 6/8 time (in the style of *comparsa*) that could last for 8, 16, or 32 measures before returning to the original tempo.

Since the *coros* ("choruses") we added often included Lucumí words, the slant was definitely Afro-Cuban. As lead singer, Nengue was usually the person who introduced the music. When he spoke into the microphone he often slurred his words, or talked in the fast-paced Cuban street rhythm with all its inflections and pronounciations. This must have been unnerving to our audiences, most of whom were not Cuban but rather a diverse mix of Latin Americans. Several times I spoke to him about the importance of clear enunciation, but he seemed unconcerned. He was used to speaking in his own way, period. I had had a similar experience with a Puerto Rican salsa singer who was insensitive to the Latino audiences in California, most of whom were from Mexico or Central and South America. Fortunately, Okan Ise continued mesmerizing crowds with its infectious rhythms and

Ex. 6.4. Juan Formell, "El carnicero," introduction.

novel sound. There had never been an all-Cuban group like this in Los Angeles. We were introducing music that was fresh and appealing. The fact that the front line of the band consisted of Afro-Cubans was in itself something new. But our material represented a dramatic break from the formulaic *salsa romántica* of the time. Soon we began to draw a loyal following of fans at shows.

Even our *chachachás* were out of the ordinary, as evidenced by the jazzy introduction (in the opening bass and piano line) to another Juan Formell piece, "El carnicero" ("The Butcher") (see ex. 6.4).

The music of Los Van Van included a variety of tempos, from *chachachá* to *guaguancó* and *merengue*. Since there were so many Formell songs in our repertory, Juan tried other methods to disguise (from any disgruntled Cuban exiles) our contemporary Cuban music. The richness of Formell's material included themes centered around domestic life. Two of the titles of Formell's songs describing life in Havana ("La Habana sí" and "La Habana no aguanta más") were changed by Oliva to "California sí" and "California no aguanta más" ("California Yes" and "California Can Take No More"). The former song revels in the beauties of the Cuban capital, the "pearl" of the Caribbean. The latter tune features a glib admonishment about the housing shortage in Havana. It bemoans the fact that so many people (from rural areas) are coming to seek a new life in a city with housing shortages. By changing both titles of the Formell songs, we were simply expressing ideas that most Californians could relate to: that is, the beauty of California and the great rise in the state's population. Thus, Juan's idea to "masquerade" these pieces by retitling them was a clever maneuver. People unacquainted with this material would assume we had composed it ourselves. While I had my own initial misgivings about this practice, I thought it prudent not to lecture Juan or the others about copyright law.

Music of Juan Formell and Los Van Van in the repertoire of Okan Ise
"La resolución," *son*
"Será que se acabó," *son*
"El carnicero" (Alina Torres), *son*
"Montuno sin complicaciones," *son*
"El mulo," *son*
"Quien bien te quiere te hara llorar," *merengue son*
"La Habana sí," *songo*
"De La Habana a Matanzas," *guaguancó*
"Fallaste al sacar la cuenta," *guaracha*
"Muévete," *songo rock*
"La Habana no aguanta más," *son*
"Danzonette," *danzón/son*
"Que Gallega de mujer," *son*
"La rumba no está completa," *rumba*
"La candela," *rumba*

One of the easier pieces to learn was "La candela." Its basic chord pattern was A minor to F Major, to G Major, and back to A minor. It was the kind of work that lent itself to elongation because the singer could make up (often right on the spot) an endless array of choruses and *pregones*. It had a very special opening, with a bass/piano figure followed by a three-part chorus (see ex. 6.5).

"Danzonette" is a classic piece that begins as a majestic *danzón* and gathers momentum after an instrumental bridge as it switches to a double-time *son montuno*. This is yet another song that lends itself to extended *pregones*, breaks, and added choruses. Typically, we would elongate the piece anywhere from six to eight minutes. It proved to be a very popular piece.

The *danzón* is derived from the French *contredanse*, believed to have been introduced by slaves and colonists in Oriente Province following the 1791 slave uprising in Santo Domingo. The term *danzón* is thought to be a composite of *danza* and *son*. José Urfé's "El bombin de Barreto" (1910) added two new sections to the *danzón*. The last section was a *montuno*, where the music would begin to swing with added horn lines and solos of indeterminate length. Aniceto Díaz wrote "Rompiendo la rutina" ("Breaking the Routine") in 1929. According to Gerard and Sheller (1998, 94), Diaz referred to this new style as *danzonette* because it featured singing for the first time in a *danzón*. Formerly a purely instrumental form, the latter *son* section would include singing along with the inclusion of claves and maracas.

Ex. 6.5. Juan Formell, "La candela," piano reduction of chorus.

Ex. 6.6. Juan Formell, "Danzonette," excerpt.

In 1989 I was quite surprised to hear another version of "Danzonette" performed in a motion picture based on the story of the first Mexican radio pioneer in Los Angeles, Pedro J. González.[12]

In the film a guitar trio (with flutist) is performing in a nightclub. A lady sings the lead vocal. The year is circa 1929. This music also begins as a *danzón* and is later transformed into a *son,* with the difference that the modern version features more elaborate and modernized instrumentation than the film version. Okan Ise enjoyed performing this song because of its dynamic contrasts and the room allowed for improvisation. I include it here to further highlight the diversity of our material (see ex. 6.6).

As in all good working relationships, there are moments of miscommunication or misunderstanding. Our dire moment of major disagreement and disaffection came during a rehearsal in the winter of 1986. We were discussing the adoption of the catchy Juan Formell piece "Anda, ven y muévete" (or simply, "Muévete"). I was not particularly fond of the simplicity of that song. Three chords (G-F-C) were repeated endlessly, only interrupted by an occasional break. It was a simple rock song that distinguished itself by the inclusion of a *tumbao* pattern on the conga drums. Harmonically, the tune was reminiscent of the Beatles. Before I had heard the original recording by Formell and Los Van Van, Rubén Blades had released his own version earlier that year (1986). The main difference between the two recordings lay in the breaks (contrasting transitions) and in the lyrics. I liked both types of transitions but preferred the Blades version of the text. Juanito was adamantly opposed to doing the Rubén Blades version, which was openly political.

In the song "Muévete" ("Move It"), Blades sings to the Latin American countries (by extension, to the people) to "move it," to rise up. On the other hand, the original Juan Formell composition has no references to other countries or to politics. It is a song exorting people to get up, to dance and simply have a good time. I felt it quite ironic that the original lyrics to the song (written in a socialist country) could be much more restrained politically than the Rubén Blades recording. I argued vociferously that the Blades version was much more interesting. If we were to do the Formell version, could we not at least include parts of Blades's text? The answer was absolutely not. As I saw that there would be no room for compromise, our discussion became more heated. I thought Juan was being stubborn, a nationalistic "purist," in rejecting the Rubén Blades version.

After things calmed down, Juan pointed out the necessity (which I had completely overlooked) of doing non-political music in the band. He impressed upon me the need to avoid making political statements. His thinking was that the group would be blacklisted by local Cuban society if we were to appear to espouse progressive politics in our music. He even feared for his family back in Cuba, that they might somehow be harmed. This was hard for me to comprehend. At that time I did not fully appreciate the importance of his decision, of how we could be impacted negatively by including political messages in our songs. I knew little of the power of the conservative Cuban community. I had failed to understand that as newly arrived members of that community, Juan and Alberto (and by extension, the rest of the ensemble) were in an extremely vulnerable position. Juan feared ostracism and retaliation. Therefore, we agreed to perform only the Formell text but also to incorporate the breaks from both the Blades and Formell versions. Musically, the result was still a win/win solution.

Choosing new material with my Cuban colleagues was not always a one-way street. They were also sensitive to my cultural background and

Ex. 6.7. "Salmo VIII," break figure.

therefore open to my own suggestions about adopting other original works apart from the Formell compositions. One such work that I brought to the group was a samba entitled "Salmo VIII," written for two trombones, violin, and flute. The piece features an introduction that culminates in a tonally ambiguous figure (see ex. 6.7).

The group demonstrated further interest in my original music, and we did some of the arranging among ourselves, dividing the tasks, each adding his own ideas. We all enjoyed learning a fast-paced *guaracha* by Pacho Alonso, "Echame a mi la culpa" ("Blame Me"), written originally by well-known Mexican *ranchera* composer José Alfredo Jiménez. We also adopted a modern Bobby Rodríguez (Puerto Rican) salsa arrangement of "El espinita" ("The Little Sliver") by Mexican Nico Jiménez, a resident of Los Angeles. Coincidentally, Jiménez happened to walk into Rosa's Place one night while we were playing the tune. He had never heard the Bobby Rodríguez version of his song, and it was quite a pleasant surprise to both of us!

By December 1985, we had begun to incorporate trombones into the group. Our first major showcase with horns came on the twenty-first of that month at a large club on Sunset Boulevard, Casa Blanca (see fig. 6.4). From that evening on we began taking too many liberties—in our enthusiasm, we stretched the songs, added more *coros* and *pregones,* more instrumental solos, and thus sowed the seeds of our own demise. The dancers were not used to these longer pieces and quickly tired out. By going against the established limitations of song duration, we were unconsciously sabotaging our goal of obtaining steady club work. But at the time we were too excited about our new sound (particularly the addition of the trombones) to care about possible excesses. That evening the core of Okan Ise was a happy lot.

Beginning of the End

The beginning of the end of Okan Ise was an incident that occurred during a Halloween dance of the José Martí Cultural Club on November 1, 1986. We were contracted to perform four sets (each about forty-five minutes long) at the Hyatt Hotel Airport Inn, on West Century Boulevard. There were more than two thousand people in attendance, including two groups of young people dressed in carnival costumes, most likely sons and daughters of the

Fig. 6.4. Okan Ise at the Casa Blanca, 5612 Sunset Blvd., Hollywood, Saturday, December 21, 1985. From left to right: Nengue, author, Ricardo, Lil Nengue, Juan, Cuco, and Alberto.

members of the Club. The first group was comprised mainly of adolescents, and the second group featured younger children who followed two young adult leaders blowing whistles to cue choreography changes. Each group appeared separately in pairs of boys and girls dancing in step in a conga line to the sounds of Gloria Estefan and the Miami Sound Machine performing "Conga." A year after its release, the song was still at the height of its popularity.[13] Therefore, both the younger and older children used the number in their routine. It seemed a little tedious, and it was almost as though in "Conga" one were hearing the anthem of this exile community.[14] The younger children continued doing choreographed routines over the sound of a *comparsa* (carnival-style music).

It was curious to observe the ethnic composition of this large group of people of all ages. In the audience there were perhaps only three or four Afro-Cubans. The largest concentration of blacks in attendance had to be the Okan Ise band members themselves, who were clearly the darkest skinned of all. Even if there had been up to twenty blacks there, that number would have constituted less than 1 percent. This was contrary to my perception of the Cuban community. I had often driven around Cuban neighborhoods in Los Angeles, noting many Afro-Cubans. In the past, I had always observed a large representation of blacks (30 percent) among salsa audiences in Oakland and San Francisco. With my awareness of the prevalence of Afro-

Cuban performers in Cuban music, it was natural for me to assume that an organization such as the José Martí Cultural Club would be quite polyglot and integrated. I was surprised to see this was not the case.

We played our first set of the evening, and the floor filled with dancers. We were careful to mix older songs with the new material. The audience seemed to be enjoying our offerings and responded with polite applause after every tune. When we finished our first set, most of the members stepped off the stage to take their break. I returned to the stage to make some adjustments and survey the crowd. The Disc Jockey played the Miami Sound Machine's "Conga" again, and a big line of dancers emerged on the floor, dancing in a line that moved all around the big hall. Suddenly, to my astonishment, the lead dancers of this line decided they wanted to dance right through the stage. The platform was instantly filled with people dancing in a path alongside of which our instruments were placed. This was most irregular—normally party revelers know better than to approach a bandstand. There are boundaries between the public and musicians that must not be broached. Most dancers know better than to jump on a stage and dance around expensive equipment. In all my years of professional performance, it was something I had never experienced. Also, there is the danger that too many people on a stage could weaken its supports. My first fear was that someone would bump into the portable synthesizer that was placed precariously on a serving stand. I was also afraid for Arte's flute, sitting unprotected on a small stand in the path of these dancers. There were drums and cymbal stands that could have been easily toppled. Juan Oliva was on the stage at that moment, and he too became very nervous about this situation. The DJ's music was blasting powerfully through speakers not more than ten feet away. I raised my voice and asked the dancers to get off the stage, but there were so many streaming through that it made my request useless. Both Juan and I loudly asked people to be careful.

The people grudgingly stepped or jumped off the stage, but without a hint of remorse. These particular revelers were the main organizing committee members of the José Martí Cultural Club. They were so incensed by our reaction to their frivolous stage dancing that they sent us packing. Juan was told in no uncertain terms that Okan Ise was through for the evening. I could not believe that we would be treated as dispensable commodities. The audience had shown their acceptance of our music, yet the attitude of the organizers was entirely condescending and racist. Once again, I understood firsthand those feelings of being denigrated and treated without respect. These people who considered themselves decent, God-fearing pillars of their community had behaved in an outrageous manner.

It was a disconcerting incident that caused its share of doubt and dissension—as a band we began to grow apart. Nengue blamed Juan for over-reacting, and now suddenly the two were in open rivalry. We tried to recover for our next performance a few days later, a benefit for El Salvador earthquake relief. But by then the band had already begun to disintegrate. Nengue was absent, and his replacement could hardly be heard at all. I had to carry the vocals. Juan also sang several numbers, but we knew we were no match for Nengue. The audience accepted us, but there was a feeling that we were no longer the same united core.

Reflections

I was a Chicano in a Cuban band, and it was a rewarding experience. For a brief moment in time, I was able to assume an identity different from my own. I learned more about the richness of Cuban culture, and it was very satisfying to perform *songo*. There were things I had taken for granted that were not true. For instance, I thought that the Cuban Revolution had eradicated racism. At the time we were learning about each other in Los Angeles, Cuba was just beginning the process of changing its demographic and cultural orientation. Perhaps it was a sense of alienation and feelings of marginality that caused Juan Oliva to abandon his homeland. Despite my sympathies for socialism, I could relate to Juan's disaffection with his country's policies. Unfortunately, in 1990, I moved back to the San Francisco Bay Area.[15] Today, time, distance, and new committments have made us all strangers again.

Curiously, during the 1990s many Cuban groups were writing songs in the style of New York salsa. Also during this decade, a number of Cuban concerts took place in San Francisco and around the country. These were times of unimagined opportunities for Cuban musicians. Los Van Van gave concerts to rave reviews on several occasions. Their music reached out to thousands of enthusiastic new fans as they continued touring the United States, including Miami. Even hardliners there could no longer manipulate laws to keep Los Van Van or any other Cuban artists away (Driscoll, Levin, Davies 2000).

By the mid-1990s, *songo* was no longer the newest attraction and sensation. A new style dubbed *timba* arrived, generating much commotion among seasoned musicians and music lovers. Unfortunately, there is still a little confusion.[16] Sue Steward describes *timba* as "concept salsa," an exhilerating, complicated style that "rubs rumba and *son* against jazz and rap" (1999, 86). *Timba* is the next generation—another new music merging various styles (even rap) and making a great impression with groups such as NG La Banda[17] and a recent young promising ensemble, Klimax.[18]

While Okan Ise represented heightened consciousness about progressive music, I do not think that our collective Afro-Cuban ethnicity ever developed into a specifically "ideological program" as suggested by Kubic (1994, 42). Curiosity and a love of progressive Cuban music enticed me into a process of discovery about the culture of *Afro-Cubanismo*. In this regard, Afro-Cuban ethnicity served as a "behavior-modifying factor" (Kubic 1994, 43) in the sense that my experiences affected personal artistic production. As a newcomer, I was accepted by my Cuban peers, and this facilitated the rich process of interactive transculturation. I began to write music in proximity to the style we were adopting. Our remakes of songs such as "Sublime ilusión," "La espinita," and "Muévete" were creative examples of stylistic change and ethnic negotiation. However, there was never a preoccupation with the identity or "proper image" of the group. On the contrary, we were always aware of our unique group identity: it was never predominantly Afro-Cuban or anything else. All band members were proud to be involved in Cuban music, period. Our shared moments of rich Afro-Cubanism came mainly during the heat of performance. Our collective spirit, the Lucumí words expressed by Nengue, his *pregones*, the *coros*, the polyrhythms, improvisations, and occasional use of *batá* rhythms and allusions to *santería* ceremony constituted our sense of Afro-Cuba. When Nengue incorporated sacred melodies and lyrics into our stage performances, we were espousing an Afro-Cuban identity. However, he could switch roles in the very next song (i.e., a *bolero romántico*) and project a more Latino persona.

Although my time with Okan Ise was brief, it left lasting impressions. My own impression of Cubans was radically challenged. For a little over two years, I felt as though I too were a little bit *cubano*, tied to the fate of several persons I called my brothers. They always considered themselves Cubans first because to them, nationality is more important than race. We were always aware of our shared *Latinidad*, but there was that Afro-Cuban side. It manifested itself primarily in the climactic reaches of our musical abandon. It became a moving instrumental spontaneity comparable to free-wheeling *toques*, the ritual possession trance states of chordal ostinato and interlocking patterns under rhythmic attack.

Richard K. Spottswood's research on early Hispanic recordings (1990) clearly demonstrates a history of collaboration between Mexicans and Cubans, although the reasons for the particular unity of Okan Ise were perhaps different from those of other ensembles. In any event, this experience leaves me with golden memories of inspired music and mutual friendship. Moreover, accummulated tapes of several of our major performances will always be a living testament to the amount of time we invested in this, our remarkable musical syncronicity, and the many ways we blended together in driving this unique musical machine (*¡y qué máquina!*).

Notes

1. The following discussion is a distillation of points in Ortiz (1965 and 1973).
2. See *Sworn to the Drum: A Tribute to Francisco Aguabella*. Produced by Tom Luddy, directed and photographed by Les Blanc. VHS video, 35 minutes (El Cerrito: Flower Films, 1995).
3. Program Hostess, Radio KCRW (89.9 FM), Santa Monica College, May 1986. Interview with Juan Oliva and Alberto Blanco.
4. Among the groups I befriended and worked with were Orquesta Bacanal, with Guillermo Loo and Carmelo Garcia (Chinese/Mexican and Dominican, respectively). Their music included Latin jazz, fusion, and salsa; Orquesta Oskardi (Columbian), *cumbias* and salsa; Edwin Blas (Puerto Rican), salsa; Bobby Matos Heritage Ensemble (Nuyorican and Afro-American), Latin jazz; Hector Rosario (Puerto Rican), salsa; Los Costeños (Honduran), *merengues* and salsa; Tamba Tropical (Mexican), *cumbias* and ballads; and Grupo Umbral (Chicano/Mexican), *nueva canción*.
5. The title was later changed to *Roots of Rhythm*, a three-part series on Cuban music and its historical influence on American culture. Howard Dratch and Eugene Rosow, *Roots of Rhythm*, Parts I, II & III (Santa Monica: Cultural Research and Communications, 1989).
6. The son of a well-known percussionist and bassist (in Cuba and Chicago), Frank Martínez, Sr. (1913–1985). Cuco's mother has been a very devoted *santera* for a long time.
7. Coincidentally, the 1983 Zaperoko release "Cosa de locos" features Juan Oliva, with whom I later worked in Okan Ise. Juan is featured on conga and *batá* drums.
8. See Ojito (2000): "Miami is deeply segregated, . . . as the roughly 7 percent of the area's Cubans who are black quickly learn, skin color easily trumps nationality." This was the second article in the series "How Race Is Lived in America."
9. Arte Webb is well known in New York salsa circles and has performed with Patato Valdez, Jorge Dalto, Roberto Torres, and has even substituted for José Fajardo. Arte is featured on the classic Ray Barretto album *Indestructible* (Fania Records 1973).
10. I worked steadily with this group from 1984 up to the time I started performing in public with Okan Ise, in the fall of 1985. Honduran music has hardly been researched and deserves separate treatment because Honduran musical preferences are quite distinct from those of other Central American countries. The favorite music of urban Hondurans is the *merengue*, of which Los Costeños performed many.
11. See Suro (1999, 165): "While the myth of Cuban Miami extols the self-reliant exile who arrived with no more than the shirt off his back and who made a fortune through brains and perseverance, the truth is that the Cubans built their enclave with massive public assistance and then continued to draw government subsidies well after they had established themselves here."
12. *Break of Dawn*, starring Oscar Chávez.
13. "Conga" was the first major national release (November 23, 1985) of the Miami Sound Machine. According to Joel Whitburn (1996, 207), the song remained in the Top Ten position for sixteen weeks. Born Gloria Fajardo (December 1, 1957), Gloria Estefan came to Miami in 1960 from Cuba, where her father was a bodyguard for President Fulgencio Batista.

14. Interestingly, major local names among Miami Cubans are primarily white Hispanics, e.g., Gloria Estefan, Henry Fiol, Chirino, and Albita Rodríguez. These people have often relied upon Afro-Cuban strains.
15. Shortly after my arrival, I joined Orquesta Gitano, a salsa group based in Watsonville. Their singer, Mario Pérez, is an Afro-Cuban who hails from Havana.
16. Robinson (2000, 1E) erroneously refers to Los Van Van as an established "timba group" that "basically invented the genre." The author speculates about whether Cuban music "so aggressively engineered to make people dance can find enough of an audience in the concert hall and the living room." My impression of the author is that he has probably had very little real exposure to Latin music in general.
17. According to Steward (1999, 86–87), José Luis Cortés is a flute player who left Irakere in 1988 "to search for the Cuban music of the future." Along the way he formed NG La Banda, a complex music "neither jazz nor salsa, but a brilliant take on each."
18. An interview with the leader of Klimax appears in web page SalsaSF: http://www.salsasf.com/Interviews/piloto_eng.html.

References

Blum, Joseph. 1978. "Problems of Salsa Research." *Ethnomusicology* 22/1: 137–49.

Driscoll, Amy, Jordan Levin, and Frank Davies. 2000. "Court Ruling Ends Dade's Cuba Policy: Massachusetts Case on Mynamar Prevents County from Enforcing Law." *The Miami Herald* (June 20): 1A.

Elí Rodríguez, Victoria. 1989. "Apuntes sobres la creación musical actual en Cuba." *Latin American Music Review* 10/2: 287–97.

———. 1994. "Cuban Music and Ethnicity: Historical Considerations." In *Music and Black Identity: The Caribbean and South America*. Edited by Gerard Béhague. New Brunswick, N.J.: Transaction Publishers/North-South Center, University of Miami.

García, María Cristina. 1996. *Havana USA: Cuban Exiles and Cuban Americans in South Florida, 1959–1994*. Berkeley: University of California Press.

Gerard, Charley, and Marty Sheller. 1998. *Salsa! The Rhythm of Latin Music*. Tempe, Ariz.: White Cliffs Media.

Kubik, Gerhard. 1994. "Ethnicity, Cultural Identity, and the Psychology of Culture Contact." In *Music and Black Identity: The Caribbean and South America*. Edited by Gerard Béhague. New Brunswick, N.J.: Transaction Publishers/North-South Center, University of Miami.

Ojito, Mirta. 2000. "Best of Friends, Worlds Apart: Joel Ruiz is Black, Achmed Valdés is White. In America They Discovered It Matters." *The New York Times* (June 5): 1.

Ortiz, Fernando. 1965. *Africanía de la música folklórica de Cuba*. La Habana: Editora Universitaria.

———. 1973. *Orbita de Fernando Ortiz*. La Habana: Unión de Escritores y Artistas de Cuba.

Robinson, Eugene. 2000. "Unique Cuban 'Timba' May Pulsate Its Way to U.S. Dance Floors," *The Miami Herald* (June 22): 1E.

Spitta, Silvia. 1997. "Transculturation, the Caribbean, and the Cuban American Imaginary." In *Tropicalizations: Transcultural Representations of Latinidad*. Edited by Frances

R. Aparicio and Susana Chávez-Silverman. Hanover: Dartmouth College, University Press of New England.

Spottswood. Richard K. *Ethnic Music on Records: A Discography of Ethnic Recordings Produced in the United States, 1893–1942*. Urbana: University of Illinois Press.

Steward, Sue. 1999. *¡Música!* San Francisco: Chronicle Books.

Suro, Roberto. 1999. *Strangers Among Us*. New York: Vintage Books.

Whitburn, Joel. 1996. *The Billboard Book of Top Forty Hits*. 6th ed. New York: Billboard Books.

7

The *Bolero Romántico*
From Cuban Dance to International Popular Song

GEORGE TORRES

W ithin the development of Latin American popular music, few genres have achieved the success of the *bolero romántico*, a genre of the
bolero repertoire. The music, which was a combination of European-style
melody and Afro-Cuban rhythm, became popular all over the world, and
the songs were translated into many different languages. The success of
composers like Agustín Lara and performers like Trio Los Panchos created a
worldwide audience for the bolero in the 1940s and '50s and made these
musicians among the most popular of their day. But even as popular as the
genre was, the advent of other dominant forms of popular music, such as
American rock 'n' roll, would eventually take the spotlight from it. After a
twenty-year lull in the *bolero romántico*'s popularity, it came back as a nostalgic tribute to the music of a golden age of romantic Mexican music. These
latter-day interpretations were less innovative than they were a panegyric
to a time in Mexico of courtship and honor.

This chapter examines the bolero from its origins as a Cuban dance, to
its appropriation by Mexican *tríos románticos*, to its resurgence among baby-
boomer artists such as Linda Ronstadt. The bolero became a vehicle for the
genre known as *tríos románticos* that was developed largely by Mexican artists
from 1944 to 1960, particularly Los Panchos and their followers, who,
through their musical innovations and international performances, were
responsible for the crystallization of the *trío romántico*. The study begins by
establishing a distinction between Spanish and Cuban boleros and then

gives some background on the development of the bolero in Cuba. Next, the Mexican appropriation of the bolero and its fusion with the *canción mexicana* is described. The study concludes with an examination of a selection of boleros by Caribbean, Mexican, and American composers and performers including Nat "King" Cole, Eydie Gorme, and Los Tri-O. The reinterpretations by these artists represent not only musical transformations of the songs themselves, but in some cases a transformation of audience: the latter constituting a type of musical crossover from a Latin American to a U.S. audience and, hence, a crosscultural phenomenon.

Spanish and Cuban Origins of the Bolero

The bolero is a Spanish song and dance form that flourished in the eighteenth and nineteenth centuries in Spain and continues to be performed in some parts of the country today. Some scholars point to a more precise origin of Mallorca, one of the Spanish Balearic islands in the Mediterranean, where it is referred to as the *bolero mallorquín* (Salazar 1988, 12). The Spanish bolero is typically in 3/4 with characteristics similar to the *seguidilla* and *fandango*, which were also very popular eighteenth- and nineteenth-century Spanish dances. As a folkloric dance rhythm, the bolero is most easily identified by the pattern of an eighth followed by two sixteenths and four eighths. Often the two sixteenths are replaced by a sixteenth triplet. This pattern is used in the rhythmic introduction to Ravel's famous *Bolero* for orchestra. The bolero as a dance was "invented" by the Spanish dancer Sebastián Cerezo around 1780 (Salazar 1988, 11).

The Cuban bolero is a duple-meter song and dance that became popular in the last half of the nineteenth century. It proceeds from the Afro-Cuban tradition, inherited from West Africa, of layers of ostinato percussion that produce a composite rhythm. In the Cuban bolero, there is more emphasis on the *tresillo* and *cinquillo* rhythms than in the Mexican variety, and the latter abandons the use of claves altogether (see ex. 7.1a and 7.1b).

The Cuban bolero is believed to have originated in Santiago de Cuba, supposedly from antecedents of the Spanish bolero. It is difficult to see the relationship between the triple-meter Spanish version and the duple-meter Cuban variety. Indeed, this has led some to speculate that the Cuban bolero has more in common with the Cuban *contradanza* and *danzón* than it does with the Spanish bolero (Kahl and Katz 2001), although one sees references to the bolero that predate the composition of the first *danzónes*. The musical differences between the *contradanza* and the *danzón* are slight. The *contradanza* (an Afro-Cuban tributary to the *danzón*) was developed in Cuba as a social dance that featured groups of paired couples. Manuel Saumell (1817–1870) was one of the more important musicians of the period and

Ex. 7.1a and 7.1b. Cuban-style bolero rhythms illustrating *cinquillo* pattern (7.1a), and *son* clave pattern with *tresillo* (7.1b).

composed some fifty *contradanzas*. The *danzón* appeared later as a partner dance for embracing couples; the first published *danzón* is credited to Miguel Failde in 1879 (Salazar 1988, 16). Another influential Cuban form was the habanera, which was popular in the nineteenth century and enjoyed much international fame. It is also a duple-meter dance, and its rhythms were characteristic of other dances as well.

The bolero, then, is the last stage in the development of these nineteenth-century genres. The first bolero in Cuba is credited to José "Pepe" Sánchez, whose "Tristezas" was written in 1885, although the term referring to a non-Spanish bolero may go back as far as 1830. At the time there was no specific structure to the bolero. Sánchez's creation included two sixteen-bar periods that were separated by an instrumental interlude known as a *passacalle*. The bolero at this time remained, for the most part, in the provinces and outside of Havana until the 1920s, at which time a newly evolving genre, the *son*, arrived on the musical scene. The *son* became hugely popular in Cuban dance halls and began to replace the *danzón*. This was beneficial for the bolero because the performances of *sones* by the Sexteto Habanero included a fusion of the bolero and the *son*: the *bolero son*. In this fusion, the band would play a moderate bolero and then go into a quicker, livelier *son*. It is because of this popularity as a dance that the bolero gained its initial celebrity beyond Cuba.

Other factors that helped elevate the popularity of the bolero were traveling orchestras and radio and phonographic performances. When the venues for performance widened, so did the popularity of the genre. In the 1920s a new form of performance furthered this trend: the *orquestas típicas* that gained popularity abroad. Cuban composer Ernesto Lecuona put together a band known as Lecuona's Cuban Boys. In the late 1920s and '30s this group made many trips to Europe, until the outbreak of World War II, when they were forced to return to Cuba. After the war, they traveled to the United States and performed in New York City. New York was a very exciting place for Latin music, and the audience there was quite receptive (Roberts 1999, 7; Salazar 1988, 36).

Advances in the media also helped encourage the widespread popularity of Cuban music. The radio allowed live and recorded music to be transmitted outside of the provinces and into the larger cities. The newly evolving recording industry also had a hand in the dissemination of Cuban music, but the close association of Cuba with Mexico had been forming musical connections going back to the nineteenth century. We shall now see how the genres that originated in Spain and Cuba made their way to Mexican soil and how Mexicans eventually appropriated and transformed the Cuban archetype into a Mexican original.

The *Canción Mexicana*

As was the case throughout much of colonial Latin America, there was an aesthetic division in music that ran along social lines. On one side was a large *mestizo* and Indian population that cultivated regional styles based on indigenous cultural patterns among the rural populations. On the other side there were the upper and middle classes that favored European style and taste. Even after Mexican independence in 1821, there was still a strong tendency among the upper classes to promote and appreciate European fashion. In music, this took the form of social dances like the waltz and the polka over the more indigenous *zapateado* and *jarabe*. Even as late as the regime of Porfirio Díaz (1884–1911), there was still a strong glorification of European musical models. In fact, it is probably safe to say that between Mexican independence and the Mexican revolution, there was very little appreciation of any "Mexican" music among the upper classes.[1]

With regard to the *canción mexicana*, it is generally accepted that there are two basic styles: one that is steeped in the *mestizo* tradition, and one that consists of songs in a *bel canto* style that were sung in the salons of the upper classes (Geijerstam 1976, 60). This second type is distinguished by some as a romantic and sentimental song that first appeared in characteristically Mexican form as early as 1830, when it was introduced to Mexico's middle-class and aristocratic circles (Mendoza 1982, 143). Musical traits include the use of tonic and dominant harmonies as opposed to the modal harmonies used in *mestizo* music, and a melodic style that showcases a strong vocal technique, such as wide leaps in the melody and cadenzas over a dominant-seventh harmony (Geijerstam 1976, 62). In any case, it seems clear that this Italianate, lyric style of Mexican song enjoyed great popularity during the last half of the nineteenth century.

In 1866, singer Conchita Méndez performed Sebastián Yradier's famous habanera "La paloma" in Mexico. This song had a profound influence on Mexican music and was eventually appropriated into the *canción* repertoire; Garrido declares that it is now thought of in Mexico as a Mexican song (1981, 17). Not long thereafter, "La golondrina" appeared, a Mexican song in the habanera style with a Mexican flavor. It is still a favorite today. The music was by Veracruz-born composer Narciso Serradell (1843–1910), with words by French poet Niceto de Zamacois and translated into Spanish by Francisco Martínez de la Rosa (Flores Longoria 1994, 28). The precise date of the song is uncertain, but it was most likely written a little before 1870 (Garrido 1981, 18). Both "La paloma" and "La golondrina" enjoyed great popularity during the last decades of the nineteenth century and, according to Garrido, were examples of songs that had a particular Mexican melos distinct from the European models of Mexican *canción* that had existed previously (1981, 18).

The last decades of the nineteenth century witnessed the formation of a uniquely Mexican song style and structure, and this important trend continued well into the first decades of the twentieth century, when Miguel Lerdo de Tejada (1869–1941) wrote the first true *canción mexicana*, "Perjura" (Geijerstam 1976, 65). However, the most illustrious contributor to the *canción mexicana* was Manuel Ponce (1882–1948), Mexico's preeminent composer during the first four decades of the century. From Ponce's oeuvre comes the most celebrated Mexican song of this period, "Estrellita" (see ex. 7.2a and 7.2b).

"Estrellita"	"Little Star"
Estrellita de lejano cielo,	Little star from a distant sky,
que miras mi dolor,	who sees my pain,
que sabes mi sufrir.	who knows of my suffering.
Baja y dime si me quiere un poco,	Come down and tell me if he/she loves me a little,
porque ya no puedo, sin su amor vivir.	because I can no longer live without his/her love.

Ex. 7.2a and 7.2b. Manuel Ponce, "Estrellita," first and last phrases, showing the melodic style of the *canción mexicana*.

¡Tú eres, estrella, mi faro de amor!	You, star, are my beacon of love!
Tu sabes que pronto, he de morir.	You know that I must soon die.
Baja y dime si me quiere un poco,	Come down and tell me if he/she loves me a little,
porque ya no puedo, sin su amor vivir.	because I can no longer live without his/her love.

In setting the poem to music, Ponce parallels the structure of the text closely. The song is a balanced binary structure that returns to the A material to close its B section, an obvious choice given the refrain-like nature of the second quatrain. The music consists of two long periods of sixteen measures, with each line of poetry set to four measures of music. The poem's first four lines (as well as the last two lines) alternate contrasting melodic shapes, while the first couplet of the second quatrain—with identical counts of ten syllables—shares identical melodic material. Ponce has set the text in a predominantly syllabic style, which was not a common trait of *bel canto*. Though not originally a bolero, this song lends itself well to the bolero style of performance and is often performed by *tríos románticos*. This affinity is due to its melodic style as well as the form of the song, which has much in common with many bolero numbers.

Mexican Appropriation of the Bolero

What were the first signs of the bolero in Mexico? The models for the dances of *habanera* and *danzón* had been around for some time, and the influence of the Italianate *canción mexicana* was already established by the time "Estrellita" was published (1912). Salazar states that the reason the bolero rose to prominence at this time was because the rhythm of the dance was easily transferable to the style of the *canción romántica* (1988, 62).

The musical connection between Cuba and Mexico dates back to the mid-nineteenth century; there was a special relationship between Cuba and the southeast Mexican state of Yucatán, which lies only about a hundred miles west of Cuba. It was most likely Cuban circus troupes and music reviews that made the Yucatán people familiar with the repertoire of *danzas, sones*, and boleros (Salazar 1988, 64; Pineda 1996, 121). There is also evidence that the first Cuban bolero, "Tristezas," was published in a Yucatán songbook in 1908, although apparently in the guise of a *guaracha* (Salazar 1988, 62). It is very likely that the Yucatán peninsula was the point of entry for the Cuban bolero. However, the first truly Mexican bolero is from the northern state of Nuevo León, written in 1919 by Armando Villareal and entitled "Morena mía" (Salazar 1988, 62). Many other boleros followed, not surprisingly by many musicians in the region of Yucatán, among whom the most renowned was Guty Cardenas (Geijerstam 1976, 64). Cardenas was a hugely popular musician who contributed a variety of hits to the early bolero repertoire, although many of his songs were famous as *huapangos*. During his very short career (Cardenas was killed in a barroom brawl in 1932 at age twenty-seven), he wrote and recorded many popular Mexican songs. Notable among his compositions are "Nunca," "Rayito de sol" (known as "Por la mañana" in its day), "Flor," and "Ojos tristes." Many of his songs have enjoyed much popularity since their composition in the late 1920s.

Época de Oro

The period from 1930 to 1960 marked the *época de oro* ("golden age") of bolero composers and performers in Mexico. It began with the work of Agustín Lara and ended with the performances of Trío Los Panchos. During the 1930s and '40s, Lara became the voice of a newly evolving Mexican middle class and influenced an entire school of both composers and performers. At the opposite end is the roughly fifteen-year reign of Trio Los Panchos as the final manifestation of the school of composition influenced by Lara.

Indeed, the most celebrated of all bolero composers remains Agustín Lara (1900–1970). His career spanned the period of the bolero's golden age, during which he wrote more than five hundred compositions.[2] As a musician, Lara was self-taught and responsible for some of the most popular Mexican songs ever. Included in his list of bolero hits are "Imposible," "Mujer," "Solamente una vez," "Perdida," "Lamento jarocho," "Nadie," "Piensa en mi," "Veracruz," "Naufragio," "Palabras de mujer," and "Jamás," to name but a few. According to Salazar, Lara did not invent anything new in bolero songwriting, but it was his successful use of harmonic and melodic formulas that made his songs attractive models for composers of succeeding generations.

Lara came into contact with many great singers who were responsible for popularizing some of his biggest hits, including Juan Arvizu, Pedro

Vargas, and Toña la Negra. Lara's musical innovations included a change from the 2/4 meter that featured a Cuban-influenced *cinquillo* rhythm, to a smoother 4/4 meter that stressed accents on beats one, three, and four (Pineda 1996, 125). Many of his compositions include a rhythmically free introductory song that is followed by and contrasted with a metrical dance section (e.g., "Noche de ronda"). Another two-part idea is beginning the first half of a song in the minor mode and then switching to the parallel major mode for the second part of the song (e.g., "Piensa en mi").

Soon after Lara, bolero composition continued to flourish with notable contributions by composers such as María Grever, Tata Nacho, Consuelo Velásquez, Gonzalo Curiel, Gabriel Ruiz, and José "Pepe" Guizar, all of whom had a significant impact on the golden age of the bolero.

The *Trío Romántico*

The style of performance initiated by Los Panchos resulted from a confluence of different influences. If one considers the performing forces from a broad perspective, one sees that the music consists of voices, chordal instruments, a lead melody instrument, and layered percussion. This distribution of forces is found in many Latin American popular-music ensembles, and I will mention several of those that played a role in the development of the *trío romántico*. Notable trios from the late 1920s and '30s included the Trío Garnica Ascencio, whose rustic sound and high-pitched voices were a big hit at the Teatro Lírico in Mexico City in the late 1920s (Rivas 1979, 159). Also from the late 1920s was Los Trovadores Tamaulipecos, a vocal group that featured virtuosic guitar playing (Rivas 1979, 159). In the 1930s, other important groups appeared that would also have a strong influence on the succeeding generation of performers, including Los Hermanos Martínez Gil (1928) and Trio Calaveras (1938). By the time Los Panchos arrived on the musical scene in 1944, there were signs that the performance of the urban bolero was returning to a guitar-based ensemble. The difference with Los Panchos and groups that followed their lead was that the singers accompanied themselves on the guitars. Also, a higher, sweeter-sounding contratenor was becoming fashionable.

The performing forces of the *triós románticos* usually consist of three guitarists, each of whom sings an independent vocal line. The instrumentation of this ensemble became standard with regard to the following features: vocals, guitars, and rhythm section. The vocals were usually three independent vocal lines that consisted of a lead tenor (*primera voz*) and two lower harmonizing vocals (*segunda* and *tercera voces*). With regard to the vocal texture, the group would usually declaim a syllabic text with the lead voice on top and the two supporting vocals underneath. Often it is the upper voice that sings the melody while the bottom voices move in stepwise motion to fit the harmony. In a typical performance, the three voices sing the song together the first time through, and the second time through the lead sings the melody text while the two lower voices hum a background harmony.

One of the distinguishing features of the ensemble is the use of the guitars as the principal accompaniment. There was in this period a type of guitar virtuosity that has remained unparalled in Mexican popular music. Generally speaking, there are two guitars and a *requinto*.[3] The *requinto* is a small classical guitar tuned a fourth higher than the standard guitar. Its name means "to tighten" or "to make taught," from the verb *requintar* (the *quinto* does not refer to the interval of a fifth). It can be plucked with either a pick or with the fingers of the right hand. If a pick is used, it is often a thumb pick. The instrument was invented in 1945 by Alfredo Gil of Los Panchos in order to play introductions and interludes on a guitar without losing any of the sustain from placing a capo too high on the neck. Since its invention and use by Gil as the melodic lead instrument, it has become standard in *trío romántico* performance practice.

All of the guitars make use of the capo in order to expedite a quick transposition without losing any of the idiomatic qualities of the instrument.[4] A typical arrangement might have one guitar without a capo (*al aire*) using a key-of-A fingering; the second guitar would play with a capo on the second fret using a key-of-G fingering; and the *requinto*, already tuned a fourth higher, would play with a capo on the second fret using a key-of-D fingering. In this way, no one player would ever play the same voicing of a chord because they were all using different portions of the guitar's diapason, thus creating a richer sound. With regard to texture, the two standard guitars play a bolero accompaniment in their respective registers while the *requinto* either plays a melodic lead or embellishes the sections between sung text (e.g., Los Panchos' recordings of "Caminemos," "Contigo," and "Sin ti"). Another option is for the *requinto* and the middle guitar to play a melodic duet while the third guitar sustains the bolero rhythm underneath (e.g., Los Panchos' recordings of "Luna lunera," "Alma vanidosa," and "Malagueña salerosa") (see ex. 7.3).

The rhythm section derives from the Cuban influence of layers of percussion that provide a composite rhythm.[5] Normally, the rhythm instruments remain those most commonly used in the Cuban *conjuntos*, namely, claves, maracas, and bongos/timbales as well as an upright bass. Earlier in the chapter, we looked at the Cuban bolero rhythm emphasizing a *tresillo* or *cinquillo* pattern. The bolero style that Los Panchos inherited from Lara smoothed the rhythm out to a gentler pattern accenting beats one, three, and four played by the bass, which replaced the clave in trio performances.

Ex. 7.3. Bolero rhythm on the guitar.

The maracas and timbales perform the same rhythmic patterns as in the Cuban varieties. This is the only style of Mexican popular music that makes use of the maracas. These generally play a common repeating pattern of steady eighth notes, while the timbales (if used) play rhythmic variations of the other repeating patterns. Sometimes the timbalero will strike the side of the drum frame with the sticks, a technique called *paila* or *cáscara*.

However, the rhythm section only served as anonymous back-up, and the focus was on the three members of the trio. Nevertheless, the rhythm section of these bolero groups was important in maintaining a steady dance rhythm, and their inclusion in recordings and in live performance was crucial to the success of the sound.

Los Panchos

If Agustín Lara was responsible for defining a standard for bolero composition, then Los Panchos were responsible for defining the standard for bolero performance in the 1940s and '50s. They were neither the first trio to come on the scene, nor did they do anything exceptional to the structure of the songs. Rather, Los Panchos's success was the result of brilliant arranging and marketing.

The group was formed by Alfredo "güero" Gil, Jesús "Chucho" Navarro, and Hernando Avilés in New York City, where they opened at the Teatro Hispano in 1944. Previous to Los Panchos, Navarro and Gil had a trio that embarked on a tour in the United States and that eventually took them to New York. After completing a radio contract with CBS, Navarro and Gil left the trio and encountered Avilés, who was also performing in New York. At first they were all playing standard guitars; however, in 1945 Alfredo Gil began using the *requinto*, which he had developed. Thus, a new sound was formed. From 1945 to 1948, Los Panchos toured the Americas, and their popularity spread throughout the Caribbean and the United States. They remained based in New York until 1948, when they accepted a slot on Mexican radio station XEW and began playing in more visible venues.

During the New York years, Los Panchos crystallized the bolero genre, which reflected the taste of the Latin American public in New York at the time (Salazar 1988, 304). Their name ("The Three Franks") was a way of using a popular Mexican name that could easily be remembered by New York audiences. Gil later recalled:

> We wanted to have a very Mexican name; we remembered our martyr of the Revolution, Francisco Madera, and the hero of the War of Guerillas, Pancho Villa, and because back then Walt Disney created his happy-go-lucky rooster, Pancho Pistolas, we didn't give it a second thought, and that's how we named the trio. (Marin n.d., 7)

The repertoire of Los Panchos consisted of compositions written by well-known composers of the period. The majority of these composers were from Mexico; however, some were from the Caribbean, most notably Puerto Rico, where the *trío romántico* was becoming quite popular. Although some of the original compositions of Navarro and Gil were very successful ("Caminemos," "Rayito de luna," "No trates de mentir"), the majority of their recorded repertoire was from golden-age composers such as Agustín Lara, María Grever, Guty Cardenas, Rafaél Hernández, José "Pepe" Guizar, and Claudio Estrada.

Bolero Poetry and Musical Style

Previous discussions of the bolero style have little to say about the music and even less about the text. In the past there has been a tendency to categorize the poetry in overly simplistic terms. Words like "sentimental" and "weepy" do little to further our understanding of the mechanics of the poetry, which, after all, is the reason there is any song to be sung.[6] The following is an examination of one of the more popular boleros, "Piel canela," with poetry and music by the Puerto Rican composer Bobby Capo.

Bolero poetry often deals with themes of bittersweet, unrequited, betrayed, or eternal love. Iris Zavala points to the extremes in bolero poetry as "magic discourses from opposite worlds of affirmations that are discretely negated: to die/to live, to love/to abhor, presence/absence, passion/jealousy" (1991, 14). The poetry in "Piel canela" reflects love and all the potential sadness of living without it.

"Piel canela"	"Cinnamon Skin"
Verso	Verse
Que se quede el infinito sin estrellas	Let infinity be without stars
o que pierda el ancho mar su inmensidad,	or let the deep sea lose its immensity,

pero el negro de tus ojos que no muera	but let the darkness of your eyes never die
y el canela de tu piel se quede igual.	and your cinnamon skin ever remain the same.
Si perdiera el arco iris su belleza	If the rainbow should lose its beauty
y las flores su perfume y su color,	and the flowers their fragrance and color,
no sería tan inmensa mi tristeza,	my sadness would not be as immense
como aquella de quedarme sin tu amor.	as that of being without your love.
Refrain	Refrain
Me importas tú, y tú, y tú,	What matters to me is you, and you and you,
y solamente tú, y tú, y tú,	and no one else but you . . . ,
me importas tú, y tú, y tú,	what matters to me is you, and you and you,
y nadie más que tú.	and no one else but you.
Ojos negros piel canela,	Dark eyes, cinnamon skin,
que me llegan a desesperar,	that drive me crazy
me importas tú, y tú y tú,	what matters to me is you, and you and you,
y nadie más que tú.	and no one else but you.[7]

The poem divides into a two-quatrain verse and a two-quatrain refrain. The phrase rhythm is distinct between the verse and the refrain with the scansion of the verses being dodecasyllabic. The refrain consists of alternating couplets, each consisting of a line of eight and a line of six syllables. Each couplet of each of the verse-quatrains alternates between a feminine and a masculine line. Rhythmically, the poem begins on two weak syllables leading to the first accent on the first syllable of the word *quede*. This is followed by the next accent on the third syllable of *infinito* and finally on the second syllable of *estrella*. The second line follows the same scansion, with the first accent of the second line occurring on the second syllable of *perdiera*. This is followed by the next accent on the word *mar*, then by the last syllable on *inmensidad*. The accents in this couplet can be seen in the following (elision of vowels is indicated by the underline between them):

Que se **que**de_el infi**ni**to sin es**tre**llas
o que **pier**da_el ancho **mar** su_inmensi**dad**

Ex. 7.4. Bobby Capo, "Piel canela."[8]

The three remaining couplets of verses one and two continue this scansion as well as the continued alternation of feminine and masculine lines. Rhythmically, the couplets may be interpreted as seen in ex. 7.4.

The phrase rhythm of the refrain departs from that of the first two verses in the poetry. The first quatrain of the refrain is an 8+10+8+6 scansion that is carefully punctuated between the words *tú* and *y* in order to avoid unnecessary elisions between syllables that would normally be joined together. As a result of this internal punctuation, the rhythm of the first line results in a series of short-long articulations (notated by an **L** for long and an **s** for short under the poetry):

Me importas tú, y tú, y tú
    L sL sL

The second line of the first couplet of the refrain brings resolution to the first line with a ten-syllable declamation; the second half of both lines is identical. The first couplet of the second quatrain of the refrain begins a scansion that consists of an 8+10 syllable count. The first of these two lines has its accents on the first syllable of *negros,* and the second syllable of *canela.* The following decasyllabic line has a cesura in between the fifth and sixth syllables (indicated here by the double slash):

Ojos **ne**gros piel can**e**la,
que me **lle**gan // a desespe**rar**,

This final quatrain of the refrain ends with the same second couplet as the first.

The poem describes a world of suspended reality. The first couplet of the verse states that a world without stars and a sea without immensity would be preferable to living without the beauty of dark eyes and cinnamon skin. The second verse conditionally states that *if* the rainbow lost its beauty and *if* the flowers lost their fragrance and color, it would not be as bad as living without love. The suspension of reality exists in the nonverifiable nature of the claims. Real or not, the claims contrast with the sentiments expressed in

Requinto

Ex. 7.5. Los Panchos, "Piel canela," introduction.

the verses of the refrain: "Nothing matters more to me than you"—with "you" repeated ten times in the first quatrain of the refrain, and four in the second, to further emphasize the sentiment.

The text speaks abstractly at first and then more inwardly as the poem continues. In the first verse, the speaking is directed outward, while in the second verse the pronoun *mi* ("my") in the third line draws the text inward to the impact on the speaker. The refrain begins the sequence of *tú*'s ("you's") that reinforce what appears to be the speaker's only desire. In a sort of self-fulfilling prophecy, the dark eyes and the cinnamon skin have indeed driven the speaker to madness, and he is reduced to repeating the most basic words and ideas.

The classic 1950's version of "Piel canela" by Los Panchos is the starting point for our study of interpretation. The piece begins with an instrumental introduction featuring a fluid *requinto* solo by Alfredo Gil (ex. 7.5). The song closely follows the structure of the poetry, and the group goes through the poem once. A *requinto* interlude that is identical to the introduction follows. The piece then returns to the first verse, skips ahead to the refrain, and omits the second verse. A striking feature of this version is the smooth blending of the three voices. The lead vocal is carefully balanced within the trio's vocal arrangement. Vocal variety is always present in Los Panchos. In the first statement of the first verse, the vocalists sing the first couplet together, but let the lead sing by himself for the second couplet. In the second statement of the first verse, Navarro and Gil hum in harmony behind the lead. At the second couplet they sing new harmonies where they had previously dropped out entirely. For the refrain they insert an interesting twist: the first three lines with *tú*'s are chanted in unison, breaking into harmony on the last line of the first quatrain of the refrain. The beginning of the second quatrain, sung to the words "ojos negros," is also harmonized, but at the return of "me importas tú" they return to the unison chant until the end of the line, opening up the harmonies on "nadie más que tú." Another striking feature of this version is the skill involved in the execution, that is, the virtuoso singing and playing by all the performers.

Once their preferred genre was established, Los Panchos rarely strayed from the bolero as the vehicle for their songs. There are cases in which they played songs in other forms, but they are rare. Even songs well known in another rhythmic form were interpreted as boleros. The group released one of the most famous songs in the tango repertoire, "El choclo," as a bolero; a well-known Cuban *son* from the period, "Me voy p'al pueblo," was also performed in a bolero rhythm. The most notable exception to this dependence on the bolero was when the group performed songs in triple-meter rhythms, the two most common being the *vals* and the "clave." The latter is a term used in connection with this repertoire to refer to a rhythm that employs the so-called clave pattern (in three) of quarter, two eighths, quarter over a half, quarter bass pattern:

```
Clave:   x      x x    x
Bass:    x             x
         1      2      3
```

This rhythm was common in the repertoire of Yucatán composer Guty Cardenas and can be heard on Los Panchos' version of "Nunca," "Rayito de sol," and "Ojos tristes."

The other common triple-meter option is the *vals*. In Mexico, the *vals* already had a long history of popularity dating back to the previous century. One of Agustín Lara's most popular songs, "Noche de ronda,"[9] has often been performed by other groups as a bolero, but Los Panchos interpreted it as a waltz. Perhaps in homage to the great composer, Los Panchos decided to leave the Lara composition in its original rhythm. Another notable performance in triple meter is their recording of "Alma, corazón y vida" by Adrián Flores Alvan.

Los Panchos were the first Mexican trio to achieve international fame. This was largely due to the availability of their music in all corners of the world. In a career spanning thirty-five years, they recorded some 2,500 songs on some 250 albums. Their international popularity is evident in the success of their numerous tours throughout North and South America, Europe, Northern Africa, and Asia. In Japan they were a huge hit, selling records by the thousands, and they made six albums in Japanese (Salazar 1988, 304). In addition to their numerous radio and television performances in Mexico and abroad, they appeared in fifty films, many of which carried the name of one of their bolero hits, such as *No me quieras tanto*, *Rayito de luna*, and *Amor de la calle*.

Immediate Followers

The influence that Trio Los Panchos had on the bolero genre was immense. Their style of vocals, guitar instrumentation, and use of the rhythm section set the standard for those who followed. Not long after their formation, trios of the same variety began to form all over Latin America, especially Mexico and the Caribbean.[10] The ensuing discussion examines some of the more popular Mexican trios that were influenced by Los Panchos.

Los Tres Diamantes were one of the first, founded in 1948 with members Gustavo Prado, Enrique Quezada, and Saulo Sedano. Prado credits the formation of their trio to the model set forth by Los Panchos: "[Los Panchos] were the first to dignify the trio genre. Before them, we only performed at *serenatas*, in bars, and we were unknown" ("Los Tres Diamantes" n.d., 6). Prado and Quezada had their own group, Trío Janitzio, and were trying to develop a reputation. After making some rather unsuccessful early recordings, they found their third member, Sedano, and performed on Mexican radio station XEW in a program of songs by María Grever. This led to their introduction to Raúl Rivera from RCA, who invited them to cut their first major recording successes, "Cuando me vaya" and "Mi canción," both by Grever ("Los Tres Diamantes" n.d., 7).

Los Tres Diamantes developed a distinct musical style of singing and guitar playing that had a sweet, lullaby-like quality. Probably their greatest success was "Usted," released in 1951, with music by Gabriel Ruiz and words by José Zorilla. One of the interesting things about this song is that the anonymous object of affection is addressed formally as "Usted" rather than "tú." Normally, intimate acquaintances would use the more familiar pronouns and verb forms.

Another popular group that followed the trend of Trío Los Panchos and Los Tres Diamantes was Los Tres Aces, which formed in 1953 with Marco Antonio Muñiz, Juan Neri, and Hector González. Their formation was the result of a successful engagement in a Mexico City brothel, La Bandida, where they were approached by Mariano Rivera Conde of RCA with an invitation to record (Salazar 1988, 316). One of their earliest successes was "Sabor a mi," with words and music by Álvaro Carillo. Musically, the style of Los Tres Aces differs from previous trios by their use of chromatic harmonies in the voices and the accompaniment, giving their music a more modern, jazz-like quality. The guitar work of Neri is very fluid and rivals the facility of Alfredo Gil. Exceptional song recordings by Los Tres Aces include "Mi último fracaso," "La enramada," "Delirio," and "El reloj." The group enjoyed much success throughout the 1950s, winning many awards and producing several gold records. But by 1959, the original trio of Muñiz, Neri, and González had disbanded. Muñiz has since put out solo albums and holds an edler-statesmen status in the Mexican recording industry, while González has tried keeping some form of Los Tres Aces together.

Influence Abroad

During the 1950s, the romantic-trio genre became popular throughout Latin America, and its influence began to spread to non-Hispanic markets. Not only Los Panchos but also Los Tres Diamantes and Los Tres Aces were international successes in North America, South America, Europe, and parts of Asia, including Japan and Indonesia, where they were especially popular. During the 1950s, the bolero found its way into mainstream American music as a representative ballad form. For example, in the 1955 musical *Damn Yankees*, there is a dance to an Americanized bolero, the now-famous "Whatever Lola Wants, Lola Gets." The bolero gradually became naturalized as a basis for romantic ballads like Patti Page's "All My Love" (Roberts 1999, 134). Indeed, the bolero rhythm became popular in the emerging rock-and-roll repertoire of the decade, featured in songs like "Venus" by Frankie Avalon and "Dream Lover" by Bobby Darin.

Although the *trío romántico*'s popularity as the supreme form of popular music in Latin America came to its close toward the end of the 1950s, the bolero found some fertile soil abroad for further growth. In the 1950s and '60s there were many recordings of Mexican boleros by American artists. The following discussion looks at two notable examples by Nat "King" Cole and Eydie Gorme.

In 1958, Nat "King" Cole released the first of two volumes of boleros, entitled *Cole Español* for Capitol/EMI Records (*More Cole Español* followed in 1962). Cole also recorded other albums that display a Cuban influence (*Rumba à la King*, which he recorded in Cuba, and *Papa Loves Mambo*). While these other albums were riding the Latin wave, *Cole Español* and *More Cole Español* showed a preference for *época de oro* standards. Most of the songs recorded on these two albums were made popular by bolero trios in the late 1940s and '50s, but their performance recalls the older, soloistic style of the interpreters of Lara's songs. There is more of a big-band sound to these recordings, complete with horn arrangements and back-up singers. While it is charming to hear Cole sing them in Spanish, the song arrangements are not very inspired. However, the success of Cole's singing in Spanish encouraged others to follow down a similar path, performing maudlin arrangements of otherwise beautiful Latin songs. Dean Martin's 1962 flop, *Dino Latino*, consists of American popular songs sung in Spanish, for example, "What a

Difference a Day Made," or songs written by Americans to satisfy current stereotypes of Latin themes, as evidenced by the embarrassingly popular "Mañana," made famous by Peggy Lee.[11] In spite of the awful treatment of Mexican and Latin music by non-Latinos, there were some other American artists who were more successful both stylistically and commercially.

In 1964 CBS released an album by Eydie Gorme (née Gormezano) and Trío Los Panchos of the more popular songs from the *época de oro* repertoire. This incarnation of the trio featured Puerto Rican vocalist Johnny Albino singing *primera voz*; he joined the group in 1958 and remained with them until 1968. The album *Eydie Gorme canta en Español* was a big seller for CBS, and the artists continued to put out a few more recordings over the next several years. The success of the Gorme/Los Panchos collaboration was twofold. First, it brought back to life the diminishing career of Los Panchos, who in the 1960s were not enjoying the success that younger, more contemporary artists were in that decade. Second, the quality of interpretation by Gorme was second to none among American performers, and her youthful sound became very popular among older fans of Los Panchos. Gorme's Spanish is good, and she brings much life to the genre in her renditions. Her interpretations are solos with understated backing vocals interspersed throughout, though at times Gorme and Albino will share an extended duet passage, and occasionally the trio is featured singing a chorus. The rhythm section is probably a little more pronounced than in older Los Panchos recordings, with timbales, congas, maracas, and stand-up bass.

The Gorme recordings of the mid-1960s represent one of the last successes for Los Panchos and the trio genre. Los Panchos and groups like Los Tres Diamantes continued to play in some incarnation or other until the 1980s, when most of the players had become too old to keep the groups going anymore. Any concertizing or recording at this point in their careers was really more of a nostalgic look at an era long past its prime. Although some groups like Los Tres Diamantes continued to make arrangements of more current material like "Theme from *Love Story*" and "The Way We Were," their older successes, like "Usted" and "Cuando me vaya" remained the mainstays of their repertoire. In the 1970s and '80s, the popularity of trios was over, and the trio genre was becoming a thing of the past. Later in his career, Gustavo Prado from Los Tres Diamantes ruefully related this in an interview:

> Unfortunately, there is no trio genre these days, [and] I am referring to the singers of the *bolero romántico*. No new groups have formed that can, in the future, fill the place of Los Tres Diamantes, or Los Panchos, Los Aces, or others. I think that this is because it is difficult to create a new style, since the above-mentioned groups include all the various styles, and younger perform-

ers run the risk that if they wind up sounding like us, the public would mistake them and they would not be able to be themselves.... ("Los Tres Diamantes" n.d., 6)

Baby-boomer Resurgence

The decade of the 1990s proved to be an interesting period for the *época de oro* repertoire. A younger generation of Latin performers was beginning a trend toward Latin stardom in ways that were entirely new. Stars like Gloria Estefan, Luis Miguel, Juan Gabriel, and Los Lobos were redefining the genre of Latin music within the context of popular culture. Throughout the decade, Latin American popular music saw a return to the golden-age repertoire by artists who grew up listening to the music of their older relatives on the phonograph at home. By the end of the decade, the repertoire was performed and released in new versions by major Latin and U.S. artists, including Linda Ronstadt, José Feliciano, Luis Miguel, Gloria Estefan, Celia Cruz, and Plácido Domingo.[12] Most of the performances on these recordings feature a solo singer accompanied by some sort of orchestral or big-band arrangement; occasionally there may be some background vocals, but the focus remains on the solo personality. Even the performances by Feliciano, who is a virtuoso guitarist himself, are heavily orchestrated and do not have any of the charm of his earliest RCA recordings, where he played and sang to a simple rhythm section.[13]

In 1998 a trio of young men from Colombia called Los Tri-O released an album entitled *Nuestro amor* that consisted of bolero medleys modeled on versions made famous by Los Panchos. The group consists of three singers—who go by their first names only, Esteban, Manuel, and Andrés—and is the realization of Colombian producer Johnny González. González was looking for three voices that would blend into a group to perform boleros in the style of Los Panchos. González auditioned singers until he found the three he wanted. Sidemen provide the guitars, *requinto*, and rhythm section, which consists of bass and percussion (drum set). The performances on *Nuestro amor* consist of versions that are very close to the original Los Panchos recordings. The vocals use the same harmonies, and Alfredo Gil's signature *requinto* lines are reproduced completely intact. There is a difference in vocal quality, in that Los Tri-O lacks the vocal blend that Los Panchos achieved, and their younger voices do not have the mature quality of the Los Panchos recordings. With regard to text declamation, Los Tri-O tend to sing everything in even rhythms, whereas Los Panchos put the rhythm of the poetry before the rhythm of the music. An example of this is in the last verses of "Contigo," where the text reads, "Y no me cansaré de bendecir" ("And I will not tire from blessing"). In the Los Tri-O version, the vocal attacks are sung on every eighth-note pulse, giving it a rather stiff declamation, whereas the Los Panchos version retains the nuance of the verse, resulting in a more rhythmic ad lib that reflects the scansion of the poetic text.

Nuestro amor was a big success in North America as well as Spain and prompted the release of another album, entitled *Mi gloria eres tú*, on which they continue to pay homage to the representative trios of the 1950s. This recording includes the use of orchestral arrangements while retaining the rhythm section and *requinto*.

If the commercial success of the *trío romántico* genre seems to have come to a halt, there is comfort in knowing that in other venues the genre is as popular as ever. For example, the trio remains the most popular ensemble for a variety of social occasions, including *serenatas*, weddings, and restaurant engagements, where they perform *al talón* (i.e., they take requests and charge by the song). The relative ease of performance, due to the portability of the group, along with a shared repertoire that was firmly established by the 1960s, makes it easy for trios to perform. There are *tríos románticos* all over Latin America and in cities in the United States that have a Latin American population. One can safely say that they remain among the most popular Latin American ensembles. It is not uncommon for musicians in Mexico and the United States to gather on a street corner until there is the requisite number of forces. The newly formed "pickup trio" will stroll from tavern to tavern, in search of requests, and because the musicians all know songs like "Piel canela" and "Solamente una vez," the pickup trio's shared repertoire will guarantee satisfaction without rehearsal.

So, in spite of the rise and fall of the bolero on the commercial charts, trios all over Latin America continue to perform *boleros románticos* from the *época de oro*, to the delight of live audiences.

Notes

1. For a discussion on the bolero and Mexican modernity, see Pedelty (1999, 30–58).
2. According to Pineda (1996), 124, many of Lara's earliest songs were lost due to the bohemian lifestyle of the composer in his early career.
3. By guitar, I mean the the modern classical nylon-string variety.
4. A capo is a device used to raise the pitch of the strings of the guitar by stopping all the strings at a desired fret. This allows the player to transpose without changing fingerings.
5. Rhythm sections are not used when trios play in a *serenata* or *rondalla* ("strolling") type of venue.
6. See Manuel (1995, 239): "The norm in most Latin music, whether weepy boleros or upbeat salsa songs, is genteel sentimentality, often idealizing women, no matter how unrealistically."

7. "Piel canela," Bobby Capo; © 1953, Edward B. Marks, Co.; copyright renewed; international copyright secured; all rights reserved; used by permission.
8. "Piel canela," Bobby Capo; © 1953, Edward B. Marks, Co.; copyright renewed; international copyright secured; all rights reserved; used by permission.
9. Cited as a bolero in Pedelty 1999, 32.
10. Cuba and Mexico already had some trios, but their style and standard varied greatly.
11. This song used the concept of "tomorrow" to reinforce the stereotype of the "lazy Latino."
12. Domingo, Pavarotti, and Carreras, as "The Three Tenors," include several Lara songs in their performances, including "Solamente una vez" and "Granada."
13. In these older recordings, Feliciano comes closest to the trio instrumentation of *época de oro* performances by using a melodic guitar introduction, rapid melodic passages between the verses, and an extended solo.

References

Flores Longoria, Samuel. 1994. *Alberto Cervantes y la historia del bolero en México*. Monterrey, Mexico: Ediciones Castillo.

Garrido, Juan S. 1981. *Historia de la música popular en Mexico*. Mexico City: Editorial Extemporáneos.

Geijerstam, Claes. 1976. *Popular Music in Mexico*. Albuquerque: University of New Mexico Press.

Kahl, Wili and Israel Katz. 2001. "Bolero." In *The New Grove Dictionary of Music and Musicians*. 2d ed. Edited by Stanley Sadie. London: Macmillan.

"Los Tres Diamantes: tres décadas de romanticismo." n.d. *Guitarra fácil* 60. Mexico City: Ediciones Libra.

Manuel, Peter, Kenneth Bilby, and Michael Largey. 1995. *Caribbean Currents*. Philadelphia: Temple University Press.

Marin, Nidia. n.d. "Los Panchos." In *Guitarra fácil* 13. Mexico City: Ediciones Libra.

Mendoza, Vicente T. 1982. *La canción mexicana: ensayo de clasificación y antología*. 2d ed. Mexico City: Fondo de Cultura Económica.

Pedelty, Mark. 1999. "The Bolero: The Birth, Life, and Death of Mexican Modernity." *Latin American Music Review* 20/1: 30–58.

Pineda, Adela. 1996. "The Cuban Bolero and Its Transculturation to Mexico: The Case of Agustín Lara." *Studies in Latin American Popular Culture* 15: 119–30.

Rivas, Yolanda Moreno. 1979. *Historia de la música popular mexicana*. Mexico City: Alianza Editorial Mexicana.

Roberts, John Storm. 1999. *The Latin Tinge: The Impact of Latin American Music on the United States*. 2d ed. New York: Oxford University Press.

Salazar, Jaime Rico. 1988. *Cien años de boleros*. Bogotá: Centro Editorial de Estudios Musicales.

Zavala, Iris M. 1991. *El bolero: historia de un amor*. Madrid: Alianza Editorial.

8

"Give Your Body Joy, Macarena"

Aspects of U.S. Participation in the "Latin" Dance Craze of the 1990s

MELINDA RUSSELL

October 1996: For months, a single dance has been nearly ubiquitous in U.S. culture. Consisting primarily of arm movements, it is performed by seniors, adults, teenagers, and children. Danced in the streets, in bars, in automobiles, at baseball games, on cruise ships, at political conventions, wedding receptions, and church picnics, it dominates many social events. Almost everywhere, it is performed and its steps are taught. Instructions for it are found on television, in the newspaper, and on sheets of paper handed out at various events. In July, three of the top one hundred singles were versions of the song accompanying this dance. It has dominated radio play in many markets and across a demographic range throughout the summer. Some stations play it again and again, even for hours at a time.[1]

Imagine a total outsider to U.S. musical culture visiting during the late summer or early fall of 1996. From one coast to the other, he or she would have found a single song and its accompanying dance—the Macarena— nearly everywhere, widely and frequently practiced, and much discussed. *Billboard*'s "Hot Single" of 1996, the Macarena broke sales records worldwide. The dance found fans across a wide spectrum of the U.S. public, and great numbers of Americans became familiar with and performed the dance.

In this chapter, I explore what seemed exceptional about the Macarena, drawing from accounts in newspapers, radio, and television, as well as from fieldwork in Minnesota and Illinois. Which elements of the Macarena contributed to its temporary ubiquity in the United States? What was the nature

172

of the "craze" for the Macarena, and how did U.S. citizens view its place in the cultural life of the country?

Macarena Basics

The Macarena was the creation of Los Del Rio, a duo from southern Spain with more than thirty albums and thirty years of performing behind them. Aging along with their formerly teenaged fans, Antonio Romero Monge and Rafael Ruiz were popular as a "nostalgia" act. Most recently, they had been sent on a government-sponsored goodwill tour in the 1980s, described by Monge: "We played to groups of aging, nostalgic Spaniards in Latin America, Norway, Belgium, the Netherlands, Morocco" (Llewellyn 1996, 102). In Llewellyn's history, as in many other accounts,[2] Monge explained that the Macarena had its beginnings at a late-1992 party in Caracas, Venezuela, where Monge complimented a flamenco dancer with words that later appeared in the lyrics.

Early in its history, the Macarena was rerecorded by the Spanish band Fangoria in the "Macarena River F-Mix," the version made popular in 1993 and '94 and revived in '95 (Llewellyn 1996, 102). A subsequent remix by the Miami-based Bayside Boys, sold in July 1995 to RCA (Castro and Salcines 1996), features a spoken voice and uses English lyrics in the verses. Most observers ascribe the intense popularity of the Macarena in the U.S. market during the summer and fall of 1996 to the Bayside Boys' remix. Interestingly, Macarena fans seemed interested in multiple versions of the song rather than insisting on one version. Still, it is the Bayside Boys' version, itself a layering of previous recordings, that is best known and received the most prominent airplay in U.S. markets.

A "Latin" Dance Craze? The Macarena as Latin American

Particularly in its early days, the Macarena was often referred to in the U.S. press and among the population as "Latin" or "Latin American." Typical headlines included: "Macarena: A Latin Dance Craze That Could Topple the Electric Slide" (Catlin 1996, E1); or "Dance Fever: Sexy Latin Moves Have Americans Hustling to Do the Macarena" (Pipp 1996, A1); or calling the Macarena a "Latin dance craze," a "frisky Latin tune" (Roberts 1996, A 01), and so on. The Macarena was marketed in the United States on "Latin" labels, appeared on "Latin charts," and was popularized in part at "Latin" venues such as Miami clubs; it enjoyed some currency in "Latin" music contexts; for example, fans performed it before a Gloria Estefan concert.

As the Macarena spread, and coverage of the craze prompted some investigation of its origins, reporters and anchors often referred to a "Spanish" song or "beat," but the "Latin" connection endured. Today the Macarena song continues to be marketed on "Latin American Dance" and "Latin Gold" compilations, and many people are still surprised to learn that the dance's originators were from Spain. Perhaps thinking of the Macarena as "Latin" is part of a more general conflation of "Spanish" with "Latin." Here and there, people seemed convinced that the Macarena had originated in Mexico or in Brazil, but most often, it was described as "Latin" or "Latin American"—this vague designation placing the Macarena's origin in a land more mythical than real, or perhaps somehow transcending place. In any case, its reception as Latin exotica situated the Macarena within a history of "dance crazes" and "fevers," and may also reflect some tension about its "foreignness." The glossing of the Macarena as "Latin American" may stem from a particular press release or other early-stage event in Macarena history (or perhaps from its early foothold in some U.S.-Latin markets), but it is also possible that as a matter of convenience, "Latin Dance craze" became a preexisting category.

Indeed, the reception of the Macarena can be situated within the history of Latin American dance crazes such as the tango, rumba, mambo, *chachachá*, and *lambada*.[3] Though it did not follow precisely the trajectory of any one of these, it has elements in common with a number of them. For example, the press coverage that John Storm Roberts cites as having "escalated the popularity" (1999, 46) of the tango functioned similarly with the Macarena. In its choreography (discussed below), the Macarena is most similar to the conga line, stressing group participation rather than couples, and utilizing simple steps designed to maximize participation.

The Inclusive Nature of the Macarena

One of the interesting aspects of the Macarena craze is the sheer number, and wide variety, of people who danced it. Indeed, its inclusivity may be one of the most exceptional things about the fad. Three interrelated elements contributed to this inclusivity: 1. the simplicity of the dance; 2. the nature of its imperative of inclusion and concomitant pedagogy; and 3. the expansion of the dance floor. After exploring these conditions contributing to the spread of the Macarena, I consider the temporary ubiquity of the dance, examine the "craze" itself, and present to the reader some of the objections raised to the Macarena.

Simplicity and Ease of Movement

The Macarena is truly quite simple, comprising only a few easily executed movements. Below, the instructions for a basic version of the dance:

Right arm straight out, PALM DOWN
Left arm straight out, PALM DOWN

Right arm straight out, PALM UP
Left arm straight out, PALM UP
Right hand touches inside of Left arm at ELBOW
Left hand touches inside of Right arm at ELBOW
Right hand behind Right back of NECK
Left hand behind Left back of NECK
Right hand on Left front HIP
Left hand on Right front HIP
Right hand on Right back HIP
Left hand on Left back HIP
Move your bottom to the LEFT
Move your bottom to the RIGHT
Move your bottom to the LEFT
CLAP and turn ninety degrees to the RIGHT
REPEAT

As you can see, if you did not already know, the dance can be taught in a minute or two. As a *Washington Post* writer put it, "it demands absolutely no grace or coordination. . . . the Macarena, is just perfect for people who can't dance" (Roberts 1996, A01). A *Los Angeles Times* writer more pointedly characterized the dance as "so simple some pets could do it" (Romero 1996, E1), while a North Carolina columnist quoted her friend as saying, "It's so easy a monkey could do it" (Rivenbark 1996, 3). The simplicity of the Macarena was central to the dance's great success. Just as Christmas carols or children's rhyming songs invite and encourage participation through simplicity and repetition, these elements fed the growth of the Macarena as a social phenomenon in U.S. culture.

To return to the hypothetical visitor to the United States, he or she might have concluded that dance in the States always involves these kinds of simple movements. But in fact, its simplicity is one way in which the Macarena is an exception to normal American dance practices. Thus, the sheer simplicity of the dance, and the ease of its movements, robbed many veteran non-dancers of a standard excuse for not participating: "I can't dance" or "I don't dance." One could "not dance" and still dance the Macarena, and verbal encouragement in this spirit was commonplace at various public venues and on television, where unlikely or reluctant dancers were urged to dance, with phrases such as "It's really easy," "Anyone can do this," or "You can definitely dance this, even if you don't dance."

Other exceptional elements deserve further examination. The Macarena dance is a sort of oxymoron: a dance without steps. Not only need one not be a dancer, or even quick on one's feet, one need not really have working feet at all. In focusing on arm movements, the Macarena permits full involvement even for a seated person; even the quarter turn at the end can be executed in a chair. In nursing homes and other facilities for people with limited movement, the dance was seen as an ideal way to get people involved, because they could literally "dance" it in their chairs, or wheelchairs. Indeed, during the height of the craze, it was not unusual to spot people, particularly in groups, performing it in their automobiles.[4]

The Macarena's focus on arm movements also meant that people could, without fear of attracting much attention, practice the dance before truly committing to it. This was possible even in a very public space, such as a club. It was not uncommon to see people checking the movements with one another, solidifying the understanding of those at the table before getting up to join others on the dance floor.

With its inclusion of so few movements, the predictability of right-left alternation, and the short cycle dictated by the music, the Macarena maximizes the opportunities to get in, or get back in, the dance. In the Bayside Boys' version, each dance cycle lasts only about nine seconds. Even in the version lasting only a little over three minutes—and the Macarena was frequently played in longer versions, or multiple times—this provided nearly two dozen opportunities to learn, practice, or perfect the dance. In practical terms, for those who have a difficult time dancing, this means that even if you do not get any steps right in the first cycle, you do not have to endure more than nine seconds of being out of sync before you get another chance. As one club owner put it: "People can make a mistake . . . but rejoin the line easily and not feel intimidated" (Romero 1996, E1).

The simplicity of the Macarena is one way in which it differs from many other dances and even dance crazes. But the Macarena was also distinguished by other exceptional qualities, including its modes of transmission and the nature of its practice in particular venues.

The Ideal of Inclusion and Its Impact on Dance Pedagogy

In addition to being quite simple, the Macarena was unusually explicit and public. That is, there were multiple, easily accessed routes to learning the dance. Moreover, these routes were not specialized but rather generally available, relying not on dance schools or private instruction but rather on dissemination through newspapers and television, among other media. Instead of a culture in which the rules and procedures of dance were rarely spoken of, but rather gleaned from direct or mediated interaction with "good" dancers, our outside visitor would have found explicit, abundant instructions. At weddings, parties, and bars, the Macarena was commonly taught by a leader who mimed the movements to the music (or before the music, in some cases) as prospective dancers copied them. In some places, dance instructions were handed out on sheets of paper or displayed on overheads. Dance instructions were also widely published in newspapers and shown on television news and entertainment programs, and were available in text and various image formats on the Internet.[5] Again, the comparison with Christmas carols is apt; they, too, are photocopied and handed out when maximizing participation is the goal of an event. The sheet of paper with Macarena instructions is an outright invitation to dance; it says, "Here's what to do," in place of the usual, comparatively hidden standards for correct dance.

More elusive than the particular practices surrounding the spread of the Macarena was a kind of spirit that pervaded many of its contexts. Namely, there was a sense that a successful Macarena is one in which the greatest number of people participate. This was true not only in the attempts at sporting, school, and civic events to set Macarena records, but also in the common contexts such as weddings, parties, and bars. As happens with Christmas carols or with singing "Happy Birthday," the culture's general preference for specialists is temporarily suspended in favor of inclusion. A successful carol or "Happy Birthday," like a successful Macarena, is one in which participation is maximized. So, just as our visitor would have found pedagogical practices somewhat exceptional, he also would have found Americans suspending critical judgment of the dance skills of their fellow human beings, preferring instead to goad, tease, beg, and cajole each other into dancing. Many factors promote this inclusivity, including the dance's repetition, its simplicity, its explicitly public pedagogy, and this wish for inclusion.

All of this represents a significant departure from pedagogical practices surrounding many kinds of social dance. While Arthur Murray and the like are available to those who wish to learn ballroom dancing, learning popular dance is largely a matter of quietly copying others who seem to be doing it right, or watching MTV at home. Other exceptions to routine dance pedagogy illustrated in the Macarena craze included children teaching adults. Just a few examples from my own town of Northfield, Minnesota: I met many parents who learned it from children—many of whom had in turn learned it in school, for instance, in Spanish classes. In the same town, Girl Scouts visited a kindergarten class to teach the Macarena. And at the Minnesota State Fair in St. Paul in late summer 1996, a group of children taught the dance to normally staid local news anchor Don Shelby on live television. The possibility of children teaching adults highlights the unusual nature of the Macarena. In contrast to the place of dance in everyday U.S. culture, the Macarena was not often accompanied by an expectation of, or even a striving for, perfection, and hence little professionalism was associated with it.

Expanding the Boundaries of the Dance Floor

There were numerous exceptional qualities in the use of space and the kinds of social interaction associated with the Macarena. Although I will deal primarily with the Macarena in bar- or nightclub-type venues, it should be remembered that one of the exceptional qualities of the Macarena is that one did not need to be on the dance floor to dance it.

This metaphorical expansion of the dance floor was echoed in smaller spaces. Interestingly, at various venues, the boundaries of the dance floor itself were extended or blurred during the Macarena. While a traditional U.S. dance floor may or may not be clearly demarcated by a change in flooring (e.g., carpeting in the rest of the bar, wood for the dance floor), there is generally a clear dancing area. With the Macarena though, these boundaries were sometimes rendered meaningless. Because it was possible to dance the Macarena from a seated position—and doing so allowed one to dance without the social declaration of dancing—it was not uncommon to see the Macarena danced simultaneously in the seating and dancing areas of a restaurant or similar venue. In outdoor restaurants, people walking by on the sidewalk sometimes danced a few steps as they heard the music. In bars or nightclubs, bartenders sometimes danced from behind the bar. All of these actions tended to blur the boundaries of the dance floor and the line between dancing and non-dancing.

The Macarena dance floor differed radically from most other U.S. dance floors, except for country line dancing. Instead of an apparently random arrangement of couples (typical in rock or ballroom), individuals were usually lined up in clearly organized positions, equally spaced from one another. This lining up blurred their organization as couples, and permitted single persons (a group normally excluded unless inebriated or otherwise exempted from following normal social-dance rules) to enter the dance floor. In many bars, and most parties or weddings, a DJ or other leader stood facing the crowd, taking them through the movements before or, in most cases, during the dance. This was repeated in smaller units on the dance floor, or in crowds where people, even if strangers, helped one another learn the movements. More informally, people also used one another as reference points, copying the person next to or in front of them, elbowing partners to point to someone who "had it" in the next row. Instead of the inward orientation of the couple on the dance floor, the Macarena featured an outward orientation toward the group. Glances, snatches of conversation, laughter, and even coaching behavior all took place on Macarena dance floors. Interaction was frequently at the small-group and large-group level rather than between individuals.

"Give Your Body Joy, Macarena"

At most dance events, at least some contingent can be counted upon to stay firmly seated, to refuse to dance through the entire event. While people sometimes try to convince their own dates or friends to get up and dance, they do not generally intrude on strangers, but the Macarena frequently provided exceptions to this rule. The Macarena was a table-clearer, getting everybody up. Where people did not immediately rise on hearing the first few bars, or the announcement of the dance, others waved them onto the floor. Strangers urged one another into joining in the dance. In two Minnesota bars visited during the craze, no one remained seated by the end of an extended playing of the Macarena; the dance crowd wooed the other people to join in. During the Macarena craze, it became unacceptable, in some places absolutely impossible, not to dance. In short, the normal option of "watching" dance events was frequently unavailable.

Club owners and DJs noticed the inclusion of "non-dancers" and the ability of the Macarena to get large groups involved. One nightclub owner observed, "People who never danced in their life—they're doing the Macarena" (Roberts 1996, A01). And in the same article, a "veteran Latin dancer" opines that "[t]he one thing is that it gets everyone involved." Disc jockeys interviewed in Minnesota and Illinois commented repeatedly that the Macarena was unmatched in its ability to get people out of their chairs and onto the dance floor, and this is echoed by DJs today who maintain the dance in the repertoire for particular occasions.

Like other aspects of Macarena behavior, these dance-floor characteristics usually disappeared without the Macarena. These contrasts were visible not just at the end of the craze, but in a single evening, as the focus shifted to and away from the Macarena. In many venues it was possible to see significant differences between the Macarena and normal dance practices. These were less obvious in line-dancing venues, where many dances share some characteristics of the Macarena. Generally, however, before and after the Macarena, no DJ taught dances to the crowds; no people visibly instructed one another on the floor; no strangers visibly commented on or laughed at each other's dancing in a move toward social connection; and no one visibly copied anyone else's dance moves.

The uniqueness and impermanence of "Macarena inclusivity" is apparent in the very temporary response of many bar, wedding, or party patrons. Having gotten up to dance the Macarena, many patrons returned to their seats for the rest of the evening, unless there was an additional Macarena. Even those who most enthusiastically participated during a Macarena would consistently turn down other offers to dance. In other words, their participation was Macarena-specific.

Maybe this is why the Macarena seemed frequently to go on forever, repeated for an hour or more. At house parties, dances, weddings, and other occasions, the Macarena was, more often than not, played two or three times in a row, just as it was played repeatedly on some radio stations. In bars and nightclubs, half-hour segments were sometimes given over to the dance. One later release of the Macarena was a seven-plus-minute "Macarena non-stop" used precisely for this purpose. This repeated playing of the dance ensures the continued participation of those who would otherwise sit down.

The Macarena was not entirely dependent on national and local media for exposure, and its popularity and ubiquity are not entirely explained by record-company hype or massive promotion efforts. In fact, what is striking about the rise of the Macarena is the grass-roots nature of its spread. While it is true that the media played an important role, the real mechanism of the Macarena's spread lay in human-to-human interaction, one person encouraging or teasing another into dancing, one person teaching another the dance, and so on. It became less permissible to say so with the waning of the craze and the rise of anti-Macarena sentiment, but the dance was fun. It offered Americans a way to connect with one another, through dancing, and to avoid many of the social risks normally attendant. If the Macarena merely conformed to and reinforced existing dance practices, it is doubtful that it would have achieved the great popularity that it did. Thus we might ask what the Macarena offered that was not otherwise available. The answer, in plainest terms: a simple, fun dance and an atmosphere of inclusion.

"Macarena Madness": The Temporary Ubiquity of the Macarena

Even with the passage of only a few years, it is difficult to recall fully the ubiquity, however temporary, of the Macarena during the late summer and early fall of 1996. It was played and danced repeatedly at events from baseball games to the Olympics to the Democratic Convention. In a single day, a normal person could easily encounter it multiple times in various settings.

The song and dance spawned innumerable parodies and contrafacta, including the Green Bay Packers' "Packerena," the Girl Scouts' " Cookarena," and a wide variety of commercials, many of them incorporating local elements. For example, the contrafacta tended to replace the lyrics with words celebrating or "spoofing" some local element, whether a rich suburb, a winning football team, or a notorious politician. Local weather and sports personalities across the country made versions of the Macarena to promote their newscasts. In Minnesota, for example, one station's sportscaster had a commercial that replaced "Hey, Macarena" with his nickname. Such contrafacta served to localize the international Macarena, particularizing it with local place names and inside jokes. "Macarena" entered the national vocabulary through these multiple routes, eventually appearing as a staple of late-night television monologues and comic repertoires.

Because of its ubiquity, the song was especially useful to politicians in portraying themselves as "of the people," not only in its use at both parties' national conventions, but in Jack Kemp's "Kemparena" (with football-throwing gestures) and Robert Dole's reference to his famed stumble from a California podium as his "version" of the Macarena. Al Gore performed a "version" at the 1996 Democratic Convention in Chicago, and local Minnesota Reform Party candidate (senate) Dean Barkly promised to do the Macarena if he received more than 5 percent of the vote, a dare offered by local candidates across the nation. Speaking on ABC's *Good Morning America* in late 1996, Hillary Rodham Clinton promised to dance the Macarena with Al Gore: "I don't know what it was, the late hour, I promised that the day after the election, Al Gore and I would dance the Macarena together."

Part of the joke of Al Gore's "Macarena" at the 1996 Democratic Convention in Chicago was that it illustrated and poked fun at his reputation as a stiff, almost wooden person:

> President Clinton asked me to speak tonight. And you can probably guess the reason why. My reputation for excitement. This is some crowd. I've been watching you do that Macarena on television. And if I could have your silence, I would like to demonstrate for you the Al Gore version of the Macarena. [Stands still, pausing] Would you like to see it again?

Perhaps the most memorable Macarena performance was the least "staged" of these, when news cameras on November 6, 1996, showed then-UN Ambassador Madeleine Albright teaching the dance to the Ambassador from Botswana, allegedly celebrating the re-election of President Clinton the day before.

Fever, Craze, Infection: Local Explanations for the Macarena

The exceptional nature of much Macarena behavior did not go unnoticed by Americans themselves, who employed a variety of explanatory strategies to account for it. Many of these strategies center on the metaphors of power in music and dance, including such ideas as "you can't help" dancing when the Macarena is playing, or "It just makes you want to dance." Both explanations focus on the individual's lack of control over the sheer force of the Macarena. Of course, in practice, what often "made" people dance was the insistence of others that they do so.

The idea of the Macarena as embodying some sort of power is also present in the most common metaphors associated with it, which are those of physical or mental disease. In these, the Macarena was an infection, a virus, or a fever sweeping the country; like other explanations, these accounts sidestep the issues of volition and situate the individual within a web of forces over which he or she has no control. The excerpt below is from a CNN newscast:

> *Bill Hemmer, anchor*: We're talking about the latest infectious dance craze, and CNN's Kathleen Barnes is on the beat.

> *Kathleen Barnes, correspondent*: The thumping Spanish beat just makes your feet want to dance, your hips swing, and your body shake all over. . . . These days, you just have to Macarena to be anybody. Instructions for the hand-jiving dance have even been published in newspapers. It doesn't matter if you haven't got it quite right—the beat will take you there. (*Early Edition*, August 21, 1996)

The absence of volition is stressed again and again in contemporary accounts of the Macarena and its spread. The Macarena is depicted as infectious, a craze, whose beat "makes" your feet want to dance and your body shake. Not only does the dance overcome a potential lack of desire to dance, but a potential lack of ability, too: "The beat will take you there," implying that the dance teaches itself.

Some sources combined metaphors of madness and disease to explain the spread of the Macarena:

> NBA Basketball fans, soccer supporters of newly crowned European champion Germany, Tour de France cyclists, and U.S. football and baseball players have something in common beyond sport: "Macarena" madness. This madness has become a fever spreading across the world, as a glance at the Hot 100 Singles chart and [other charts shows]. . . . For anybody who has had enough of "Macarena" and its simple but contagious dance, which was "invented" spontaneously in Mexico and Miami, the news is that there is more to come. Much more. (Llewellyn 1996, 7)

The centrality of these explanatory devices can be seen even in a cursory examination of contemporary news accounts. By far the most common noun associated with the Macarena was "craze," with "madness" and "fever" trailing behind. From the earliest accounts detailing Miami-club exposure to the Macarena, around January and February of 1995, these words were already associated with the dance, as in "Macarena Madness Now Has the Floor," and "Macarena Dance Craze Hits Miami" (Navarro 1995A, 1995B).

"Craze" may just refer to the popularity of the dance, but it could also be argued that "fever," "infection," along with "craze" all connote a passing fad.

Hence, we find it funny that people once called color pictures, automobiles, computers, and television "crazes," because those people misidentified the future centrality of these cultural objects. How were observers of the Macarena sure at its beginnings that it was a craze or fever? After all, until it ended, why was it not possible that the logical outcome of Macarena popularity might be a spate of additional easily learned, widely taught line dances? How was it that headlines did not read "Revolutionary Macarena May Change U.S. Dance for Foreseeable Future"? This outcome was clearly unlikely precisely because of the many ways in which the Macarena violated the real values surrounding dance in U.S. culture. The preemptive labeling of the dance as a "craze" was the culture's promise to itself that these exceptions would not last, that they would not truly interrupt the traditions of dance culture that they seemed to topple. Craze, infection, and fever all served to frame the Macarena experience—and its implied values—as temporary.

Negative Responses to the Macarena

The two most polarized responses to the Macarena, embracing or rejecting it, are only the most obvious. Between those poles lie a variety of possible positions. Some people will not dance no matter how many "rules of the dance" are suspended, and no matter how much encouragement or pressure exists. Others simply would not participate in the Macarena precisely because of its popularity: if so many people are doing it, it must be worthless. For some people, not knowing the Macarena, not unlike the "Kill your television" bumpersticker, was a testament to their place outside the mainstream, immune to the fever.

CNN's "Macarena Wrap Up" (September 19, 1996), provided an overview of the Macarena's temporary dominance in popular culture "just in case you were on another planet." On this program, a few celebrities gladly admitted to having participated in the dance, some even proud of their early knowledge, like actress Geena Davis: "I knew the Macarena back in January, so, you know, I feel like I'm really ahead of the game." Those on the hipper end of the continuum implied or demonstrated contempt. For example, comedienne Janeane Garafolo said, "I find that it says a lot about a person . . . how enthusiastic they get about the Macarena." And sports star Dennis Rodman commented disdainfully, "Macarena? Please. You couldn't pay me to do that." Such comments deliberately placed the speaker apart from the craze and its adherents.

After leading 51,000 Yankees fans (she claimed) in the Macarena, Chita Rivera began to explain the dance to host Scott Simon in August 1996, on NPR's *Weekend Edition*:

Rivera: It—you have not tried it?

Simon: I sure have not.

Similarly, an excerpt from the introduction to CNN's coverage of the Macarena three days earlier may illustrate the same phenomenon, or at least Hemmer's co-anchor hinted at it ("La Macarena Dance Craze" 1996):

Bill Hemmer, anchor: They say when you hear it, you can't sit still, and they say when you do it, you just can't get enough.

Catherine Callaway, anchor: Are you implying you've never done this?

Bill Hemmer: I have not, no.

To be sure, there must be many people who never tried the dance. But in the *Weekend Edition* interview quoted above, Chita Rivera exposed a phenomenon familiar to students of the Macarena:

I can guarantee you that, people say it's ridiculous and stupid, if they go to a party you can bet your bottom dollar they know it. They did it in their closet. Ha! They learned it in their bathroom!

Similar dissembling is anecdotally related on one of the anti-Macarena websites, now defunct, in which a writer complains that a mandatory office meeting was called wherein the Macarena was taught, ostensibly as a "morale-building exercise." The writer and a few other employees declined to participate. He or she notes that "[c]uriously, after the meeting, the number of admitted 'Macarenia-ites' declined drastically, and suddenly no one would admit to having done it."

Avoiding or eschewing the Macarena was one possible position, but another was to object to it more actively. The Macarena was considered unpalatable by many people, for widely varied reasons. Some objected to the simplicity of the dance, some to its very popularity—the fact that others were excited about it. Still others objected to what they saw as the advancement of moral turpitude in its lyrics, particularly in the Bayside Boys' version. These objections help situate the Macarena within a web of reactions to it, and they also provided occasions for people to articulate what they saw as the basic rules underlying dance in our culture.

Moral Objections to the Macarena

Moral objections to the Macarena sometimes addressed the dance movements, but most often centered on the lyrics, usually those of the Bayside Boys' remix. Many people found the Macarena's lyrics disturbing. It is important to point out that the vast majority of Macarena dancers were utterly unaware of the lyrics, except for the "Macarena" portion. Lyrics were not included in many of the most commonly sold versions of the recording. Still, in video, on websites,[6] and sometimes in newspapers, the lyrics gained exposure. The narrative is open to interpretation but implies that the speaker enjoys teasing men. Most scandalously, a spoken portion mysteriously asks, "Now come on, what was I supposed to do? He was out of town and his two friends were soooo fine." And in the very beginning of the song, the singer claims, "They all want me, they can't have me," and later promises that "if you're good, I'll take you home with me." The juxtaposition of these narrative elements with the exhortation in the chorus to "Give your body joy, Macarena" was especially troubling to some observers.

In public commentary, church sermons, and letters to the editor, people implored their fellow citizens to listen more attentively, as in the editorial "The Macarena is no innocent dance; How can we ignore the song's blatant call for infidelity?" (Calkins 1996, A10). Concerned by the "glorifi[cation]" of "giving your body joy and good things," and of "partying hard," the writer insisted, "[t]hings like the Macarena insidiously eat away at the values and character we want our children to have, like caring, honesty, respect, responsibility, integrity, trustworthiness, fairness, and citizenship." As with many such writers (see also Roybal 1996 and Hoffman 1996), Calkins was particularly upset by the use of the Macarena by and in front of children.

The matter of sex and the Macarena, though, is more complex than a casual look at the lyrics might indicate. First, consider that in the Bayside Boys' version there are three English verses but sixteen units without English-language content, eleven repetitions of the Spanish chorus and five of an instrumental substitute. English lyrics are thus present for only a small portion of the song, and this means that the sexual content, scandalous or not, is only a small part of the song. Much more importantly, many people seemed to miss the Macarena's "blatant call for infidelity" entirely. "What are the words to the song?" wrote one citizen to *The Houston Chronicle*, "They sing them so fast I can't understand them" (Hoffman 1996). "Da da da da da da da da da da Macarena" was by far the most common understanding of the rapidly sung English lyrics.

Whether the cause was the speed of the vocals, the mix of English and Spanish lyrics, or the noise of the context, many people were not aware of the English lyrics, let alone cognizant of their specific content. Yet, even assuming people heard the lyrics, it is not clear that the "call for infidelity" or the "three-timing" referred to by writers is wholly evident. "Move with me, chant with me, and if you're good, I'll take you home with me," and "He was out of town and his two friends were soooo fine" seem transparent enough, but what does one do with the first line: "I am not trying to seduce you" and with "they all want me, they can't have me"? It seems safest to conclude from the total narrative that Macarena is a skilled flirt.

The juxtaposition of the dance and the lyrics is particularly interesting. While the song is ostensibly about touching other people, perhaps even a few other people, the dance is entirely about touching oneself. However, it is also about doing so in a group, touching oneself in a crowd of other people doing precisely the same. Jane Dark (1996) examined this irony in her *Village Voice* article:

> When you do the Macarena you get all the partners you ever dreamed of, with only one catch: no touching. This was true of the Bus Stop and the Twist before it—and is nearly matched by the current outburst of scheduled "YMCA" voguing at ballgames. But the formula is pure Hula Hoop: shake your love like James Brown, but only within a whirling circle of suburban plastic inviolability. And of course, exactly this mix of sexual insinuation and absolute denial explains the whole Regis and Kathie Lee thing.

This "mix of sexual insinuation and absolute denial" is embedded in the Macarena, from its lyrics ("I am not trying to seduce you") to its movements (reaching out, then embracing oneself, then grinding one's hips), to its social enactment (in which strangers reach out to strangers, but only to join them in creating separate "whirling circle[s] of suburban plastic inviolability"). Not hearing or understanding the lyrics is a further step in being able to repudiate any sexual content.

Anti-Macarena Websites

From the early stages of the Macarena craze, in the winter and spring of 1996, Macarena websites began to appear, with instructions and lyrics. Nearly as quickly, anti-Macarena websites were up as well. In some cases, people with personal Web pages simply added their thoughts about the Macarena, but others were wholly devoted to eradicating, or at least speaking out against, the dance. There were the HateMac page, the Macarena Sucks page, the Macarena-Free Zone, That Damn Macarena, the Dead Laszlo Institute, and many others, evincing stances varying from good-natured ribbing to murderous rage.

Moral objections were not evident on any of these pages. Rather, writers tended to deride the dance's simplicity or popularity. Many correspondents seemed most intent on having others understand the inferiority of the Macarena. Thus, the Macarena was not a "real" dance; it was "inane," "simplistic," "stupid," or "mindless," as in these two excerpts from the *Sacramento Bee* Macarena-Free Zone (now defunct, but then at Sacbee.com). In one, a prickly student at a Fred Astaire Dance Studio is:

absolutely appalled that people come in the door (in the middle of my lesson!!!) to ask if we teach the Macarena!!! First of all, if you want to pay $66/hour to learn such an inane dance, sure we'll teach you, but can't you just get drunk at a bar and imitate everyone else.... Now we have half the floor full of nitwits flailing their arms about and the other half doing real dancing.... What is the world coming to?

In another anecdote, a University of Illinois freshman relates her satisfaction in not having participated in a "New Student Week" Macarena:

... they started playing that horrific music and recruited some cheerleaders and other university employees ... the MC kept encouraging the crowd, imploring them to dance so that we could set a record.... But much to my delight, there was dead silence. People were shocked at this grotesque display of mindless pop culture. No one danced, save for one poor girl who had probably just crawled out from under a rock.

Here and there, a writer warns of the grave physical threat hidden in the craze: "My mom did the Macarena and now has permanent back problems. She also hurt her knee (tore the cartilage) and had to have an operation on it." Many people felt compelled to convey only their complete rejection of the Macarena, resulting in such pithy contributions as, "I have never done the Macarena and I never will!!!" (Sacbee.com 1996)

In particular, many writers objected to the presumption of people they considered unfit for dance in doing the Macarena, and regretted the permission to perform that such people seemed to feel. The Sacbee.com site, while less caustic than many, featured some comments in this general vein. One terrorized report, signed "forever traumatized," was an autobiographical tale of a girl brought to an "adult party and forced to witness adults dancing." Here are two further examples:

People say that anyone can do the Macarena. That's the problem. The truth is that not everyone can dance. Give the people a standard set of moves to follow and they'll be attempting it on a dance floor.

... much to my dismay, my 50 year old dad starts doing the Macarena in front of his 17 year old son. This thing has just got to stop!

"Non-dancers" and adults are here depicted as groups unwelcome to dance, and who normally know their place. The Macarena, though, has upset the normal order of things, making them feel free to dance. More specific objections to people "not meant to dance" are found in this account of a mandatory office-meeting Macarena, from a now defunct anti-Macarena site:

Now it was time to watch almost everyone (except for a few of us rebels) contort their bodies to the mind-numbing, brain-washing melody that is that song. Let me tell you, this is in the midwest, so there are LOTS of bodies that were never meant to wiggle and squirm. A few looked like the momentum they'd mustered would keep them jiggling for hours.

And similar sentiments are found in this example from the Sacbee Macarena-Free Zone:

> This is my horror story. At our annual church picnic last week, a few of the elder members decided it would be fun to do . . . the Macarena. They played it six times, and I was forced to watch as people about 100 years old and 400 or more pounds wiggled and jiggled, contorting their humongous bodies into the different positions of the hated dance. It was hell on earth!

In these comments, which echo the kind of objections heard at the local level, the very inclusivity of the Macarena is under attack. In these accounts, elderly people and overweight people are dancing, and they are doing so publicly. That these objections appear on anti-Macarena sites, rather than anti-elderly or anti-obesity sites, reinforces the idea that the "permission to dance" felt by these groups was Macarena-specific. Thus, the contributors seek to eradicate the dance, seeing it as the cause of, rather than just an instance of, loosening standards for dance participation.

Macarena for All?

As the craze waned, the cultural pendulum as it related to the Macarena shifted at different points in different cities and in individual lives. At some point, for most people, it was important to know the Macarena, and at some later point, it became important to leave it behind. To put it differently, at one point (and we must remain vague because the point is both geographically localized and individual) knowing the Macarena was a measure of one's awareness of cultural trends and at another point, dancing it was a measure of just the opposite. Thus, the onset of the Macarena was greeted at one week's baseball game with cheers and participation, and at the next, with boos. To cite another cultural indicator, here are two examples mentioning the Macarena from the "Top Ten List" on CBS's *Late Show with David Letterman*. The first is from December 30, 1996, the second from February 18, 2000.

> *From a top ten list of "Dave's New Year's Resolutions"*: Learn how to do this "Macarena" thing before the craze passes.

> *From a top ten list of "Things that sound cool when sung by a barbershop quartet"*: Last night we saw a man doing the Macarena, so we beat him to a bloody pulp.

Among such cultural insiders as those who watch the *Late Show*, the Macarena craze had largely passed by December 1996. So the first one pokes fun at the craze and at Letterman's implied "outsider" status, while the second makes fun not of the Macarena or of Letterman, but of "a man doing the Macarena," who meets a grisly fate. Perhaps the hostility of the line reflects only its search for comic value and should not be overexamined. In any case, making fun of the Macarena in 2000 was a rather cheap shot. It is part and parcel of a "craze" that the object becomes not just passé but laughable.

An examination of the Macarena craze reveals that tension about how U.S. social dance really works is evident in the simultaneous popularity and widespread derision of the dance. I have attempted here to explore the question of "What made everyone dance the Macarena?" But this implies a different question: "What keeps everyone sitting down the rest of the time?" The answers lie, at least in part, in a cultural repression of dance accomplished by the professionalization, specialization, and segmentation of dance. These are augmented by the social risks encountered in many dancing contexts. While many people are undeterred by these barriers, many others are not; the Macarena was notable for the way it seemed to open these gates.

The implantation of this "foreign" matter caused many to attempt modifications, trying to reshape the Macarena in a more familiar image. I have already argued that the simplicity of the Macarena was key to the other elements of its exceptionality, such as its explicit pedagogy and its encouragement of participation. In other words, explicit pedagogy and encouragement do not help some potential participants if the dance itself is complicated. Thus, the addition of any steps, especially complex steps, to a dance consisting mostly of arm movements is a significant change, in itself precluding many of the aspects of Macarena behavior. In some dancing circles, various steps were added to the basic Macarena sequence. To do so sometimes eliminated potential dancers, for example those "dancing" from a seated position.

Many people were content to do the Macarena as taught, or with slight, consistent variations; others found greater revisions necessary. Thus, in ballroom-dance circles (where sharp divisions were sometimes found between those eschewing the dance entirely and those interested in making it more worthy of their attention), there were some movements to make a "ballroom Macarena," with various versions incorporating some of the original arm movements. Transforming the Macarena from an individual or line dance into a couples dance is only one of the changes in such a scenario.

Elsewhere, similar debates occurred. Some line-dancing venues were among the first champions of the Macarena, but they were also places where the tension between professionalization/specialization and inclusion were evident. One solution was to have some people dance a "simple"

Macarena and others a more elaborate one, using the same floor. Another was to have "basic" Macarena early in the evening and more complex versions later on, or to alternate them. One favorite complication was to dance the Macarena at two or three times normal speed, a practice that quickly excluded all but the most nimble dancers. The increased tempo eliminated the option of simultaneous "basic" and "complex" participation.

Added steps and other movements toward specialization in the Macarena were not limited to specialized dance venues. In many places, some tension existed between the participatory nature of the Macarena and the normal practices surrounding and underlying dance. At a "World's Greatest Macarena Jam" held at a local festival in Decatur, Illinois, in 1996, for example, the ostensible goal was participation. A notebook was even available for participants to sign in, and efforts were made to solicit the participation of those in the crowd. Yet the dance itself was taught only once, in somewhat fragmented form. After a few cycles (very few, by Macarena standards), the DJs began playing the Macarena at double and triple time, and even referred to a "winner."

"Correcting" or "fixing" the dance, setting up anti-Macarena websites, and speaking out against the dance were all occasions to articulate some unwritten (and not necessarily unanimously held) rules about dance culture in the United States. These unwritten rules indicate preferences for complexity, specialization, and the exclusion of certain groups from the dance floor. Inclusion is not a particular goal of many dance contexts in the United States, or at least there is no trace of the elements that seemed to foster it in the case of the Macarena.

Where the goal is inclusion, the Macarena sometimes survives, generally in the company of the Hokey Pokey, the Chicken, the Locomotion, and the Electric Slide. The Macarena remains a staple at many weddings, bar mitzvahs, and some community events, and maintains a presence on cruise ships and in similar vacation settings. Anticipation of the celebration of the millennium caused many writers and those in the music industry to search for another "Macarena," seeking the inclusive experience it seemed to engender. The "Milly" in Chicago and "Mambo No. 5" were both frequently cited as heirs to the Macarena, and Los Del Rio offered "Baila, Baila" in order to "produce a 'Macarena' effect" (Llewellyn 1999), but none approached the Macarena's level of participation. As with many elements of culture, knowing the "recipe" (in this case, simple movements, public pedagogy, catchy tune) does not guarantee production of the desired result. Perhaps the most elusive element of the Macarena, an ingredient beyond manufacture, was the temporary desire of many Americans to dance together.

"Give Your Body Joy, Macarena"

Notes

1. An eleven-hour Macarena at a southern Maryland radio station in late August 1996 jammed not only the station's phone lines but local 911 lines (see Yorke 1996).
2. Llewelyn's history is the most straightforward and comprehensive I have found. See also the accounts by Castro and Salcines and by Dark, which give additional details on the genesis of particular versions.
3. All but the *lambada* are discussed in Roberts (1999).
4. Bill Heavey (1996) gives a descriptive contemporary account of a three-hour vacation drive during which his daughter and her best friend did the dance in the back seat "about 6,000 times," and a vacation where nearly every event could send the girls into the dance.
5. Most web-based Macarena instruction sites are no longer accessible, but one still available as of this writing is http://www.megalink.net/~dale/macarena.htm.
6. http://www.geocities.com/Paris/2583/macarena.html and http://www.online-fans.de/Lyrics/macarena.htm remain available.

References

Calkins, Nancy. 1996. "The Macarena is No Innocent Dance; How Can We Ignore the Song's Blatant Call for Infidelity?" Editorial, *Greensboro NC News & Record* (September 21): A10.

Castro, Peter and Marisa Salcines. 1996. "Don't Blame It on the Bossa Nova. The Likely Culprit Is . . . Macarena Madness." *People* (August 19, 1996): 76.

Catlin, Roger. 1996. "Macarena: A Latin Dance Craze That Could Topple the Electric Slide." *The Hartford Courant* (July 17): E1.

Dark, Jane. 1996. "The Popular Crowd: Macarena Mania Sweeps the Globe." *Village Voice* (August 20): 59.

Heavey, Bill. 1996. "The Girls of Summer: One More Trip to the Beach. And, Uh, One More Macarena." *The Washington Post* (September 11): D9.

Hoffman, Ken. 1996. "Original 'Macarena' Lyrics Are Not So Squeaky-Clean." *The Houston Chronicle* (October 9): 2.

Levin, Jordan. 1995. "Miami Dance Clubs Help Expose New Latin Acts." *Billboard* (February 11): 1.

Llewellyn, Howell. 1996. "BMG's Macarena Fever Spreads Around the World." *Billboard* (July 27): 7.

N.A. 1996. "Hollywood Minute." *CNN Headline News* (January 6).

N.A. 1996. "La Macarena Dance Craze Sweeps the Globe." *CNN Early Edition* (August 21).

N.A. 1996. "Macarena a Hit at Convention." *Washingtonpost.com* (August 29): 9:24 EDT.

N.A. 1996. "Macarena Wrap Up." *CNN Headline News* (September 19).

Navarro, Mireya. 1995a. "Macarena Madness Now Has the Floor." *The New York Times* (December 27): A 10.

———. 1995b. "Macarena Dance Craze Hits Miami." *Rocky Mountain News* (December 31): 38A.

Pipp, Tracy L. 1996. "Dance Fever: Sexy Latin Moves Have Americans Hustling to Do the Macarena." *The Detroit News* (June 12): A1.

Rivenbark, Celia. 1996. "Macarena Madness Usurps Hokey Pokey Passion." *The Houston Chronicle* (September 12): 3.

Roberts, John Storm. 1999. *The Latin Tinge: The Impact of Latin American Music on the United States*. 2d ed. New York: Oxford University Press.

Roberts, Roxanne. 1996. "Want to Dance? Get in Line! From Day Camps to Nightclubs, the Macarena Is a Hands-Down Hit." *The Washington Post* (August 1): A01.

Romero, Dennis. 1996. "Lining Up and Letting Loose: It's a Little Hand Jive, A Little Hokey Pokey and Lots of Fun." *The Los Angeles Times Home Edition* (August 19): E1.

Roybal, David. 1996. "Are They Really Listening to 'La Macarena'?" *The Sante Fe New Mexican* (October 11): B1.

Sacramento Bee Macarena-Free Zone: sacbee.com/smile/macarena/macarena.html.

"Weekend Edition." 1996. *National Public Radio* (August 24).

Yorke, Jeffrey. 1996. "Dance Crazed: A Station's Nonstop 'Macarena' Creates Publicity and Alarm." *The Washington Post* (September 3): C07.

Part III

Globalization and Mass Mediation

Brazil and Peru

9

Music and Place in the Brazilian Popular Imagination

The Interplay of Local and Global in the Mangue Bit *Movement of Recife, Pernambuco, Brazil*

PHILIP GALINSKY

This chapter looks at the recent *mangue bit* (or just *mangue*) movement of Recife, capital of Pernambuco State in Northeast Brazil, focusing on the relation between music and place.[1] Formed in Recife in the early 1990s as a cultural response to a debilitating socioeconomic situation, *mangue bit* refers to both the ubiquitous mangrove swamps on top of which the city is built—emphasizing a strong grounding in the local environment and traditional culture of the region—as well as to the "bit" of computer technology—an embrace of the global, modern, and universal. Articulated primarily in pop music but also later expressed in theater, dance, cinema, fashion, and the visual arts, the *mangue* project symbolically involved planting a satellite antenna in the mud of the region and picking up signals from the rest of the world. Accordingly, the movement advocates the active use of technology in its blending of once-obscure regional folk-music styles and national popular music with a wide variety of global pop genres.

The two pioneering *mangue* bands are Nação Zumbi ("Zumbi Nation"), founded by the late frontman, vocalist, and composer Chico Science, and Mundo Livre S/A,[2] founded and led by guitarist-vocalist-composer Fred Zero Quatro. Chico Science was the undisputed leader of the *mangue* movement and arguably the most innovative Brazilian pop musician of his generation before his untimely death in early 1997 in a car accident at age thirty. A tremendously charismatic role model for a young subculture in Brazil, Chico assimilated and embodied in his dress, music, behavior, and even his nickname the fusion of the local and global. Chico Science and Nação Zumbi (hereafter referred to as CSNZ) updated the foreign sound-scape of Brazilian pop by blending soul, funk, rap, Jamaican *raggamuffin*, psychedelic rock, heavy metal, electronic dance music, and other global trends with local styles. They inspired many regional (and some national) rock and fusion bands, while simultaneously helping to revitalize Pernambucan folk music and dance traditions. Indeed, since the 1990s such styles as *maracatu, côco, embolada,* and *ciranda* have been enjoying unprecedented popularity among people of various social classes in Pernambuco, and some credit Chico Science personally for much of this newfound interest.[3] In short, *mangue* has reinvested Pernambuco, a materially impoverished state rich in folk and popular culture, with a renewed value and sense of pride, placing it firmly on the world map of pop music.

Together with related projects (such as the work of Nação Pernambuco and Mestre Ambrósio), *mangue* spawned an entire "new music scene" in Recife, the so-called *nova cena musical,* which has become one of the most critically acclaimed in Brazil. *Mangue*'s merging of the rustic and old with the modern and new has made its mark on the history of *Música Popular Brasileira* (MPB, or Brazilian popular music, a catch-all term for post-bossa nova pop). Indeed, critics have hailed *mangue* as the most significant trend in MPB since the groundbreaking *tropicália* ("tropicalism") movement[4] of the late 1960s, which made the "cultural cannibalism," or *antropofagia,* of the Brazilian modernists into a norm for pop music in the country. *Mangue* has also gained international renown, particularly through CSNZ, the most influential band to come out of Pernambuco in the last several decades.

The first part of this chapter provides an ethnographically informed history of the *mangue* movement and related "new music scene" of Recife, highlighting how people have used music and other elements of expressive culture to change the place in which they live. The second part explores the new cultural identity and relation between local and global that have emerged with the movement. I argue that in its heightened sense of both local and global, *mangue* exemplifies a recent challenge to older notions of the link between popular music and Brazilian national identity.

A History of the *Mangue* Movement and *Nova Cena Musical*

Concentrating on the bands CSNZ and Mundo Livre S/A, this section provides a history of *mangue* and the *nova cena musical* of Recife.[5] Not only are these bands central to the *mangue* movement, but they (particularly Nação

Zumbi) also exerted a profound influence on the subsequent music scene. But if CSNZ was the most influential and arguably the most original group to emerge from this scene, the *nova cena* has also relied on a strikingly diverse array of groups and artists.[6] These range from folk performers and associations to young regional-rhythms bands to fusion groups to rock (mainly punk, hard-core, or heavy metal) and rap outfits. The following is a sampling, as of 1998, of some important names, besides the two bands featured here, that have formed part of this scene: Mestre Ambrósio, Cascabulho, Devotos do Ódio (recently shortened to Devotos), Via Sat, Coração Tribal, Faces do Subúrbio, Sheik Tosado, Eddie, Maracatu Nação Pernambuco, Dona Selma do Côco, Lia de Itamaracá, Zé Neguinho do Côco, Mestre Salustiano, Maracatu Nação Estrela Brilhante, Comadre Florzinha, and Chão e Chinelo.

Setting the Scene: Recife in the 1980s

Journalist José Teles[7] locates the origins of the *mangue* movement (which he prefers to call a scene) at the end of the 1970s or beginning of the '80s. At the time, the military government, in power since 1964, began to ease censorship, allowing for a tentative opening of the ports and consequently a "timid but very important rebirth of pop art in the country." Teles points to several manifestations of this pop culture, such as a renewed interest in beat literature (*On the Road* first appeared in Brazilian translation during this period) and the availability of imported records in national editions (previously such records would be sold only in record import shops in the wealthier Southeast of the country).

In the 1980s, there was a boom in Brazilian-made rock, centered in southern cities such as Rio de Janeiro, São Paulo, and Brasília. Meanwhile in Recife, some middle-class students at the Federal University of Pernambuco were introducing themselves to beat literature, the cyberpunk fiction of William Gibson, and the sounds of Joy Division, New Order, the Smiths, Bauhaus, Siouxie and the Banshees, and Pil, among other groups. These students produced a program on the University radio called *Décadas* ("Decades"), on which "future manguegirls and mangueboys [the local term for adherents of the movement] began to tune into other sounds." Several of the *mangue* movement's figures, such as DJ-journalist Renato L. (Renato Lins), Herr Doktor Mabuse, and Fred Zero Quatro, were part of the *Décadas* team. According to Teles, *Décadas* was important for the development of *mangue* because it showed that "there was space to create a music outside of the parameters desired by the FM stations and multinational record companies, and even as such to make friends and influence people."

Mundo Livre S/A.   Fred Rodrigues Montenegro (a.k.a. Fred Zero Quatro) is one of the primary figures behind the *mangue* movement and the frontman of the band Mundo Livre S/A.[8] Before Mundo Livre, Fred participated in three successive punk or post-punk bands: Trapaça ("Swindle"), Serviço Sujo ("Dirty Service"), and Câmbio Negro H.C. ("Black Market Hard-Core").[9] At the time, in the early 1980s, there was a tiny nucleus of bands of this type in the city. This early punk phase lasted only about a year, however, because there was no space for this kind of music in Recife, and the bands had nowhere to play.

In the beginning of 1984, Fred quit Câmbio Negro and reunited the old members of Trapaça (which included Fred on guitar, Fred's brother Fábio on bass, Neguinho on drumset, and Avron on *guitarra baiana*[10]) and founded Mundo Livre S/A. Fred describes the concept behind the band:

> The idea was to make a sound that was at the same time new wave but with many ingredients of the samba. So . . . another brother of mine was always at the show [and] we invited him to play *tamborim, agogô* [percussion instruments typical of samba]. We wanted to make a fusion, a bridge between Johnny Rotten [of the Sex Pistols punk band] and Jorge Ben [a pioneering Brazilian pop musician who fuses funk, soul, and samba] and Moreira da Silva [a samba musician from the 1930s and '40s], understand? . . . It would be a type of new wave but very Brazilian, really very Brazilian, that would be identified neither as rock nor as MPB.

Although the band had no intentions of becoming professional in the beginning, Mundo Livre slowly built a name for themselves, despite the fact that the rock public in Recife at the time preferred to hear cover songs of famous English-language bands. Moreover, according to Zero Quatro, there was no musical infrastructure in Recife during this period:

> Until 1988 more or less . . . Recife was a place that had no [music] circuit. There wasn't any place to record a good tape, there wasn't any place to buy good instruments, no place to play, there was nowhere to rehearse, there were no sound engineers, no music producers, no impresarios, nothing!

Nevertheless, the band held onto the hope that someday they might get a break. Zero Quatro notes that the bleak economic situation in the 1980s in Recife, which had and still has the highest levels of unemployment in the country, was stimulus enough to maintain a band that at least had some name. Indeed, the alternatives were even less desirable.

Around 1987, two years after Brazil's return to civilian rule, dozens of other rock bands spread throughout Recife, many of them playing heavy metal or hard-core. According to journalist José Teles (n.d., 13–14), these bands had trouble finding places to play. Curiously, one of the most popular venues for this crop of '80s groups was at a dance academy directed by a rock enthusiast named Lourdes Rossiter: the Espaço Arte Viva, located in the chic beach neighborhood of Boa Viagem.

Nação Pernambuco.   About two years after the emergence of this underground hard-core and heavy-metal scene, a group of middle-class youths known as Nação Pernambuco ("Pernambuco Nation") began to recreate interest in the regional folk culture and, in particular, an important local Afro-Brazilian drumming and dance style called *maracatu*. Technically referred to as the *maracatu de baque virado* ("*maracatu* of the turned rhythm"), this style has gone from being largely disregarded to becoming one of the preeminent sonic emblems for the new Pernambuco.[11] Part of the credit for this turn-around, and for a recent revalorization of the local culture, could be attributed to Nação Pernambuco, although some people on the scene may dispute such a claim. According to Recife journalist Pedro Rampazzo,

> In December of 1989 a kind of group different from anything that already existed in the city emerged in Olinda, Pernambuco [Olinda is a colonial city next to Recife]. A group of young men and women of the middle class were getting together to play and dance *maracatu*, a rhythm until then performed only by traditional groups or by artists such as Alceu Valença, Geraldo Azevedo, Elba Ramalho, and Quinteto Violado. Even though they were not a traditional group, they called themselves Maracatu Nação Pernambuco. The first shows or open rehearsals, as they were known, happened outside in the historic section of Olinda and attracted large numbers of people, young people of the middle class, who in the large majority were friends of members of the group. Among these young people was Francisco de Assis França, or Chico Science, as he would come to be called in the near future. Nação Pernambuco innovated in bringing to the public a rhythm that before that time [1989] had been performed exclusively during the Carnival season. (n.d., 5–6)

The culture that Nação Pernambuco represents has traditionally been the provenance of the *maracatus nação* ("*maracatu* nations"), old associations based in poor areas of the city that have a direct connection to an Afro-Brazilian religious and cultural heritage and parade as a syncretic royal court during Recife's Carnival. Although Nação Pernambuco is a folkloric troupe and not a traditional "nation," it nonetheless has brought the local culture to a wider audience in Pernambuco, Brazil, and the world.[12]

Chico Science and Nação Zumbi.   While Nação Pernambuco was helping to rejuvenate local music through the formation of a folkloric association, the *mangue* project, and particularly CSNZ, adapted the influence of local styles into a contemporary pop format and brought the regional culture more fully into the age of the Internet. Band members combined straw fisherman hats of the region with Ray-Ban sunglasses, *bombo* drums of the *maracatu* with electric guitars and samplers. They used a vocabulary tied to the environment (e.g., swamps, rivers, mud, crabs, vultures, etc.) and infrastructure (e.g., bridges) of the port city.

The idea of associating the local term *mangue* ("mangrove swamp") with music came from Chico Science, a pivotal figure for whom the black urban style of New York in the late 1970s and early '80s was just as natural as the regional folk rhythms of his native Recife. Chico Science was born Francisco de Assis França in 1966 to a home of the lower middle class in the Rio Doce neighborhood of Paulista, a city on the periphery of Olinda. Whereas Fred Zero Quatro gravitated toward punk and new-wave, as a preadolescent and teenager Chico enjoyed black popular music from the United States, particularly of the 1970s and '80s. Chico favored the classic funk sounds of James Brown, Curtis Mayfield, and Funkadelic and the early hip-hop of Sugar Hill Gang, Kurtis Blow, and Grand Master Flash, among other groups (Teles n.d., 8, 10). As a pre-teen, he would take part in the so-called *bailes funk* ("funk parties") that happened on the outskirts of the city (Pires 1998). In 1984, as the breakdance phenomenon hit Recife, Chico and his inseparable friend Jorge du Peixe joined the *Legião Hip Hop* ("Hip-Hop Legion"), one of the major street breakdance groups of the city (Teles n.d., 8). Aside from international black music, another crucial formative influence on Chico was the local folk culture as well as the rock music that his brothers listened to.[13]

In 1987, as various groups were emerging in the city, Chico and Jorge du Peixe joined the rock cover band of guitarist Lúcio Maia, called Orla Orbe, which they inflected with a funk influence (Teles n.d., 8). Orla Orbe was succeeded in 1989 by Loustal, whose name was inspired by a famous French cartoonist whom Chico admired (Teles n.d., 8). In 1989, Fred Zero Quatro met Chico Science. He says:

> When I saw Loustal's show for the first time, I thought, damn, I really identi-fied [with them], with a lot of identification with the sound of Mundo Livre because it was rock, there was an electric guitarist there and such, but the drummer was already adding heavy doses of *frevo*, *ciranda* [two regional folk styles]. And we [Mundo Livre] had this history with the samba, an idea from a long time ago and such. So I perceived that there was a possibility for the first time for a more cohesive scene to happen. (Zero Quatro 1998)

Aside from a musical affinity based on a merging of local and global, Zero Quatro felt also that the geographic gap between his and Chico's band (which were based out of opposite ends of the city) was a useful condition for forging a wider scene:

> And we even realized that, as there was this geographic distance, if we did shows collectively, produced shows of the two bands, uniting the audience of one band with that of the other, we could increase our public. And so since 1989 there was a desire to create a scene in the city—a movement. (Zero Quatro 1998)

Although Loustal and other bands in the late 1980s already experimented with Pernambucan folk elements, it was not until Chico Science solidified a stronger musical link to the local black culture and a social connection to the poorest communities of Recife that Nação Zumbi and a new musical movement were born. In 1990, Gilmar "Bola Oito" ("Eight Ball Gilmar"), a colleague at Chico's government agency job, introduced Chico to a local *bloco afro* (Afro-Brazilian cultural group) called Lamento Negro ("Black Lament"), based in the very poor Peixinhos neighborhood on the periphery of Olinda (Teles n.d., 8).[14] At the time, Lamento specialized in the *samba-reggae*, a nationally popular musical hybrid formulated in Salvador, Bahia, in the 1980s; they also worked on grass-roots cultural education together with Daruê Malungo, a center for the support of poor communities based in nearby Chão de Estrelas (Teles n.d., 8).

Along with Jorge du Peixe, Chico began to attend Lamento Negro's rehearsals, initiating a series of musical experiments. The group that was originally called Chico Science and Lamento Negro at first utilized percussion and vocals (still with a strong influence of the Bahian-style *samba-reggae*), later adding Lúcio Maia on guitar and Alexandre Dengue on bass from Chico's band Loustal. The modest debut of the band occurred at the Espaço Oásis in Olinda on June 1, 1991 (Teles n.d., 11). Only friends showed up for the gig, but according to Teles, "all confessed that they were surprised with [the band's] unusual [musical] alchemy" (Teles n.d., 11).

The first printed article about Chico came out in the local Recife paper that day, advertising the event as the Black Planet party. It was to feature DJs Renato L., Dr. Mabuse, and Chico spinning black sounds such as soul, reggae, hip-hop, jazz, *samba-reggae*, funk, Jamaican *toast* and *raggamuffin*, and a performance by Loustal/Lamento Negro of *mangue*, which Chico defined at the time as "a mixture of *samba-reggae*, rap, *ragamuffin* [sic] and *embolada*," the latter being a musical-poetic form of Northeast Brazil (article reproduced in Teles n.d., 2). Describing his musical outlook, Chico commented: "It is our responsibility to recover the rhythms of the region and add them together with a musical vision of the world" (Teles n.d., 2). Indeed, due to Chico's interest in reclaiming an unsung Pernambucan musical heritage, the band soon left behind the influence of the Bahian *samba-reggae* in favor of Pernambucan styles.[15]

The concept of the *mangue* served as both the local geographical setting on which the members of CSNZ literally lived and as a symbol for cultural and musical diversity that Recife could show Brazil and the world. As Fred Zero Quatro explains:

> So there was this story that Chico was from . . . Rio Doce, the people of Lamento Negro were from Peixinhos. It's that the whole area is in mud, the land of *mangue* and such. And when Chico went to do the promotion of a party, of a show, he would say, "It's going to be the greatest *lama* [mud], the greatest *mangue* [swamp]" and such. So this thing was created. [Renato and I] would meet with Chico and call him *"mangueboy."* . . . [The sound of CSNZ] was a great musical formula, it was a great musical synthesis, very cool and irresistible, but it also had to be very well accessed so as not to come out of here as a thing, a band from Recife, something exotic like that. Because, damn, [it was] perfect to construct from there a scene based on diversity, because Recife has much diversity and such. And the thing would have much more weight united with Mundo Livre, because Mundo Livre has a totally different history, messing more with samba, to show that Recife really is something, that there was a scene that even had a much bigger potential than something restricted just to Chico Science and such. And we knew there really was all this potential here in Recife. (1998)

Initially, Chico adopted the term *mangue* to describe the blending of various styles he discovered with Lamento Negro and eventually the fusion sound of his band Nação Zumbi (Lins 1998). But other members of the *mangue* movement defined the term less by particular musical characteristics. As DJ-journalist Renato L. explains:

> Originally, when this whole story began here in Recife at the beginning of the '90s, *mangue* was a label that we used for a type of cultural cooperative . . . that united some bands [particularly Nação Zumbi and Mundo Livre S/A], some visual artists, some journalists, some unemployed. And the idea, the label *mangue* emerged because Recife is a city that is constructed on top of the *manguezais* ["mangrove swamps"]. Our idea at the time [in the early '90s] was to try to create a cultural scene here in Recife that was as rich and diversified as the *mangue* swamps, because the swamps are perhaps the ecosystem that has the greatest biodiversity of the planet. So the idea was to create a cultural scene . . . that had the same diversity, that wasn't tied down to a single rhythm, a single style, or single fashion. So we made use of that label [*mangue*], it fit well with this idea. . . . A bit motivated by the work . . . of the cooperative . . . a musical scene was born here in Recife. And the press began to label the whole scene *"mangue."* So today there is a certain confusion

between *mangue*, this cooperative . . . in the beginning of the '90s and the *mangue* that the press and the people call this new scene of Recife. (1998)

Perhaps partly as a result of Chico's initial use of the word to describe a particular beat or genre, the Brazilian press began to talk of a *mangue beat*—which was, in fact, a corruption of an earlier name for the movement: *mangue bit*.[16]

Beginning in 1991, shows began to appear with the *mangue* label: Viagem Ao Centro Do Mangue ("Journey to the Center of the *Mangue*") and Mangue Feliz ("Merry *Mangue*," which was a play on Natal Feliz, or Merry Christmas) (Zero Quatro 1998). The *mangue* public began to grow, and, according to Fred Zero Quatro, "everything was contributed spontaneously in the city to create a complex scene" (Zero Quatro 1998).

The Beginnings of a "New Music Scene"

Paulo André Pires, the future manager of CSNZ, opened his record store, Rock Xpress, in December 1989 and began to involve himself in local music production. By his own account, he "has accompanied, perhaps more than anyone, the evolution of this scene" (Pires 1998). Recalling its origins, Pires asserts that:

> At that time . . . in 1990–91 the pop scene of the city practically didn't exist. There existed a more underground scene of thrash and hard-core bands, and punk rock, too. The Devótos do Ódio ["The Devotees of Hate," one of the most important bands on the current Recife scene, now known simply as Devotos], for example, dates back to this time. . . . (Pires 1998)

Suffering from its own insularity, this nascent scene in Recife began to benefit from the arrival in Recife of some new media, such as MTV at the end of 1991 and São Paulo's Rádio Rock, one of the biggest rock stations in Brazil, in 1992 (Pires 1998). MTV brought information to the local bands and enabled them to see what was happening in other parts of the country, while Rádio Rock:

> gave hope to the bands of playing someplace. Because the local radio stations, in the great majority, ignored this music that is produced here. There were never great spaces for this music in its own state. (Pires, 1998)

The Manifesto Mangue

As a new music scene was emerging in Recife, Francisco França (baptized by Renato L. with the pseudonym "Science," referring to Chico's predilection for experimenting with the "alchemy" of sounds), Fred Zero Quatro, and Renato L. came out with the *Manifesto Mangue*, entitled *Caranguejos com cérebro* ("Crabs with Brains"). Written by Fred Zero Quatro (a journalist by trade) and distributed to the press in 1991, the manifesto consists of three parts (reproduced in Teles n.d., 5–6). "Mangue—the Concept" presents Recife's *manguezais*, swamps of tropical and subtropical plants, as "symbols of fertility, diversity and richness." "Manguetown—The City" points to the pernicious effects of Recife's modern growth as *the* metropolis of the Northeast: economic stagnation, destruction of the *manguezais*, the worst unemployment in the country, more than 50 percent of the population living in slums, and the distinction of being classified as the fourth worst city in the world to live in, according to an institute of population studies in Washington, D.C. "Mangue—the Scene" suggests that the solution to this condition is to "inject a little energy in the mud and stimulate what fertility still remains in the veins of Recife." Calling themselves a "nucleus of pop ideas," the *mangueboys* aimed to "engender an 'energetic circuit' capable of connecting allegorically the good vibrations of the *mangue* with the world network of the circulation of pop concepts." Their symbol is a parabolic antenna sunk in the *lama* ("mud") of Recife, picking up signals from around the world, or a *caranguejo* ("crab") remixing the album *Ánthena* by the Euro-tech group Kraftwerk on a computer.

The image of the crab has become a metaphor for the movement, often appearing in the lyrics of CSNZ songs. Inspired by the ideas of Recife writer-nutritionist Josué de Castro (see Castro 1970), who described the interconnected life cycle of crabs and fishermen in the region, the *mangue* adherents imagine themselves as "crabs with brains"—people in touch with and able to transcend their environment or see a way out of their predicament. *Mangue* has become a remarkably creative and self-aware vehicle for young people in Recife of various social and racial backgrounds to come together, creating a scene that has helped rechannel energies in the city.

The Consolidation of Recife's "New Music Scene"

With the launch of *mangue*, various other pop bands appeared and began to play small shows in venues such as Soparia in the Pina neighborhood (which in 1998 was still the primary club for local bands on the scene). According to Paulo André Pires, these events "didn't attract more than 200 people; it was very much an alternative thing." At the end of 1992, Rádio Rock went off the air, leaving "zero space for the Pernambucan bands" (1998).

Impressed with Nação Pernambuco's revalorization of Pernambucan culture among young people in Recife, Pires invited them in 1993, along with twelve local rock bands (eleven of them without a recording), to perform at what became the first edition of an annual music festival in the city that

Pires created and produced called Abril Pro Rock ("April for Rock") (Pires 1998). Seen as the largest showcase for young bands in Brazil, Abril Pro Rock draws international as well as regional and national artists. This landmark event in Pernambucan music united an audience of 1,500 people to see only local bands—which had not been done before—serving as a launching pad for CSNZ and Mundo Livre S/A (Pires 1998). The two bands went on tour together in southern Brazil, leading to their first recording contracts, CSNZ with Sony, and Mundo Livre with Banguela, a Brazilian label (Pires 1998). Both groups' debut albums were released in 1994.

Featuring an erratic line-up in the beginning, CSNZ narrowed down to eight members before the recording of its debut CD: Chico Science, vocals; Alexandre Dengue, bass; Lúcio Maia, guitar; Gilmar Bola Oito, Gira; and Jorge du Peixe, *bombo* drum (culled from the *maracatu*); Toca Ogan, percussion; and Canhoto, snare drum (later replaced by Pupillo on drumset). The title of the band's CD, *Da lama ao caos* ("From Mud to Chaos"), refers to the chaotic, sprawling metropolis of Recife that was erected on top of the region's mud. The album is a volatile mixture of regional Pernambucan rhythms and styles—such as *maracatu*, *ciranda*, *côco*, and *embolada*—with heavy rock guitar and funk grooves, among other influences. Paulo André Pires assesses the impact of the band in the beginning:

> Until that time in Brazil there didn't exist a rock band with [Afro-Brazilian] drums [the *bombo* drums of the *maracatu* style] in its formation. And a lot of people thought it was strange in the beginning. (1998)

Despite this initial shock on the part of some listeners, including prominent local musicians, the Brazilian press recognized the importance of *mangue* right from the start.

With the release of their CD, CSNZ embarked on their first international tour in five European countries and the United States, where they opened up for MPB star and *tropicália* pioneer Gilberto Gil at the 1995 SummerStage Festival in New York's Central Park. Back home in 1995, CSNZ was the biggest draw for that year's April for Rock Festival, which had been expanded to four nights with a total of 8,000 ticket buyers (Abramo 1997, 76). Meanwhile, aside from Soparia, the club Moritzstadt (named after the colonial Pernambucan Dutch leader Maurice, who advocated cultural liberty) became another important locale in Recife's downtown. In its heyday, Moritzstadt featured two to three *mangue* shows per night for twenty to five hundred people, as well as DJs who would play jazz, R&B, hip-hop, punk, and *mangue* (Filho 1998).

Beginning in 1995, the "Minster of Information" of the movement, Renato L., led a radio program on Rádio Caetés FM in Recife called "Mangue

Beat," which was heard between 8:00 and 9:00 P.M., Monday through Friday. The role of this program was to provide a space on the air for Recife's bands and to give exposure to various world trends (e.g., African, Arabic, avant-garde electronic music, etc.) that do not usually circulate in the Brazilian mass media (Lins 1998). In 1995, *mangue* also appeared in cyberspace with the launch of its manifesto. Since then, various websites have emerged based on *mangue* and the Recife scene, including Manguetronic, an Internet radio program hosted by Renato L. (www.uol.com.br/manguetronic; other useful sites include www.terra.com.br/manguenius and www. aponte.com.br).

In 1996, CSNZ released its even more exploratory, critically acclaimed second CD, *Afrociberdelia*, toured Europe, and appeared, along with fellow Pernambucans Mundo Livre and the folkloric Banda de Pífanos Dois Irmãos de Caruaru, in Brooklyn's Prospect Park as part of New York City's Brazilian Music Festival. The band was also one of the national attractions that year at the Hollywood Rock Festival in Rio. In cinema, the Pernambucan film *Baile perfumado* by Paulo Caldas and Lírio Ferreira—the winner of the Festival de Brasília in 1996—has a soundtrack by Chico Science, Fred Zero Quatro, and Siba of the band Mestre Ambrósio. By 1996, CSNZ had conquered a niche in the fickle Brazilian pop-music circuit while gaining critical acclaim and audiences throughout Brazil and the world.

The Recife Scene Loses Its "Greatest Exponent"

Early in 1997, CSNZ played its last show for the Recife public at the Clube Portugûes.[17] Then, on February 2, while driving his Fiat Uno from Recife to Olinda, Chico Science hit a pole and died almost instantly. News of Chico's death quickly reached the national media, forcing the country to recognize what it had lost. Before his death, the band would play for audiences of about 1,000 to 1,500 people, mostly poor and middle class; after the massive media coverage of Chico's passing, "the rich people recognized and started to like him" (Filho 1998). According to Chico's father, his son's popularity tripled after his death (França 1998).

Chico remains a guiding spirit—even a martyr—of Recife's music scene. Many Recife bands these days either copy Chico's concept or are directly or indirectly indebted to his influence. Youths who attend shows wear Chico Science T-shirts, as well as those of other popular national and international rock bands; some wear the straw fisherman's hat and Ray-Ban sunglasses he made popular. All around Recife, graffiti art also pays homage to him. The use of baseball caps, certain expressions (e.g., *fique antenado*, "stay connected," derived from the antenna symbol), and the formation of one's hands into the shape of crab claws are all part of a fascinating youth subculture in Recife that emerged from its "swamp" movement. Visual artists and designers have claimed to create *mangue* styles, and *Zambo*, the first dance-theater piece inspired by the *mangue* movement, debuted in Recife in 1998.

Meanwhile, despite the loss of its foremost musician, Recife's current music scene continues to evolve, gaining more and more attention outside of Recife. In 1997, the Pernambucans Mestre Ambrósio, Cascabulho, the Banda de Pífanos Dois Irmãos de Caruaru, and Lenine (with percussionist Marcos Suzano) participated in an expanded five-day Brazilian Music Festival in New York City at Central Park's SummerStage. The entire festival was filmed and edited by HBO Brazil and later rebroadcast on the U.S. Public Broadcasting System television station. The program was dedicated to Chico Science. After a hiatus, Nação Zumbi resumed touring and recording.

Changes in the City

Although Recife is still home to some of the worst poverty and social problems not only in Brazil but also the world, things have improved slightly since the 1980s. Parts of Recife have undergone drastic changes, although the recent development in the Northeast generally has only significantly benefited the region's affluent population (see Page 1995, 195). Many of CSNZ's songs, such as "A Cidade" ("The City"), critique the widening social gap in Recife.

Even if life mostly continues as it always did for the vast majority of city dwellers, the *mangue* movement and *nova cena musical* have nonetheless contributed to important changes in both poor and middle-class communities as well as altered the public image of the city. There appears to be a new-found feeling of pride in the city. As local producer Zé da Flauta told me, the self-esteem of northeastern Brazilians, and particularly Pernambucans, has augmented notably in the last several years (1998). Many attribute this new self-esteem in Pernambuco to Chico Science. As Pires comments:

> I think that Chico really helped this question of the *periphery* [the outskirts of the city where poor communities live]. He is very much respected by the youth of the periphery because, like them, he was a young, lower-middle-class guy from the periphery who lived in low-income housing and who managed to make his international career viable. So it's as if he were a symbol for a guy who overcame his situation in life, who managed to go from nothing, from zero money to a very successful artistic career in the little time that it existed. (1998)

Indeed, many young people in Recife are making viable careers in music these days, and by showing that this was possible, Chico Science became a role model for impoverished youth.

Pupillo, drumset player for Nação Zumbi, believes Chico's greatest contribution was the fact that, as a humble man from the periphery of the city, he accomplished what someone with more money could not have done (1998). As both Pupillo and Renato L. (1998) reported, Chico assumed his "Brazilianness" and his "Pernambucanness" in the wake of an era, the 1980s, in which (rock/fusion) bands largely copied what came from abroad.

An overlapping counterpart to the *mangue* movement has developed in the *favelas* of Greater Recife. *Favelas* are poor squatter settlements in urban areas of Brazil, often perched on hills called *morros*. Two neighborhoods have emerged as important musical/cultural centers: the aforementioned Peixinhos and the Alto José do Pinho. Peixinhos is home to Lamento Negro, which has supplied Nação Zumbi and other bands on the scene with their drummers. The Alto Zé do Pinho (as it is popularly known) boasts the city's best-known hard-core and rap groups (Devotos and Faces do Subúrbio, respectively), and it is also a stronghold of regional folk culture. Producer Zé da Flauta claims that the Alto Zé do Pinho contains forty-two bands, while there are more than forty in Peixinhos (1998). As he explains: "[The Alto Zé do Pinho and Peixinhos] only appeared in the newspaper, on the radio, and on television when there was news of criminals. . . . Today, the people of [these neighborhoods] stand out in the social columns of the newspapers, in the cultural sections. . . . According to the data of the military police of the state, the occurance of criminality in [the two neighborhoods] has diminished by 55%. And so I ask, 'What other kind of social work could the government do in a place like this to obtain such a result?' No other, no other. It's the power of the music. So the power of music is doing very important social work in these places" (1998). The Alto Zé do Pinho is now seen as safer and better off than it used to be. As one of the designated hip spots for aficionados of Recife's new cultural scene, including among the middle class, the neighborhood is emblematic of the positive changes in the city that *mangue* and the "new music scene" in Recife have helped produce.

The Interplay of Local and Global in *Mangue*

The *mangue* movement is representative of a recent trend in Brazil (and worldwide) that some may call postmodern: an increasing emphasis on locales within nation-states and an increased interaction of such locales directly with the rest of the world. Indeed, in some sense, *mangue* bypasses Brazil in its construction of identity. Recall that the symbolic image of the movement is an antenna sunk in the mud of the region, receiving influences from the rest of the world. These influences are figuratively incorporated into the *mangue* and mixed with local traditions, yielding new hybrids that are projected not only to Brazil but even more back out to the rest of the world. This final section explores the relation between local and global in *mangue*, suggesting what this relation might say about the question of national identity in Brazil.

First, *mangue* must be understood within a wider context of regional and national cultural dynamics. Pernambuco and the Northeast are claiming space in the Brazilian cultural identity. To understand this dynamic between regions of Brazil, one has to consider the great socioeconomic differential between a poorer northern and wealthier southern Brazil, the significant cultural divisions among the diverse regions, and the traditional dominance of the South, particularly the city of Rio de Janeiro, in representing the cultural identity of the country. Suffice it to say that *mangue* reflects and embodies a current assertion of pride in being a Northeasterner and a Pernambucan. Many regard the Northeast as the cultural heart of Brazil, the region where the nation's most important traditions (including the samba) were first manifest, as well as a source of some of Brazil's most important musical and cultural developments. But while it reconnects with what many may regard as the "true essence" of Brazilian national culture, *mangue* can also be seen from another perspective as a salient example of how Brazil is becoming more consciously pluralistic and decentralized. It shows how, in part through alliances to global music, technology, and other cultural practices, certain established Brazilian nationalistic images and identities have been challenged.[18]

Since the 1930s, Brazilian national identity has been influenced by the work of the Recife sociologist Gilberto Freyre, whose notion of *mestiçagem* ("miscegenation") has served as a cornerstone of Brazilian modernist thought. A celebration of racial mixing, Freyre's *mestiçagem* praised the African and indigenous, as well as the European, components of Brazilian society. With *mestiçagem* has come the concept of "racial democracy," the assumption that the social and genetic intermingling initiated by the Portuguese has resulted in a state of racial harmony in which social class, but not race, is perceived to affect one's status in society (Margolis 1992).[19] Though it still holds powerful sway among Brazilians of all colors, "racial democracy" has for decades come under attack as a myth that disguises and even propagates racial discrimination in the country.

As home to the largest African-descended population outside of Africa, Brazil has witnessed a growing black-pride movement, particularly since the 1960s. With the easing of censorship in the late 1970s and the return to civilian rule in 1985, a focus on subaltern groups and expressions of racial and class difference (supposedly postmodern traits) have begun to be articulated more clearly in Brazilian popular music (e.g., in the political music of the *blocos afro* of Bahia, in Rio de Janeiro samba, and in Brazilian rap). These recent assertions of race and class consciousness have emerged concurrently with an increased influence in Brazil of various global popular styles of the

African diaspora such as soul, funk, reggae, and rap (which may or may not be explicitly "resistant").

Mangue shows an affinity with some of these recent musical trends in its strong social criticism, an emphasis on class difference, and a valorization of black or mixed-race and lower-class cultural forms within the nation and globally. In a general sense, then, *mangue* offers a challenge to the nation through participation in a more open, social critique via popular culture in post-dictatorship Brazil. However, the movement does not represent an assertion of racial politics the way some Brazilian rap and *bloco afro* material does. Rather, *mangue's* challenge to the authority of the nation has more to do with a new emphasis on, and relation between, the local and the global than with racial, ethnic, or class politics. The name Nação Zumbi refers to the Afro-Brazilian "nations" as well as the legendary Brazilian leader of black resistance, Zumbi; yet the band is racially mixed and does not espouse a divisive racial ideology. The way in which the *mangue* movement draws from Recife's various races and classes speaks to the overriding importance of revitalizing the city in a cooperative, inclusive effort and spreading its culture and message throughout Brazil and internationally.

The work of CSNZ is sonic and visual evidence of the role of Recife citizens as global cultural navigators. As Frederick Moehn points out, "to be Brazilian is not in contradiction with being of the world, it is precisely to be of the world. . . . Rather than viewing local musical traditions and values as unchanging, or as losing ground to some kind of homogenized global mass culture, [MPB artists such as Fernanda Abreu and Chico Science] assert that the way Brazilians 'mix' will always be unique" (2001, 268). Indeed, Brazilian musicians since the 1990s have increasingly asserted the local identity of their music (in whatever way they see or hear this identity) as they raid the global soundscape and reach international ears. In stark contrast to the typical framing of the Brazilian-cultural-identity debate as a dichotomization of "national" versus "international" music, or even the portrayal of foreign styles as a means of "opting out" of a rigid, national "consensus culture" that masks deep social inequities (see Yúdice 1994), the case of *mangue* and other cutting-edge MPB presents instead a mutual affinity and overlap among local and global musics.

Of course, this has been a model for avant-garde pop in the country at least since bossa nova. But in the case of CSNZ, Carlinhos Brown, and some other contemporary MPB artists, this process is taken to extremes. The music of Chico Science, for example, is arguably even more "local" and more "global" than much MPB—that is, at once more firmly situated in a specific regional context and more open to the culture of the world, particularly that of a global youth culture.

But where does this leave the question of Brazil in this debate? As suggested earlier, in some sense, *mangue* bands are bypassing the role of the nation in determining the identity of their music. A similar notion is present in the work of Rio-based MPB artist Fernanda Abreu, who positions Rio de Janeiro, rather than Recife, as the "crucial conduit for groove circulation" (Moehn 2001, 260). In interviews, Chico Science said that his band needed to gain an international career to avoid having to play certain prescribed kinds of music in Brazil.

At the same time, Fernanda Abreu, like some of my consultants in Recife, has stressed "the idea that, starting in the 1990s, Brazilian Pop Music mixes, in a more effective manner, 'Brazil' in its language" (from a press kit, publicity office of Fernanda Abreu, 1998), quoted in Moehn 2001, 262). Brazil is a regionally divided country, where there are pronounced cultural and musical differences (as well as rivalries) among states. As such, pop musicians in the country choose to define their local heritage differently, depending on where they come from. This situation allows for the diversity of Brazilian culture while it refuses a rigid definition of what it means to make Brazilian music (either as circumscribed by the music industry or cultural critics). Since the 1990s, there has been an increased diversification of popular styles based on different regional and artistic perspectives.

But more than this, in a postmodern way, *mangue* positions Recife and Pernambuco rather than Brazil as the most salient markers of its identity. Thus, while modernity legitimized the uniform authorities of nation-states, postmodern thought shifts emphasis to the community—or, more precisely, to *communities* (Bauman 1992, 35–36). This, of course, does not discount *mangue's* relation to Brazil or MPB, but rather reveals a dramatic shift in emphasis. That has not been the case with the samba, bossa nova, or *tropicália*. Both the urban samba and the bossa nova are inextricably tied to one city, Rio de Janeiro. In part because of Rio's role as cultural capital of the nation, both of these styles—particularly the samba—came to speak for Brazil or to represent it in some way to the outside world and to itself. Although at first it was considered radical, *tropicália*, too, has come to be a widely accepted marker of a Brazilian national identity. But *mangue* charts a new course. Although it has resonated throughout Brazil and has come to be associated on some level with the nation in the minds of listeners, *mangue* is a regionally based trend. It points to popular music's shrinking ability to represent the nation as a completely unified entity, and its expanding ability to represent specific regions or communities within nations and across them.

But concurrent with this increased emphasis on the local is an emergence of the global, though not as the foreboding homogenizing agent so feared by many scholars and musicians alike. Indeed, as Nação Zumbi and other bands put Pernambuco on the world musical map, they have also mapped music of the world onto Pernambuco in a mutually beneficial process. The relation between local-global, traditional-modern, and domestic-foreign elements in *mangue* is symbiotic, integrated, and overlapping (see Galinsky 1999, 160–65). The movement is evidence of the increased importance of both the evermore particular "local" and the evermore universal "global" in popular music and ideology, revealing the articulations of these elements within each other, and a blurring between them. For instance, in *mangue* the local *maracatu* rhythm is no longer exclusively local but projected into a globalized sound that is imagined as "universal"; at the same time, global styles such as rock and rap have been reconstituted as local Pernambucan expressions in *mangue* and Recife's new music scene. Not rejecting a sense of national identity by any means, *mangue* retains the prerogative to employ modernist and nationalist discourses (such as *mestiçagem* and *antropofagia*) as well as nationally associated cultural forms such as the samba among a host of others in the shaping of its hybrid sound, style, identity, and ideology.[20]

In conclusion, music and place in contemporary Brazil have formed a special relationship as imagined by popular musicians. In the case of Recife, devotees of the *mangue* movement have constructed a new image and feeling about themselves and their city (*manguetown*) based on music and other elements of expressive culture, in the process helping to change their sense of identity and place. The relation between this locale and its music is not easily subsumed within a "national" framework. Rather, *mangue* and the Recife scene have, through technology (e.g., the Internet), become a part of the world's music on their own terms, enabling more of a sense of local empowerment (see Galinsky 1999, 221–23). Local musicians in Recife, many of them from an underprivileged social background, are actively and critically part of a wider system that until recently was out of reach. They are projecting their own sense of themselves and their sociocultural situation into a network of information that has made them a part of the world—and the world a part of Recife—as never before.[21] In turn, this unprecedented dynamic interaction with a global system has had a reinvigorating impact on local realities in Recife and Pernambuco.[22]

Notes

1. This article is based on my doctoral dissertation in ethnomusicology from Wesleyan University (1999), which is the first academic work on the *mangue* movement in English. I conducted the research for the dissertation and this article in Greater Recife between January 27 and June 25, 1998. I am very grateful to my adviser, Gage Averill, and the rest of my dissertation committee for their guidance. I deeply

appreciate the many consultants in Recife who helped me with my research; some of them appear in the references below. The Joaquim Nabuco Foundation in Recife kindly hosted me as a visiting scholar from March through June, 1998.

2. Mundo Livre means "Free World," and "S/A" is a business acronym standing for *Sociedade Anônima* ("Anonymous Society"), which indicates that the owners of a company are not known.

3. The *côco* is an Afro-Brazilian song-and-dance genre of the Northeast. *Embolada* is an improvised poetic vocal style, also of the Northeast, often performed as a contest between two singers. The *ciranda* is a typical northeastern dance formed by a circle of participants who hold hands and move slowly in a counterclockwise direction. I describe the *maracatu* later on.

4. Led by composer-musicians Caetano Veloso and Gilberto Gil, *tropicália* borrowed from Oswald de Andrade's "Cannibalistic Manifesto" (1928), which urged the voracious assimilation of foreign culture into a new Brazilian synthesis. *Tropicália* was the first movement to mix rock 'n' roll with local Brazilian styles and other influences (McGowan and Pessanha 1998, 84). On *tropicália*, see, for example, Béhague (1973); Perrone (1989); Dunn (1992, 2001a, 2001b); and Marzorati (1999). See Galinsky (1999, 87–99), for a comparison of *mangue* and *tropicália*.

5. This history is indebted to Recife journalist José Teles's *Meteoro Chico* (n.d.), which traces the career of Chico Science. The first codified history of *mangue* is synthesized here with the perspectives of various local musicians, producers, and others whom I formally interviewed in Recife.

6. Although the press and many people in Recife refer to the entire "new music scene" as *mangue*, some members of this scene do make distinctions between *mangue* and other kinds of projects. See Galinsky (1999) and Murphy (2001) for some of these distinctions.

7. All of the information and quotations in this section ("Setting the scene: Recife in the 1980s"), except for my own interspersed comments, are derived from Teles (n.d., 13–14).

8. The following information and quotations in the "Mundo Livre S/A" section are derived from my interview with Fred Zero Quatro (1998). Fred's pseudonym (Zero Quatro, or "Zero Four") comes from the last two digits of his identification number.

9. Hard-core (or hardcore) is a substyle of rock that came after punk; it is sometimes called "post-punk."

10. The *guitarra baiana* is a miniature electric guitar used in Bahian pop music.

11. There are, in fact, two distinct styles that share the name *maracatu*. The *maracatu de baque virado* is a coastal rhythm and dance performed by Afro-Brazilian "nations" in Recife. The *maracatu de baque solto* ("*maracatu* of the free, alone or loose rhythm") is associated with Afro-indigenous groups in the forest area of Pernambuco, inland from the coast (Zona da Mata). For more information on *maracatu*, see Guerra Peixe (1980 [1955]); Silva (1988); Real (1990); Pinto (1994 and 1996); and Galinsky (1999).

12. Other subsequent middle-class *maracatu* bands as well as traditional *maracatus nação*, such as Estrela Brilhante, have also recently found a place in Recife's "new music scene." *Nação* ("nation") originally referred to an ethnic or pseudo-ethnic grouping of Africans in Brazil during the slave period (see Kubik 1979). The term has since come to identify cultural affinities as opposed to ethnic affiliations (ibid.; Browning 1995, 23). The *maracatu* "nations" of Recife purportedly originated in

213

the practice of crowning a "King of the Congo," a ceremony in which a slave would be designated and legally sanctioned to "rule" over the black population in colonial Brazil (see Guerra-Peixe 1980; Silva 1988; and Real 1990).

13. As producer and former CSNZ manager, Paulo André Pires recalls, "Across from [Chico's] house in the street there was a *ciranda* [a type of circle dance from Northeast Brazil]. So for him diversion was *cultura popular* [folk or lower-class culture] and he had this in the soul really, in the blood as we say here" (1998).

14. *Blocos afro* ("Afro blocs") are Afrocentric cultural groups that perform in the Carnival of Salvador, Bahia, and other Brazilian cities (see Crook 1993). The *bloco afro* Olodum is famous, among other things, for having created and popularized a recent hybrid genre called *samba-reggae*.

15. Maureliano, former member of Lamento Negro and percussionist for the band Via Sat (from "via satellite"), which was formed in the wake of Nação Zumbi, assumed an important didactic musical role in Nação Zumbi's formative period. He taught the future members of the band some local folk styles and created at least one of their signature rhythmic fusions (a hybrid funk-*maracatu*) (see Galinsky 1999 for more in-depth musical analysis of CSNZ).

16. The story goes that upon learning of the movement, journalists in the South of Brazil heard the word "bit" as "beat," since the two words have the same pronunciation in Portuguese, leading them to call the movement "*mangue beat*" (Zé da Flauta 1998; Tenório 1998). Not surprisingly, this in turn has compelled many to believe erroneously that there is one particular musical genre or rhythm called "*mangue beat*." Nonetheless, *mangue beat* has since become the more common term, even among members of the Recife scene.

17. Paulo André Pires called Chico the scene's "greatest exponent" (1998).

18. See Vianna (1995) for a discussion of one dominant national project (that of Gilberto Freyre and the Rio de Janeiro samba) and how this has been challenged in recent decades.

19. It is not possible here to provide an in-depth discussion of racial issues in Brazil. For more information on this subject, see Degler (1971); Skidmore (1974); Fontaine (1985); Margolis (1992); and Winant (1994).

20. In a certain sense this approach may be considered postmodern. According to Frederick Buell, "Modernism becomes one more code afloat in the hyperreal sea of codes that the postmodern sponsors" (1994, 332).

21. I do not mean to deny that globalization has had negative effects worldwide. Rather, I am emphasizing here the optimism with which many on the Recife scene view the potential of globalization in the construction and marketing of their music and identity.

22. In line with my conclusions here and with the work of Averill (1995) and Monson (1999), Kenneth Bilby (1999, 285–86) reasserts the importance of the local in globalizing patterns in his discussion of Surinamese popular music.

References

Abramo, Bia. 1997. "Da lama à fama." *República* (July): 74–77.

Averill, Gage. 1995. "Haitian Music in the Global System." In *The Reordering of Culture: Latin America, The Caribbean and Canada in the Hood*. Edited by Alvina Ruprecht and Cecilia Taiana. Ottawa: Carleton University Press, 339–62.

Bauman, Zygmunt. 1992. *Intimations of Postmodernity*. London and New York: Routledge.

Béhague, Gerard. 1973. "Bossa & Bossas: Recent Changes in Brazilian Urban Popular Music." *Ethnomusicology* 17/2: 209–33.

Bilby, Kenneth. 1999. "'Roots Explosion': Indigenization and Cosmopolitanism in Contemporary Surinamese Popular Music." *Ethnomusicology* 43/2: 256–96.

Browning, Barbara. 1995. *Samba: Resistance in Motion*. Bloomington: Indiana University Press.

Buell, Frederick. 1994. "Postmodernism and Globalization." In *National Culture and the New Global System*. Baltimore: Johns Hopkins University Press, 325–43.

Castro, Josué de. 1970. *Of Men and Crabs*. Trans. from Portuguese by Susan Hertelendy. New York: The Vanguard Press.

Chico Science & Nação Zumbi. 1995. *Da Lama Ao Caos*. Sony CD-81594/2-464476.

———. 1996. *Afrociberdelia*. Sony Latin CDZ-81996/2-479255.

Crook, Larry N. 1993. "Black Consciousness, *samba reggae*, and the Re-Africanization of Bahian Carnival Music in Brazil." *World of Music* 35/2: 90–108.

Degler, Carl N. 1971. *Neither Black nor White: Slavery and Race Relations in Brazil and the United States*. New York: The Macmillan Company.

Dunn, Christopher. 1992. "Return of Tropicália." *Afropop Worldwide*. Produced by Sean Barlow for World Music Productions. Public Radio International (November 18).

———. 2001a. "*Tropicália*, Counterculture, and the Diasporic Imagination in Brazil." In *Brazilian Popular Music and Globalization*. Edited by Charles Perrone and Christopher Dunn. New York: Routledge, 72–95.

———. 2001b. *Brutality Garden:* Tropicália *and the Emergence of a Brazilian Counterculture*. Chapel Hill: University of North Carolina Press.

Filho, José Antônio de Souza. 1998. Interview by the author, June 5, in Recife.

Flauta, Zé da. 1998. Interview by the author, February 5, in Recife.

Fontaine, Pierre-Michel, ed. 1985. *Race, Class, and Power in Brazil*. Los Angeles: UCLA Center for Afro-American Studies.

França, Francisco (Chico Science's father). 1998. Interview by the author, May 30, in Olinda.

Galinsky, Philip. 1999. "'*Maracatu Atômico*': Tradition, Modernity, and Postmodernity in the *Mangue* Movement and 'New Music Scene' of Recife, Pernambuco, Brazil." Ph.D. diss., Wesleyan University.

Guerra-Peixe, César. 1980 [1955]. *Maracatus do Recife*. São Paulo: Ricordi Brasileira Editôres.

Kubik, Gerhard. 1979. *Angolan Traits in Black Music, Games and Dances of Brazil*. Lisboa: Junta de Investigações Científicas do Ultramar.

Lins, Renato. 1998. Interview by the author, January 30, in Olinda.

Margolis, Mac. 1992. "The Invisible Issue: Race in Brazil." *The Ford Foundation Report* 23/2: 3–7.

Marzorati, Gerald. 1999. "Tropicália Agora!" *The New York Times Magazine* (April 25): 48–51.

Maureliano. 1998. Interviews by the author, April 13 and May 22, in Recife.

McGowan, Chris and Ricardo Pessanha. 1998. *The Brazilian Sound: Samba, Bossa Nova, and the Popular Music of Brazil*. Philadelphia: Temple University Press.

Moehn, Frederick. 2001. "'Good Blood in the Veins of this Brazilian Rio' or, a Cannibalist Transnationalism." In *Brazilian Popular Music and Globalization*. Edited by Charles Perrone and Christopher Dunn. New York: Routledge, 258–69.

Monson, Ingrid. 1999. "Riffs, Repetition and Theories of Globalization." *Ethnomusicology* 43/1: 31–65.

Murphy, John. 2001. "Self-Discovery in Brazilian Popular Music: Mestre Ambrósio." In *Brazilian Popular Music and Globalization*. Edited by Charles Perrone and Christopher Dunn. New York: Routledge, 245–57.

Page, Joseph A. 1995. *The Brazilians*. Reading, Mass.: Addison-Wesley Publishing.

Perrone, Charles A. 1989. *Masters of Contemporary Brazilian Song: MPB 1965–1985*. Austin: University of Texas Press.

Pinto, Tiago de Oliveira. 1994. "The Pernambuco Carnival and its Formal Organizations: Music as Expression of Hierarchies and Power in Brazil." *Yearbook for Traditional Music* 26: 20–39.

———. 1996. "Musical Difference, Competition, and Conflict: The Maracatu Groups in the Pernambuco Carnival, Brazil." *Latin American Music Review* 17/2: 97–119.

Pires, Paulo André. 1998. Interview by the author, March 6, in Recife.

Pupillo. 1998. Interview by the author, March 9, in Recife.

Rampazzo, Pedro. n.d. "A influência dos ritmos regionais na música pernambucana dos Anos 90." A paper for the journalism course of the Universidade Católica de Pernambuco—UNICAP.

Real, Katarina. 1990. *O folclore no carnaval do Recife*. 2d ed. Recife: Editora Massangana, Fundação Joaquim Nabuco.

Silva, Leonardo Dantas. 1988. "Maracatu: Presença da África no carnaval do Recife." *Folclore* 190/191: 1–10.

Skidmore, Thomas E. 1974. *Black into White: Race and Nationality in Brazilian Thought*. New York: Oxford University Press.

Teles, José. n.d. *Meteoro Chico*. Recife: Editôra Bagaço.

Tenório, Hamilton. 1998. Interviews by the author, April 13 and May 22, in Recife.

Vianna, Hermano. 1995. *O mistério do samba*. Rio de Janeiro: Zahar.

Winant, Howard. 1994. *Racial Conditions: Politics, Theory, Comparisons*. Minneapolis and London: University of Minnesota Press.

Yúdice, George. 1994. "The Funkification of Rio." In *Microphone Fiends: Youth Music and Youth Culture*. Edited by Andrew Ross and Tricia Rose. New York and London: Routledge, 193–217.

Zéro Quatro, Fred. 1998. Interview by the author, March 10, in Recife.

10

Popular Music and the Global City

Huayno, Chicha, *and* Techno-cumbia *in Lima*

Raúl R. Romero

In the late 1990s there were two developments that captured the public's attention in Peru. One was the rise and fall of the corrupt Fujimori regime, a decade of concealed political dictatorship and systematic human-rights violations. The other was the rise of *techno-cumbia*, a musical style based on the *cumbia* from Colombia characterized by the extensive use of electronic instruments (electric guitars, electric drums, and synthesizer). Coming from the less affluent social sectors, *techno-cumbia* broke social and ethnic barriers for the first time to become the favorite dance music for all Peruvians, poor and rich, plain and sophisticated, villagers and cosmopolitans.

Music and politics had seldom been connected by social analysts and journalists in Peru, but this time both dimensions shared front pages, television broadcasts, public debates, and even presidential campaigns.[1] While Alberto Fujimori and his unethical politics led the country to the near destruction of its formal institutions (judicial system, electoral council, military and political parties) and systematically ignored the voices of civil society, *techno-cumbia* was seen by many as a spontaneous expression of the people. The degree of public participation and social interaction connected with *techno-cumbia* music, spectacle, and performance grew in inverse proportion to the decreasing democratic channels though which the people could express themselves in local and national governments. The dark figures of the national congress and the military, representatives of a dying dictatorial regime, stood in stark contrast to the self-made performers who, rising from humble homes, had become celebrities and role models for the general public. Popular music, therefore, presented a different view of the nation's future.[2]

In this chapter I discuss the reasons for *techno-cumbia*'s success in Peru, tracing its recent history and musical antecedents. The overall framework of my argument will be the process of globalization, since I think that it is imperative to view the rise of this musical style as the result of transnational processes of cultural exchange. *Techno-cumbia* has become a case study in ascertaining whether globalization has a positive or a negative impact on local culture. The current discourse of globalization switches back and forth between the celebration of global currents, on the one hand, and the criticism of its homogenizing trends, on the other (Jameson 1998, xiii). The former views globalization as a process that has definitely shaped the new century, building a new world order in which interdependence is the norm. Borders and customs are gradually replaced by free and open markets. Thus products, services, and cultural goods appear to circulate widely throughout the world; people no longer are predestined to live and die in their village, but move around the world as part of the massive international migrations of the modern era. The mass media reach all corners of the earth, and for the first time in world history everyone can witness in real time a war, a concert, or a coup d'état. And though cable TV and incessant radio broadcasts of "Top 40" hits may not exactly be considered dialogical media, the advent of the Internet has provided the means for an interactive exchange of ideas and images around the world.

On the other side of the spectrum are the ones who consider that globalization is nothing new, taking into account that multinational exchange of goods and services has existed for centuries (Hannerz 1996, 18). It is just a new-fashioned rhetoric behind which homogenizing forces hide. It is a facade for neoliberal politics and the economic expansion of the industrialized countries into the rest of the world. In this view, globalization only benefits the powerful countries, which control media and communications, to the detriment of sovereign local and national cultures. In the cultural arena, globalization is understood as Americanization, and the invasion of McDonald's and Burger King parallels the rising ratings of MTV and the dominance of Hollywood films in the world market.

Through which lens should we see the rise of new transnational musics such as *techno-cumbia*? Is it a bona fide appropriation by the popular sectors of the global trends that are available in the free world, or the result of the imposing homogenizing forces of the mass media? Is it a welcome contribution to the cultural diversity of Latin America, or does it represent the forces of hollow commercialism and escapist entertainment? Is it what

Marxists would have called an alienated cultural form, or what postmodernists would label as cultural appropriation? Whatever the final interpretation may be, the indisputable certainty is that *techno-cumbia* is the result of transnational influences and that its success in Peru reflects the good or bad consequences of globalization.

In order to understand this process, I first examine its immediate background, starting with the success of the commercial *huayno* since the 1950s in Lima (Núñez and Llórens 1981; Turino 1988). It was one of the first cultural expressions of a subaltern group to appropriate urban and media spaces previously used only by the elites. The commercial *huayno* contributed to building a market for popular musics based on regional traditions, primarily among migrants from the Andes. In the late 1960s, when the commercial *huayno* was still at its peak, the *cumbia* began to gain wide acceptance, adopting a variety of regional and cultural styles. In the 1980s, one of these regional styles, later labeled as *chicha* music, blended *huayno* with *cumbia* and produced a danceable and fashionable musical form that attracted hundreds of thousands of young migrants and migrant descendants. It became the most popular music in the nation (Turino 1990; Hurtado 1995). In the late 1990s, the rise of *techno-cumbia* found a consolidated urban market ready to be exploited. This was formed primarily by what urban sociologists have intuitively called "emergent classes," "informal sectors," or "new *Limeños*," referring to a social sector made up primarily of non-traditional *Limeños*: the population that migrated to Lima from the provinces after the 1950s (or were born in Lima to recent migrants), and who did not integrate fully into the cultural trends or residential patterns of the traditional elite sectors.[3]

The Rural *huayno* and the Culture Industry: How Local Became National (1950–1980)

Why did a rural genre like the *huayno* became a commercial success in urban Peru?[4] This accomplishment was the direct result of the sudden development of an internal urban market comprised of Andean migrants since the 1950s. Until that decade, internal rural-urban migration had been limited to the provincial elites, for example, landowners, tradesmen, and trained professionals (Altamirano 1984). But beginning in the '50s, migration reached massive proportions. In search for better employment opportunities and improved services (e.g., health and education) and in the midst of political and economic unrest, hundreds of thousands of migrants flooded to the cities, especially Lima. Lima had more than a half million inhabitants by the 1940s, but by 1956 its population had more than doubled, to 1,200,000 (Matos Mar 1966, 23). Most of this growth was due to migration from the Andean areas, and it continued after the '50s. Peru's population went from being 73.1 percent rural in 1940, to a record 53 percent urban by 1972 (Cotler 1978, 290). This rural-to-urban transformation of the country's demographics generated serious social problems, since the national economy and social planning were not ready to absorb such an expansion.

As a result of this lack of planning, the migrant population coming from impoverished social sectors (primarily from the peasantry) lived in *barriadas* (squatter settlements), later to be called *pueblos jóvenes* ("young towns"). Gathered in informal associations, most of the migrant crowds had organized massive illegal land invasions and built shantytowns. The first homes to be erected in the barriadas were shacks made of fragile and unprotected *esteras*, a material useful only in an environment like Lima, a city where rain is rare and meager. Gradually, thanks to communal lobbying and with state support, most of these shantytowns were able to secure urban services, like electricity and water sewage, and improve the materials of their households. By the 1970s former *barriadas* like El Agustino and San Cosme were considered working-class suburbs, with paved roads, restaurants, and plenty of business, thus becoming examples to follow.

The city of Lima was changing radically. The "city of kings," always proud of its colonial heritage and creole culture and home of the nation's political and financial elite, was witnessing a literal invasion of its hinterland by Andean peasants. Hernando De Soto estimated that in 1981, the city of Lima would have had only 1,445,000 people, instead of the 4,000,000 that were officially counted, if migration had not occurred since the 1940s (1987, 8).

The *pueblos jóvenes*, and the urban spaces surrounding them, became the new settings for cultural production as well. As the population in these shantytowns increased, so did the demand for Andean music, the main cultural expression that the migrants brought to the cities. Having had to leave behind other cultural habits like clothing, language, and food in their quest to adapt to urban habits and strategies, music was one of the cultural manifestations that could still express their identity, regional nostalgia, and their resistance to full cultural integration into urban life and values. Thanks to the new demographics, the Sunday gatherings in *coliseos* (sports stadiums adapted to musical festivals, or in other cases just circus tents) became the favorite places to perform and listen to live music and recollect regional emotions. Soon, the morning hours of AM radio stations were rented by migrant entrepreneurs in order to air regional musics and community messages, thus becoming the most important medium for migrant interaction and communication, in the absence of other means, such as newspapers and magazines for example (Lloréns 1991). In the realm of commercial LP recordings of Andean music, the *huayno* was the most popular genre and soon became a cultural symbol in its own right.[5]

During the "golden age" of commercial Andean music (1950–1980), almost 50 percent of total record sales fell in the "folklore" category (meaning Andean music), signaling the importance of this market. But by the late 1980s, this figure had dropped to 20 percent, primarily due to changes in market demand and increasing cassette piracy.[6] By this date, *chicha* music began to outsell commercial *huayno* music, which, while not completely disappearing from the scene, now maintained a low profile. The success of the commercial *huayno*, however, had established pioneering trends. It was the first traditional music genre to jump from a local setting to national contexts. It was also the first to adopt the use of amplification, stage performance, and electronic reproduction in order to transcend its locality. The intensive use of AM radio and the distribution of commercial recordings provided the *huayno* with a solid urban presence, though its market was limited to migrant sectors.

In terms of style, the urban *huayno*, disseminated through staged live performances, radio broadcasts, or commercial recordings, introduced a previously unknown performance technique to rural musical expressions: a solo singer accompanied by a musical ensemble (with the aid of amplified sound). The notoriety of the soloist allowed a selected few of them to achieve celebrity status among their followers, thus breaking the metaphors of anonymity and communality that had heretofore identified Andean folklore. *Huayno* recording initiated personalized urban success, the appropriation of modernity, and the conquest of the city. In comparison with *chicha* music and *techno-cumbia*, however, the urban commercial *huayno* was musically conservative. The traditional *huayno* remained almost intact in its structure and form, while the musical accompaniment that became most common was the regional *orquesta típica* ("traditional orchestra") from the central Andes, comprised of saxophones, clarinets, a harp, and a violin. The appeal lay, therefore, in the combination of a singer and an orchestra, and the obvious requirements of the performance format (stage, live broadcast, or recording).[7]

Perhaps the most important consequence of the appearance of the Andean "star system" was that it was an order that transcended local and regional barriers and expanded into the national context. Before its emergence, regional musics were produced and used by their own community; now, people from different regions would become consumers of a single recording star. Such a phenomenon could be seen, for example, in the music of Pastorita Huaracina ("Shepherdess from Huaraz") and Jilguero del Huascarán ("Goldfinch of the Huascarán"), who were linked to the regional styles of Ancash, and the Picaflor de los Andes ("Hummingbird of the

221

Andes") and Flor Pucarina ("The flower from Pucará"), who were linked to Wanka folklore from the central Andes. Despite their allegiance to the musical style of one particular regional culture, their followers originated from diverse regions of Peru and learned to appreciate their style through radio, live shows, and records. This first attempt at crossover between local styles and tastes was far from a process of homogenization. It was evident, however, that the migrant lifestyle in the city had begun to create the conditions for cultural interaction and the breaking down of local singularities, in favor of a supra-regional identification process.

The other relevant outgrowth of this was the development of a consumer market for the urban *huayno* as a commodity. The newly arrived population constituted a new market to be exploited by the record companies (transnational and local), major and modest entrepreneurs, and the artists themselves. The market for urban *huayno* was part of an "informal economy" consisting of *vendedores ambulantes* ("street vendors"), family shops, and clandestine businesses located on the outskirts of the city, in the *pueblos jóvenes*, and sometimes in downtown Lima (as in the case of street vendors and informal flea markets like the *Mercado Central* or *La Parada*). Record executives knew before the sociologists that the market for urban *huayno* music resided in the informal sectors, that is, in the new neighborhoods, some of them still *barriadas*, and others austere but large working-class suburbs. That is why they never advertised Andean records in the middle- and higher-class districts of Lima, but only in poor settlements of the southern and northern city limits.

As already mentioned, among the most renowned recording stars of this time were singers Picaflor de los Andes, Flor Pucarina, Pastorita Huaracina, and Jilguero del Huascarán (pseudonyms alluding to animal or flower figures, metaphors frequent in Andean popular poetry). These singers were just a chosen few from hundreds of performers who were trying to make a career from music. The case of Picaflor de los Andes (Víctor Alberto Gil Malma) is emblematic (see fig. 10.1). He began recording relatively late in life. Born in 1929 and raised in Huancayo, the thriving commercial center of the Central Andes, Picaflor did what many peasants from that region do as adolescents: he worked in the nearby mining centers to supplement the limited income that came from agricultural or cattle-raising activities. In his thirties he attempted to try the incipient but rewarding record industry in Lima. In 1959, when the commercial *huayno* was flourishing, Picaflor went to the capital to participate in a contest organized by Radio Excelsior. Four years later Picaflor saw his first hit record, "Aguas del Río Rímac" ("Waters of the Rímac River"), released and distributed. Subsequently, each of his fourteen long-play recordings was a huge success, and he became famous

Fig. 10.1. *Huayno* singer Victor Alberto Gil Malma (Picaflor de los Andes) dressed in a regional outfit from the Central Andes.

among his fellow migrants. He died in 1975 while touring La Oroya, a mining town center near Huancayo. The vehicle bringing his remains to Lima had to stop in every town along the way, for everyone around the Central Highway (a geographical strip strongly influenced by the regional culture of the valley) wanted to see him and pay their respects. His body was mourned at the *Coliseo Nacional* in Lima, where he and many of his colleagues had spent unforgettable music sessions.

Picaflor's musical style had adopted the fundamental traits from the regional music of the central Andes. The *orquesta típica* was the chosen instrumental ensemble, and the power of its sound and timbre tainted the entire cycle. The modern saxophones and clarinets would mix with the colonial harp and violin, resulting in a regional expression which, due to its popularity, was accepted as a musical *lingua franca* by people from different regions. The same musical format, in terms of style, was adopted by many of his fellow musical singers-celebrities, which determined the prevalence of this style.

The *huayno* market rapidly grew in different directions and diversified itself, adapting to different generational groups, regional origins, and musical tastes. *Huayno* was the favorite music of the newly arrived migrants into Lima in this period. Though migrants from the 1950s onwards held the urban *huayno* as their main regional referent, they also demanded other musical styles that would diversify their worldviews and express their multicultural experience in a city like Lima. Their progeny would have other needs and demands as well. And there was an emerging market that was ready to accept creative musical styles from the various sectors of Lima.

The Advent of the *Cumbia* in Peruvian Popular Music (1960s–1970s)

While commercial *huayno* continued to congregate multitudes, another musical genre from a neighboring country began to gain popular acceptance around the late 1960s, the *cumbia* from Colombia. The *cumbia* had evolved in Colombia in a fashion similar to that of the *huayno* in Peru. From local, rural communities, it had developed into urban dance music, sold in commercial recordings and widely consumed in the cities of the nation at large. Like the Mexican *ranchera* and the Argentinean tango, the Colombian *cumbia* soon became an exportable cultural commodity and invaded foreign markets and international radio waves (Wade 2000, 174).

It is not surprising that in Perú the *cumbia* would gain rapid popular acceptance. After all, in the 1950s, the urban population of Lima had enthusiastically received the Cuban rumba, the Dominican *merengue,* and Perez Prado's mambo. What distinguished the *cumbia* was that it gained acceptance in the rural areas as well. On the coast and in the Andes, brass bands in peasant towns began to perform *cumbia*s as dance music in regional festivities. Regional markets throughout Peru, located primarily in the capitals of the provinces, sold LPs of famous *cumbia* artists, thus disseminating it further.

Soon local musicians began playing and recording *cumbia* music. Sustained by their live performances and extensive touring around the country, these performers achieved great popularity and sold many records. These groups came from everywhere in Peru, but some of the most conspicuous came from the area surrounding Huancayo, in the Mantaro valley in central Peru. Groups like Los Demonios del Mantaro, directed by Manuel Baquerizo and featuring two saxophones and Latin percussion (timbales and bongos), played a straightforward *cumbia* faithful to the style of Colombian ensembles. One of their songs, "La chichera," became a big hit in the late 1960s and is often cited as one probable origin of the term *chicha* as applied to the style of the Peruvian *cumbia* (Hurtado 1995, 11–12).

Enrique Delgado and Los Destellos

It was another local *cumbia* group that would make a definitive mark on the so-called Peruvian *cumbia*. Founded in Lima by Enrique Delgado in 1968, Los Destellos featured two electric guitars, electric bass, and a set of timbales. Congas and bongos were incorporated afterward and, in the mid-1970s, the electric organ (see fig. 10.2). This instrumentation reflected as well the strong influence of rock, pop, and tropical (Caribbean) music on the Peruvian *cumbia*. Lima, after all, was a cosmopolitan city in which movies, television, radio, and other media provided access to global musical and cultural currents. Beatles LPs, for example, were sold in Lima almost at the same time of their release in Great Britain, and were aired by local radio stations. Delgado, the lead guitar, mixed purely instrumental *cumbia*s with vocal renditions. In the former repertory he would play the entire melody with his characteristic clean, open, and slightly resonating sound. In the latter, his guitar would fill the melodic pauses of the singer with riffs and countermelodies. This style of guitar playing would influence other Peruvian *cumbia* groups well into the 1980s, especially those involved with *chicha* music. In the introductions and various interludes, Delgado's guitar announced the main theme, and its presence was overwhelming throughout the entire song. The instrumental interludes were of such proportions that they could be thought of as contrasting melodies in themselves (like a second theme). In the instrumental tunes, the guitar was the only leading instrument. For example, in "Caminito Serrano," composed by Delgado himself and one of Los Destellos' most popular hits, the entire melody is played by the guitar, including riffs and interludes. Its melody was not Andean, though the title ("Mountain Road") alludes to the Andean region.

225

Fig. 10.2. Los Destellos, a Peruvian-*cumbia* group in 1994. Director Enrique Delgado is seated in the center.

But Enrique Delgado's contributions went beyond performance styles. In terms of repertoire, Delgado also introduced diverse regional musical roots in his songs, thus anticipating the variety of musical styles that Peruvian *cumbia* would exhibit in subsequent years. While Los Destellos would play mostly straightforward *cumbia*, usually referred as *cumbia costeña* ("coastal *cumbia*") by its followers, they also introduced songs with Andean overtones, like the *huaynos* "Valicha" and "Carnaval de Arequipa," and Amazonian (jungle) imagery, for example, "La charapita." As it evolved in the 1970s and '80s, the latter types of repertory became known to the public as *cumbia andina* ("Andean *cumbia*") and *cumbia selvática* ("jungle *cumbia*").

Enrique Delgado's personal life story reflects this cultural diversity. He was born in coastal Lima but performed commercial *huayno* music as the lead guitar for Andean recording star Pastorita Huaracina. In fact, his first instrument was the mandolin, which in Peru is considered a folk instrument since it was introduced by the Spaniards in the sixteenth century. His father, from the southern province of Cuzco, was a regional musician himself and a performer on the traditional Andean *charango* (small guitar). Enrique Delgado's personal experience reflects an important cultural and generational change. Instead of following in his parents' footsteps and sticking to traditional patterns, he preferred to experiment with the urban, popular and "modern" *cumbia*.[8] Peruvian journalist Pablo O'Brien sums up the situation in eloquent fashion:

Fig. 10.3. *Chicha* group Los Mirlos, in a recent performance. Influenced by the success of *techno-cumbia* groups, they have added female dancers in their presentations.

The new style created by Los Destellos gradually became more elaborate. Mixing rhythms of different musical traditions, especially the Colombian *cumbia*, the *huayno*, rock, and *nueva ola* [pop music], it rapidly connected with the sentiments of the new Limeños, those youngsters who were the offspring of migrants and did not feel themselves to be outsiders or insiders. They identified with the *huayno* lyrics, which they had listened to along with their parents. But the nostalgia and grief of its rhythm troubled them, and they preferred the joy of the *cumbias* and *guarachas*, despite the fact that their lyrics did not tell them anything. (1999)

Enrique Delgado's contributions have not gone unnoticed. He is widely recognized by all the performers I have talked to as the father of the Peruvian *cumbia*. Among these performers is Jorge Rodríguez Grandes, who founded the well-known group Los Mirlos in 1973 (see fig. 10.3). While Los Destellos was considered a coastal *limeño* group, despite Delgado's Andean heritage, Los Mirlos stressed their identification with the Peruvian jungles. Rodríguez Grandes was born in Moyobamba, a city in the middle of the Peruvian Amazon forest. His father was a businessman and an accordion player from Rioja, a nearby town. Jorge grew up watching his father playing the *chimaycha* and *pandilla*, traditional genres from the Peruvian Amazon. Rodríguez Grandes openly acknowledges the regional identification that his music was seeking by describing it as *cumbia amazónica* ("Amazonian *cumbia*"), and by being outspoken about his commitment to his regional roots: "I have spoken to my jungle, to all immigrants from Peru." The titles of his most successful songs are emblematic, for example: "Contigo a la selva" ("With You to the Jungle"), "Fiesta en la selva" ("Festival in the Jungle"), and "El poder verde" ("The Green Power"). The overall presence and popularity of Amazonian *cumbia*, however, was limited in this time, in which coastal *cumbia* was prevailing. It would only be in the late 1990s that Amazonian symbols and imagery would reappear.

Cumbia Finds the *Huayno*: *Chicha* Music in the 1980s

In the thirty years that had passed since the 1950s, Peru, and especially Lima, experienced crucial changes. The shantytowns that appeared as a result of massive illegal invasions of migrant families had developed into prosperous working-class neighborhoods. The economy of these informal sectors was experiencing a sudden yet consistent expansion, providing support and resources to migrants, their families and their progeny. By the 1980s, Lima was a city already conquered by newcomers from the provinces. Their suburbs occupied most of the metropolitan area, its constituents outnumbered traditional *Limeños*, and their "way of life" painted the whole city life with new colors. By 1984, roughly 80 percent of Lima's population, most of which were first- and second-generation migrants, lived in *pueblos jóvenes* and working-class neighborhoods, while only 20 percent lived in middle-class and affluent suburbs, strongholds of traditional *limeño* families (Matos Mar 1984, 67).

A market had been forged and it was ready to admit a product that would express the aspirations and values of the sons and daughters of the first migrants who had arrived in the capital during the 1950s. Though in the 1970s this market was still incipient and dominated by coastal groups performing Peruvian *cumbia*, the 1980s witnessed the ascendancy of groups incorporating Andean musical elements into the *cumbia*. In particular, the *huayno* made a comeback in the form of a melodic frame and singing style beneath which *cumbia* patterns were exposed: a style which was referred as to *música chicha*. Many of the songs were *huayno*s adapted to the rhythm of the Peruvian *cumbia*, and in the case of original songs, the Andean flavor was evident in the singing style, the inner rhythmic pulse (compatible to that of the *huayno*), and the musician's movements on stage. Even its lyrics were similar in character to the *huayno*'s, dealing primarily with romantic love and only secondarily with other themes relevant to the everyday life of Lima's migrants, for example, social, political, and labor issues (Hurtado Suarez 1995, 52).[9]

The increase in sales and overall presence of performers of *chicha* resulted from the advent of a new generation of Andean residents in the capital city: the offspring of the first wave of migrants that arrived in the 1950s and '60s (Turino 1990; Hurtado 1995). To be sure, though *chicha* music was the most expressive of the manifestations of this new social sector, it was certainly not the only one. Social analysts have used the term *chicha* to describe the culture of migrants in Lima, characterized by survival strategies, informal procedures, and emergency arrangements. Its main symbols being the *pueblos jóvenes*, the *micro* (a small van used as the principal means of transportation), and the *vendedor ambulante*. *Chicha* music was, indeed, the most structured and powerful language that these sectors could use to express their creativity.

Among the many groups that appeared, Los Shapish was the most celebrated *chicha* ensemble in the 1980s. It was the first one to break previous record sales and to have an impact on the media, appearing in newspapers and television interviews. Its founder, Jaime Moreyra Mercado, was born in 1952 to a family of southern Andean migrants. He was brought to Lima at the age of six, to attend junior and high school. In 1974, he entered the National University of Engineering, where he used to listen to salsa stars such as Willie Colón and Hector Lavoe, *cumbia* from Colombia, and Peruvian *cumbia* groups like Los Destellos, Los Ecos, and Los Diablos Rojos. He lived in the *cono norte* (an area north of Lima in which many *pueblos jóvenes* are located), where he founded Los Elios in 1973, a group devoted to Peruvian *cumbia* and featuring three guitars, three percussion instruments, and one singer (no keyboards were yet used). In 1977 he traveled to Huancayo, the second largest market for Peruvian *cumbia*, and formed a group called Melodía, which had moderate local success. In 1981 he and the singer Julio Simeón, nicknamed Chapulín, formed Los Shapish.

Los Shapish followed the model of Los Destellos in terms of overall musical format and style. They continued to use two electric guitars, one electric bass, and Latin percussion (timbales, congas, bongos and cowbell), but they added keyboard. If the latter was a synthesizer, its use was limited, since it was usually programmed as an electric organ. The main characteristic was the clear, undistorted sound of the electric guitar, sometimes uplifted by the "wa-wa" effect. One of its most conspicuous traits was the singing style of the singer Chapulín, who sang in an Andean style with a tense vocal production and emotional restraint. Their first hit record was an adaptation of the popular *huayno* "El Alizal" into a *chicha* song, renamed "El Aguajal." Jaime Moreyra recalls his beginnings in Huancayo and also the role of "El Aguajal" in the group's career:

> We began playing in Huancayo in front of 200, 250, 300 people. In the region of Mantaro there existed great support for this music. We began in 1981, and

in 1982 "Radio Moderna" awarded us a special prize for the song "El Aguajal." This song was recorded at the suggestion of the producer, and also because it was a blend of *chicha* and *huayno*. We recorded it to go beyond the realm of "El Alizal," which was popular folklore, but not fashionable among the kids of migrants.[10]

Los Shapish was the first group from the working class to attract the attention of the visual and print media: newspapers, radio, and television programs reported on the enormous recognition that they were receiving. Besides its social origins, the fact that a local group would garner the amount of attention usually reserved for foreign musical groups was surprising. The main focus of the news, however, was on the social and ethnic roots of the group. The general opinion was that their artistic merit was debatable, their technology poor, and their craft merely instinctive. *Chicha* music was seen from above, and it was still considered an underground and marginal (if boisterous) phenomenon. But its success was obvious. Official culture (intellectuals, mass media, and public opinion) had to take notice of such a phenomenon, but it was undeniable that the main media channels were still inaccessible to *chicha*. Using alternative routes, *chicha* music occupied specific AM radio programs, and their records were produced by small independent companies. In the 1980s, cassette piracy was widespread throughout the nation, and most *chicha* was disseminated through cheap and accessible audio cassettes on almost every street corner in business districts. Live performances, however, were at the core of the *chicha* business. Since it was a highly danceable form, the *bailes sociales* ("social dances") became the favorite type of gathering (see fig. 10.4). Different type of locales, restaurants, parking lots, public and private yards were rented to host *bailes sociales*, especially on weekends. Attended almost exclusively by young, unmarried men and women, they took place especially in the *cono norte* and *cono sur* (northern and southern outskirts of the city), and in downtown Lima.

Los Shapish was only the group that made much impact on the media, due in part to the charisma of its two leaders, Jaime Moreira and Chapulín. But hundreds of other *chicha* groups entered the marketplace, and some were as talented as Los Shapish, such as Chacalón y la Nueva Crema, Alegría, Génesis, and Vico and his group Karicia.

Techno-Culture and the Rise of a New Middle Class (Late 1990s)

In the 1990s, the desire to live "in modernity" got a boost from the neoliberal politics of President Fujimori. As soon as he took power, thanks to a democratic election process in 1990 (before his regime turned into a dictatorship through a self-inflicted coup d'état in 1992), new Shell and Mobil

Fig. 10.4. A *chicha* music *baile social* in an empty lot in a working-class neighborhood. Lima, 1984.

gas stations were built throughout the city. Modeled exactly after their American equivalents, their lights, colors, coin-operated machines, and 24-hour service became symbolic of modern Lima. Cellular phones became so cheap that they were given out for free. In less than a year, McDonald's had opened their first store, followed by Burger King, Blockbuster Video, Citibank, and Telefónica (the gigantic multinational phone company from Spain that had won the bid over AT&T to take over the entire telephone system in the nation). Images of modernity pervaded the entire city. I still remember how I, from the window of my middle-class apartment in Lima, saw a construction worker earning a minimal salary talking through his cell phone while holding a brick in his other hand. The leader of the left-wing terrorist group Shining Path (*Sendero Luminoso*) went to prison in 1992, and soon afterward terrorism ceased, giving citizens a new sense of security. The Internet industry in Peru grew much more rapidly than in other countries in the region, and underdevelopment was a thing of the past, or at least it seemed to be. This was the sociopolitical context in which *techno-cumbia* rose in the late 1990s.

As the name suggests, *techno-cumbia* is based on the *cumbia* from Colombia, performed by a lead singer or vocal group, accompanied by electric guitars, electric drums, and synthetizers. The prefix "techno" suggests no stylistic relation to the techno movement that originated in Detroit in the late 1970s, although it derives from this usage. In Detroit, techno referred to a specific development in R&B characterized by innovative and experimental electronic arrangements and the use of sequencers. The term has been used freely in a variety of Peruvian musical genres since the 1980s simply to denote the use of electronics. The mere utilization of electric guitars in a folk-genre such as the *huaylas* (a regional variety of the popular *huayno*), for example, prompted the record industry to label it *techno-huaylas* in the early 1990s. Thus, record producers attached the techno prefix to *cumbia* when electronic instruments became predominant in those ensembles.

In the early '90s, sales of *chicha* began to decline. The excitement experienced for over a decade moderated. The *bailes sociales* decreased in both intensity and frequency, and *chicha* groups were no longer a novelty to the media. This apparent decline was similar to the one experienced by the commercial *huayno* in the 1980s. With the disappearance of the LP format and the increasing demand of a second generation of migrants, the *huayno* recording stars began to maintain a low profile. It is important to stress, however, that neither the urban *huayno* nor *chicha* passed away; they just consolidated their popularity after a period in which they were constantly in the spotlight. There are still *festivales folkóricos* ("folklore festivals") throughout Lima, in which *huayno* singers attract considerable crowds. The old *Coliseo* no longer exists, but any court, playground, or stadium serves just as well, since every weekend a different locale may be rented for this same purpose. One can still buy records of urban *huayno*, in the voices of new performers such as Amanda Portales and "Chato" Grados. Affordable prices of digital technology have allowed a fluid production of CDs since 1998, when local entrepreneurs finally imported the first industrial duplicating machines. *Chicha* groups like Los Shapish and Alegría are still playing around the country and releasing commercial recordings. They no longer occupy center stage, but they have not vanished altogether from the scene.

Rossy War and the Ascendancy of *Techno-cumbia*

The emergence of *techno-cumbia* in Peru was as swift as it was unexpected. It happened through the remarkable success of a hit record from singer Rossy War (née Rosa Guerra) in 1998 (see fig. 10.5). Her single "Nunca pensé llorar" ("I Never Meant to Cry"), composed by her husband/producer Tito Mauri, broke record sales, became a familiar tune for several weeks on the majority of radio stations, and made her a frequent guest on television shows. This time something was different, however: Rossy War's music was being accepted by all social sectors, not only by migrant or working-class groups. Even when the media reported on her music, they did it with admiration and respect, in contrast to the prejudiced and high-brow attitude to which *chicha* had been subjected. In the elite circles of Lima, Rossy War's

Fig. 10.5. Rossy War, the biggest star of *techno-cumbia* in Peru.

performances were greeted with curiosity rather than suspicion, and soon even the most lavish parties in the most affluent suburbs were playing Rossy War's *techno-cumbia*. How was this possible?

Rossy War was born in a small village in Madre de Dios, a region in the tropical forest of the Peruvian Amazon. She grew up watching Mexican films and singing *rancheras* and Peruvian creole songs. At age five, she began to sing in public, and at fifteen she was singing with a local group in the city of Puerto Maldonado. At 17 she moved to Vitarte, a factory town close to Lima. In 1984 she began her professional career as a singer in the group Los Bio Chips, from Chimbote (north of Lima), where she met her husband, Tito Mauri, the group's producer. Rossy War began touring extensively in several provinces of Peru and neighboring countries. In 1993 she released her first recording, "Como la flor" ("Like the Flower") in Chile, and another one in Bolivia in 1996, entitled "Cositas del amor" ("Love Affairs"). In 1997 she and Alberto Mauri formed her current musical group, La Banda Caliente, with whom she continued building a loyal following throughout southern and northern Peru. Once having conquered the provinces, their own record company, the independent Fama Records, released in Lima in 1997 what would be her biggest-selling album, which included her hit "Nunca pensé llorar." It was even broadcast on radio stations that normally aired rock, salsa, or pop.

Rossy War's short yet intense music career serves us as background for explaining why a working-class music, like the Peruvian *cumbia*, evolved from being a marginal cultural expression to mainstream dance music, from low culture (accessible to some) to mass culture (accessible to everyone). The following are four reasons this process came about.

1. De-Andeanization. Rossy War's *techno-cumbia* left aside any musical references to the Andean *huayno*. Her singing style was influenced by pop music, especially by the Mexican singer Ana Gabriel, and had no relation with *chicha* singing style. If previous *cumbia* types had adapted known *huayno*s to the *cumbia* format, or had composed *cumbia* melodies with a *huayno* feeling, Rossy War did not follow this trend. Moreover, she accentuated other non-Andean elements, such as the incorporation of salsa *montunos* and intensive use of synthesizers, which detracted from the prominent role that the lead guitar had played in previous *cumbia* styles.

2. Sensualization. Dance would play a more prominent role than before. In *chicha* the musicians would take a few synchronized steps right and left during their performance, but their movements were not choreographed in a strict sense. Rossy War performed with two female dancers, who performed in light clothes using sensual movements, such as expressive pelvic gestures and intensive hip rotations. The attire worn by Rossy War and her

dancers represented a radical departure from previous styles and reinforced the erotic quality of her performances on stage. Having been born in a city surrounded by the Peruvian jungle, Rossy War emphasized proudly her Amazonian heritage. One of her favorite performance garments was a stylization of traditional Amazonian dress.

3. Globalization. Besides the native Amazonian dress, Rossy War's most frequent attire was one very similar to Selena's, the Tex-Mex pop star. Dressed in black, short pants and tight blouse, with a black hat, Rossy War simulated a Peruvian Selena, pop star, global icon, and Hollywood symbol. Rossy War's competent voice quality and its resemblance to Ana Gabriel's helped to make people view her as a singer with global qualities. The association with the Amazonian jungle, which was stressed through photographs, dresses, and paraphernalia (as well as by self-proclamation), also enhanced her global persona. The Amazon jungle crosses national borders in South America, covering parts of Bolivia, Peru, Ecuador, Colombia, Venezuela, and Brazil. Moreover, the "exotic" quality of the Amazon jungle could symbolize all the jungles of the world. The increasing popularity of *techno-cumbia* in neighboring countries like Bolivia, Chile, and Argentina also reinforced the transnational quality of the genre.

4. Mass mediation. *Techno-cumbia*, of Rossy War's variety, became highly mass-mediated. Radio, television, and the recording industry focused on the *techno-cumbia* as the most profitable music business in recent times. Shortly after the huge success of Rossy War's *techno-cumbia*, independent producers began to assemble groups of young *techno-cumbia* singers, in imitation of groups that the Mexican pop industry had marketed so effectively in Latin America. Aimed directly at the teenage market, and with the help of highly qualified professional arrangers and studio musicians, these groups (Skandalo, Tornado, and Zona Franca, to name a few) have grabbed an important share of the market.

Immediately after Rossy War's success, other performers of *techno-cumbia* were discovered by the media and the recording industry. Some of these performers had been on the road even longer than Rossy War, and had evolved through different musical styles along the way. Armonía 10, for example, was founded in Piura, a northern province 1,000 kilometers north of Lima, in 1972. After going through different stylistic stages, Armonía 10 is now one of the most recognized and musically diversified representatives of the *techno-cumbia* phenomenon. Keeping the same improvised riffs that characterized the Colombian *cumbia* groups from the 1970s, Armonía 10 added influences from the Latin American *balada* pop, Caribbean salsa and *montunos* (especially in the role of the keyboards and brass breaks). Their most striking difference from other *techno-cumbia* groups is their conformation. They use a section of

Fig. 10.6. *Techno-cumbia* singer Ruth Karina, center, with her dancers dressed with out-fits reminiscent of the jungle.

brass instruments (trombones and trumpets), which provides added strength to their arrangements, and feature four singers that lead the group in their live performances. Their vocal style remains interestingly close to that of *chicha* musicians, along with the performance style of the electric guitar. In fact, their style has been referred as *norteño* ("northern") by some followers.

A female singer who followed in the footsteps of Rossy War is Ruth Karina, who began as the lead of the well-known group Euforia (see fig. 10.6). Also born in an Amazonian municipality (Pucallpa), she began her career in Iquitos, the most important fluvial port and city in the Peruvian tropical forest. With the group Euforia she achieved moderate success, but it was when she started her own solo career that she became a celebrity, just like Rossy War two years before. Using the Amazonian jungle imagery more intensively than even War herself, Karina dressed her four dancers in feathers and very short bikinis ornamented with "jungle" paraphernalia. In her choreography, she further cultivated the use of unabashedly sensual motions, especially pelvic ones. But rather than scandalizing the audience, these dance movements became very popular among all age and gender groups. The use of jungle imagery was also evident in her video clips, shot in Iquitos. It was clear that Karina's producers wanted her to be identified with the jungle. But she introduced a new musical element in her career.

Trying to distinguish her repertoire from Rossy War's, she turned to Brazilian popular music, in particular the *toadas* from the Amazonian northern states. The feeling and rhythm of the *toadas* (a lively and highly danceable blend of Brazilian music, salsa, Caribbean beats, and pop) were very compatible with *techno-cumbia*'s pulse. So it was not very difficult for Karina to sing *toadas* and still pass as a *techno-cumbia* performer (even when pirated copies of the original Brazilian *toadas* could be found locally).

Local or Mass Culture?

Are the emergent social sectors of Lima being creative and inventive, or are they just creating "bad copies" of the originals? Should we be grateful to globalization for enabling local cultures to reinforce their identities through the revitalization of their cultural expressions? Or does *techno-cumbia* demonstrate the evils of globalization, its capacity to impose dominant prototypes on local cultures out of a sense of urgency to be global and cosmopolitan?

Whatever the case, *techno-cumbia* in the 1990s constituted more than an ephemeral fashion among young people. The avalanche of this music in the media was overwhelming. For the first time in the twentieth century, a cultural product of a subaltern group came to occupy center stage, front pages, and prime-time television in a strongly divided country like Peru. Previous cultural expressions from the "new *Limeños*" had never received such preferential treatment. Instead, they had been viewed by the official culture with disdain, as lowbrow entertainment or picturesque folklore. The urban *huayno* and *chicha* had been seen in such a light until the appearance of *techno-cumbia*. This shift was not merely a change of attitude but resulted from the slow but steady growth of an internal market and consumer pressure, geared toward the generation of alternative cultural expressions. Without doubt, the strongly neoliberal politics of the 1990s accelerated a dynamic by which a multiclass and multiethnic majority, rather than a privileged elite, would influence market decisions and media attention. This outcome would not have been possible without the growth (however unequal) of marginal social sectors of Lima and the transformation of their status, from displaced and poor to resident and solvent. Popular music and transnational exchanges have indeed played a crucial role in the dynamic of urban culture and social genesis.

Notes

1. In the 2000 presidential elections, incumbent President Alberto Fujimori composed a *techno-cumbia* song and used it as the main theme for his campaign. Entitled "El Chino" ("The Chinaman," his nickname), it was played during all his public meetings and danced to by Fujimori himself and his running mates.

2. Recent accounts of the Fujimori regime have analyzed the political and social consequences of the public policies implemented in last decade. See Bowen (2000); Degregori (2000); and Rospigliosi (2000).
3. Sociologist Aníbal Quijano theorized in the 1970s about the "emergent social groups" (1980). De Soto coined the term "informal sectors" to refer to the same social group (1987), and Gonzalo Portocarrero introduced the description of "new *Limeños*" when speaking about these social sectors, a definition that posed a challenge to urban sociologists (1993).
4. The *huayno* is the most popular song and dance throughout the Andean countries. The music of the *huayno* is generally in duple meter, and its inner pulse is highly syncopated. The redundant rhythmic figure that characterizes it consists of an eighth and two sixteenth notes, or a sixteenth-eighth-sixteenth figure.
5. There are numerous recordings of the music discussed in this chapter. The first four titles cited here are widely available; the others (of *chicha* and *techno-cumbia* music) might be difficult to obtain outside of Peru. *Huaynos & Huaylas: The Real Music of Peru* (Globestyle Records CDORBD 064, 1991); *Huayno Music of Peru*, vol. 1: 1949–1989, vol 2: 1960–1975 (Arhoolie Productions, 1989/91); *Chicha Belén: The Drink, the Culture, the Music* (TUMI CD045, 1994); *Picaflor de los Andes* (Bodas de Plata CD-VIR 1403, n.d.); *Una hora con Los Destellos* (IEMPSA 77.15.1276, n.d.); *Historia musical de Los Shapish de Chapulín y Jaime Moreyra* (El Virrey COL-1362, n.d.); *Rossy War y su banda Kaliente. Lo mejor de la ronquita de la technocumbia* (Fama Record/IEMPSA IEM 0390–2, 1999); *Ruth Karina y su grupo Pa'Gozar. Sangre caliente* (IEMPSA IEM-0416–2, 2000); *Armonía 10 (Piura, Perú). La Primerísima* (IEMPSA IEM-0345, 1998).
6. Official and exact figures of record sales in Peru are generally classified and therefore hard to procure. The information provided here was obtained through various interviews with recording executives, but especially with Ezequiel Soto, a sales executive with IEMPSA in Lima, in 1986.
7. For more information on the *orquesta típica* and music from the Mantaro valley, see Romero (2001). For surveys of Andean traditional music, see Romero (1998 and 1999), and Turino (1998).
8. Personal data on Enrique Delgado and other musicians was obtained during interviews with the performers themselves or their relatives. I thank Carlos Baldeón for his assistance in conducting some of the most fruitful sessions. Other biographical information was available in advertising brochures and web pages of the artist-management firms.
9. For an extensive study and collection of lyrics of Andean songs, especially the *huayno*, see Montoya (1987).
10. From an interview cited in Hurtado Suárez (1995, 20).

References

Altamirano, Teófilo. 1984. "Regional Commitment among Central Highland Migrants in Lima." In *Miners, Peasants and Entrepreneurs: Regional Development in the Central Highland of Peru*. Edited by Norman Long and Bryan Roberts. Cambridge: Cambridge University Press.

Bowen, Sally. 2000. *El expediente Fujimori: el Perú y su Presidente 1990–2000*. Lima: Perú Monitor.

Cotler, Julio. 1978. *Clases, estado y nación en el Perú*. Lima: Instituto de Estudios Peruanos.

Degregori, Carlos Iván. 2000. *La década de la antipolítica: auge y huida de Alberto Fujimori y Vladimiro Montesinos*. Lima: Instituto de Estudios Peruanos.

De Soto, Hernando. 1987. *El otro sendero: la revolución informal*. Lima: Instituto Libertad y Democracia.

Hannerz, Ulf. 1996. *Transnational Connections: Culture, People, Places*. New York: Routledge.

Hurtado Suárez, Wilfredo. 1995. *Chicha peruana: música de los nuevos migrantes*. Lima: ECO:Grupo de Investigaciones Económicas.

Jameson, Fredric. 1998. Preface to *The Cultures of Globalization*. Edited by Jameson Fredrick and Miyoshi Masao. Durham, N.C.: Duke University Press.

Lloréns, José Antonio. 1991. "Andean Voices on Lima Airwaves: Highland Migrants and Radio Broadcasting in Peru." *Studies in Latin American Popular Culture* 10: 177–89.

Matos Mar, José. 1966. *Las barriadas de Lima 1957*. Lima: Instituto de Estudios Peruanos.

———. 1984. *Desborde popular y crisis del estado: el nuevo rostro del Perú en la década de 1980*. Lima: Instituto de Estudios Peruanos.

Montoya, Rodrigo, and Edwin Luis. 1987. *La sangre de los cerros*. Lima: CEPES/Mosca Azul/Universidad Mayor de San Marcos.

Núñez Rebaza, Lucy, and José Antonio Lloréns. 1981. "La Música Tradicional Andina en Lima Metropolitana." *América Indígena* 41/1: 53–74.

O'Brien, Pablo. 1999. "Grandes momentos de la música tropical peruana." *Somos* 643 (magazine of *El Comercio*, March 3).

Portocarrero, Gonzalo, ed. 1993. *Los nuevos Limeños: sueños, fervores y caminos en el mundo popular*. Lima: SUR Casa de Estudios del Socialismo/TAFOS Taller de Fotografía Social.

Quijano, Aníbal. 1980. *Dominación y cultura: Lo Cholo y el conflicto cultural en el Perú*. Lima: Mosca Azul.

Romero, Raúl R. 1998. "Peru." In *The Garland Encyclopedia of World Music. Vol. 2: South America, Mexico, Central America, and the Caribbean*. Edited by D. Olsen and D. Sheehy. New York: Garland Publishing.

———. 1999. "Andean Peru." In *Music in Latin American Culture: Regional Traditions*. Edited by John Schechter. New York: Schirmer Books.

———. 2001. *Debating the Past: Music, Memory and Identity in the Andes*. New York: Oxford University Press.

Rospigliosi, Fernando. 2000. *Montesinos y las fuerzas armadas: cómo controló durante una década las instituciones militares*. Lima: Instituto de Estudios Peruanos.

Turino, Thomas. 1988. "The Music of Andean Migrants in Lima, Peru: Demographics, Social Power and Style." *Latin American Music Review* 9/2: 127–50.

———. 1990. "Somos el Peru: *Cumbia Andina* and the Children of Andean Migrants in Lima, Peru." *Studies in Latin American Popular Culture* 9: 15–37.

———. 1998. "Quechua and Aymara." In *The Garland Encyclopedia of World Music. Vol. 2: South America, Mexico, Central America, and the Caribbean*. Edited by D. Olsen and D. Sheehy. New York: Garland.

Wade, Peter. 2000. *Music, Race and Nation: Música Tropical in Colombia*. Chicago: University of Chicago Press.

11

Viral Creativity

A Memetic Approach to the Music of
André Abujamra and Karnak

JOHN MURPHY

etaphors that leap from biology to computing to the humanities and back are a symptom of these times, and few are more potent than those of the virus and the gene. News stories from the summer of 2000 underscore the prevalence of this imagery: efforts to sequence the human genome were complete; an e-mail virus spread worldwide from the Philippines; and concern over genetically modified crops was widespread. It is against this backdrop that humanists and social scientists are attempting to explain the spread of cultural information by turning to memetics, an outgrowth of evolutionary biology.

The new information technologies have changed the conditions for the ownership of intellectual property, and prompted new concerns over the ways it circulates. These concerns are reflected in studies of the global circulation of music and other elements of culture (Appadurai 1990; Slobin 1993), the appropriation of local musics by artists whose commercial reach is global (Feld 1996 and 2000; Zemp 1996), digital sampling (Porcello 1991), and globalization and diasporic connections (Monson 1999). The terms of this inquiry are usually borrowed from the marketplace. Despite the interest of ethnomusicologists in musical performances and not only musical products, the units of reference (if not analysis) are the same as those used for commercial purposes: the song, the CD, and, on a more general level, stylistic designations that also serve as marketing categories, such as *Música Popular Brasileira* (MPB, or Brazilian popular music) and rock.

Musicians who make frequent use of sampling and stylistic borrowing challenge those who would interpret their music: what is the best way to understand music whose most salient feature is its broad range of stylistic reference, parody, and sampling? Is it productive to continue to focus on the song, the CD, and conventional style categories as our units of reference? Are there other levels of analysis, other metaphors, that can explain how musical ideas circulate?

This chapter explores the proposition that the metaphor of the meme and the loose collection of ideas called memetics can be useful for the study of popular music. A melody, a sample, a quotation, a rhythmic feel, a timbre, a harmonic voicing: all are prime examples of memes, or units of cultural meaning. A meme is copied when one person passes it on to another. The greater the "longevity, fecundity, and copying-fidelity" of a meme (Dawkins 1989, 194), the faster and more widely it is transmitted. The meme concept will be explored more fully below. The musical context for this discussion is the work of the Brazilian band Karnak, led by André Abujamra, who has become well known and widely praised for his creative use of sampling and the broad range of stylistic references in his music. On *Karnak* (1996) and *Universo umbigo* (1998), Abujamra and his group combine samples of a wide variety of Brazilian and global styles. Their third CD, *Estamos adorando Tokio* ("We're Adoring Tokyo"), was released in November 2000, after this chapter was completed; a CD released in Europe, *Original*, combines tracks from the first two. My intent here is not to prove or disprove a memetic theory of music, but to try out the meme idea as a model of musical structure and transmission.

André Abujamra and Karnak

André Abujamra is a composer of music for films, theater, and television, and a former member of the duo Os Mulheres Negras ("The Black Women") and the group Vexame ("Shame"). He formed Karnak after traveling with a theater group to Spain, Greece, and Africa, where he recorded many musical samples (Gilman 1998). The group's music blends samples with eclectic playing by Abujamra (vocals, guitar, samplers, and other instruments), Lulu Camargo (keyboards), Kuki Stolarsky (percussion), Carneiro Sândalo (percussion), James Muller (percussion), Eduardo Cabello (guitar), Serginho Bartolo (bass), Marcos Bowie (trumpet), and Hugo Hori (saxophone). A large number of guest artists appear on *Karnak* and *Universo umbigo*, including Chico César (voice), Lulu Santos (guitar), the bands Pato Fu and Mestre Ambrósio, traditional musicians such as the *maracatu* group of Mestre Salustiano of Olinda,[1] and Abujamra's father and three-year-old son (liner notes; Gilman 1998).[2]

Abujamra has written emphatically in the liner notes to both CDs that Karnak is not "world music," but a "pop band."[3] Its orientation toward the pop market is reflected in the consistently danceable grooves, the memorable melodic hooks, and the length of each song (typically around four minutes). Yet, a pop listener's expectation of stylistic consistency is soon challenged by the diversity of each album. The range of styles includes reggae, rock, samba, funk, frevo, African pop, swing, and country and western.[4] The basic instrumentation of guitar, bass, keyboards, drums, and horns is augmented by a wide variety of percussion, and either live or sampled flute, organ, accordion, rabeca, shenai, erhu, xylophone, mbira, Hawaiian slide guitar, cello, vibraphone, and Scottish bagpipes.

Abujamra dislikes the label "world music" because, in Brazil, it has the connotation of music based on research into the music of a culture other than one's own. "We are already mixed," he says, and "my research was never in music, it was always in the area of human relationships."[5] He looks for human elements in music and chooses those to include in Karnak's music simply because he likes them. He makes his own version "from my own antenna." He prefers to call Karnak a pop band or a band from São Paulo. While the jacket copy of Karnak's Tinder Records release compares the band to Frank Zappa and the Mothers of Invention, Abujamra states that he was never much interested in Zappa's music. By contrast, he is very interested in that of Beck, and the two artists share many similarities in their approach to lyric writing and use of samples.

The approach to recording taken with the first CD was modeled on the mixes in rap recordings by using loops. The result was "pretty modular, almost like a mantra," according to Abujamra, and was difficult to reproduce in live performances. For the second CD, they wanted something "more visceral, stronger," and to do so they recorded the drums and percussion last. With the third CD, *Estamos adorando Tokio*, Abujamra is acting on a belief that many more people are doing now what he did in 1994, with loops and layers. He is trying to make an "old school" (his term) recording, with all of the parts recorded live in the studio and then edited with his layered approach. While the trademark opening of false spoken Russian has been retained, on the rest of the CD there is less use of false languages. In a move to reach new audiences (the band has toured the United States and Europe), there are two songs sung in English and one in Spanish. The emphasis on group interaction is intensified in the band's live shows, which, according to Abujamra, feature extended improvisations that approach free jazz.

While most of each of the songs on *Karnak* and *Universo umbigo* are in Portuguese, Abujamra shows an intense interest in languages and voices by including spoken texts in real and/or invented versions of Spanish, Russian,

Arabic, English, Italian, Japanese, Hebrew, Croatian, German, and Devadara (an invented "Karnakian" language). Most of the texts are short samples used in the introduction to a song. André's father, Antônio, reads the poem "Os três mal amados" by Jõao Cabral de Melo Neto in "Num pode ser" on *Universo umbigo*. English appears in the lyrics of several songs, most memorably in "Candelara" (*Universo umbigo*), a meditation on the cruelty of the strong toward the weak in which a diabolical voice states, "Now I understand the violence," and "Why do you beat this guy? 'Cause I'm stronger."

The contemplation of humankind's place in the world is the thread that connects the songs on *Universo umbigo*, which literally means "Universe Navel" or "Navel of the Universe." The title track makes fun of self-absorption: "Não somos nada / Nós somos tudo / Nós somos o umbigo do Mundo!" ("We're nothing / We're everything / We're the navel of the World!"). "Candelara" criticizes the prevalence of violence in present-day society, and ends with an expression of pity for the children of Brazil: "o Karnak fica com pena das crianças do Brasil" ("Karnak feels sorry for the children of Brazil").

A text by Aguinaldo Rocca in the liner notes of *Universo umbigo* describes the intent of the CD in terms that are compatible with the memetic approach:

> a Karnakian being doesn't think logically. He wants pop with the pleasure of doing things differently. A mixture of bubblegum with nitroglycerine in the arteries. Each member of the group carries this mixture in his genetic code. . . . There's always one more virus between play and eject than we imagine.

Abujamra's lyrics are distinguished by their vividness and rhymed opposite terms. In this they resemble the *quadras* of traditional Brazilian poetry and song. An example from *Karnak*:

"Balança a pança"	"Shake Your Belly"
De um lado o ódio,	From one side, hatred,
do outro lado tem amor,	from the other there is love,
desse lado tem justiça,	from this side there is justice,
desse outro tem a dor.	from that side there is pain.

And one from Universo umbigo:

"O mundo muda"	"The World Changes"
Eu era pobre e hoje eu sou rico,	I was poor and now I'm rich,
eu era feio e hoje sou bonito,	I was ugly and now I'm handsome,
eu era rico e hoje sou pobre,	I was rich and now I'm poor,
eu era escravo e hoje eu sou nobre.	I was a slave and now I'm a nobleman.

Many of the sampled voices and musical extracts are identified, but none are cited as used with permission. The *Karnak* liner notes acknowledge samples this way:

This CD uses samples of Banda de Pífanos de Caruaru, Maracatu rural do Mestre Salustiano de Olinda, Os Mulheres Negras, an Arabic street ensemble, and a Tuvan throat singer, among others. Ninety percent of the samples were recorded by André Abujamra during his travels around the world.

The much-traveled obbligato part from "Wimoweh," or "The Lion Sleeps Tonight," shows up in "Lee-o-dua" on *Karnak*. The Tuvan overtone singing in "Comendo uva na chuva" ("Eating Grapes in the Rain"), on *Karnak*, seems to have been sampled from the Smithsonian/Folkways CD *Tuva: Voices from the Center of Asia* (Alekseev, Kirgiz, and Levin 1990): track 3, "Sigit 'Alash,'" sung by Margen Mongush, and track 18, "Kargiraa 'Artii-Sayir,'" sung by Vasili Chazir. Both have been shifted up a minor second. This sample became part of the song in 1992 or '93, when Abujamra and keyboardist Lulu Camargo were working on it and Camago played a tape of Tuvan singing. Abujamra liked the sound, and it fit the key of the song, so it was included. To this day he is unsure why it appealed to him. To try to explain, he offered a quotation by Picasso: "First I find, then I seek."[6] "Comendo uva na chuva" also includes the tune "Chattanooga Choo-Choo," which Abujamra included because he likes big-band music and is fond of that tune, and a song with the lyrics "Hare Krishna." *Estamos adorando Tokio* has fewer samples than either of the band's first two CDs.

Brazilian audiences react to specific aspects of the band's presentation by age, according to Abujamra. Pre-college fans are attracted by the band's costumes, which include a wide variety of hats. College-age and older listeners react more to the lyrics and the music. Eighty percent of listeners, by Abujamra's estimate, think the band is amusing, but he emphasizes the current of seriousness that is discernible beneath the band's extroverted musical exterior, to which he feels insufficient attention has been given. The lyrics of the first two CDs are "sad, bitter," he says, and those on the third CD are even more so. "Maria Inês," for example, sung in the style of a northeastern ballad, tells the story of an abused woman who goes on a murderous and ultimately suicidal rampage rather than suffer more abuse.

Critical reaction to Karnak's music, not surprisingly, has stressed the band's diverse range of sources. *Karnak* was named one of the fifteen most significant Brazilian popular music recordings of the last thirty years by Brazilian music journalists (Gilman 1998). In a review of a performance in New York's Central Park, Jon Pareles wrote that the band blends its diverse sources into a coherent whole, and "makes complex music sound lighthearted" (1998). In a review of *Karnak*, Will Hermes catalogs the sampled musical styles and languages and concludes that "*Karnak* has an unmistakable integrity despite the sharp turns" from one style to another (1997). Cliff Furnald finds the combination of styles on *Karnak* to be "sometimes droll, sometimes jarring," but concedes that "the groove is irresistible, the music is exciting and at times it is indescribably perfect" (n.d.).

Although the emphasis on diverse stylistic references and sampling might lead one to suspect that it masks a lack of substance, there is a consistently critical and playful artistic sensibility at work in Karnak's music. Repeated listening yields a sense of a musical palimpsest, a complex layering of musical and linguistic ideas. On *Universo umbigo*, the bonus track that begins eleven minutes after the end of the listed final track, "Boiadeiro," which lasts six minutes, does the seemingly impossible, given what has gone before: it introduces a new sound. After a collage of sounds already heard on the CD comes an mbira ostinato over which is layered a lyrical string/synthesizer passage.

The Memetic Approach

The word "meme" was coined by Richard Dawkins in *The Selfish Gene* (1989) [1976], which explained to a non-specialist audience the new view of evolution centered on the gene, rather than the organism, as the unit of natural selection. Dawkins intended the concept of memes and their replication to demonstrate that other entities besides genes could be considered replicators, and gave as examples "tunes, ideas, catch-phrases, clothes fashions, ways of making pots or of building arches" (1976, 192). The value of the gene-centered view of evolution is that it enabled biologists to explain, among other things, altruistic behavior, like that of worker ants, whose labor benefits not their own offspring but those of their siblings.

In *The Extended Phenotype*, Dawkins explains how the effects of genes extend beyond the organism to the environment, and suggests a flexible way of viewing these three levels that avoids attributing conscious agency to the genes. An organism's phenotype is its body, which is shaped by genes. An extended phenotype is an alteration of the environment that can be shown to have positive effects on the replication of that organism's genes (1982, 199); examples could include a beaver's dam or a wasp's nest. To explain the shifting perspective on genes, organism, and extended phenotype, Dawkins uses the model of a Necker cube: a two-dimensional design formed by two overlapping squares. Viewers perceive it as a cube extending toward them, or away from them, in alternation, but never both at the same time. His explanation of the analogy is worth quoting at length because I will suggest a similar shifting of perspectives between the levels of musical meme, song, and style:

To return to the analogy of the Necker Cube, the mental flip that I want to encourage can be characterized as follows. We look at life and begin by seeing a collection of interacting individual organisms. We know that they contain smaller units, and we know that they are, in turn, parts of larger composite units, but we fix our gaze on the whole organisms. Then suddenly the image flips. The individual bodies are still there; they have not moved, but they seem to have gone transparent. We see through them to the replicating fragments of DNA within, and we see the wider world as an arena in which these genetic fragments play out their tournaments of manipulative skill. (1982, 4–5)

For music, the "mental flip" is between the levels of song, musical meme, and style. From the point of view of the song, the juxtaposition of samples in Abujamra's music may seem incongruous or contrived, because we are used to thinking of a song as one thing, or perhaps as three: music, lyrics, and arrangement. From the point of view of the meme, a song is a convenient vehicle for transmitting memes, and the juxtaposition of diverse memes within one song is not an aberration but a normal practice. Musical styles can be reconceived as meme complexes or collections of memes that get transmitted together.

While the concept of memes continues to be debated by evolutionary biologists, and may ultimately be discarded as the relationship between the brain and consciousness is better understood, scholars in philosophy, psychology, and cultural studies have found it useful as a way to conceptualize the spread of ideas. Philosopher Daniel Dennett uses memes to explain the circulation of ideas in culture: "A scholar is just a library's way of making another library" (1995, 346). Ideas spread not because they are good, but because they are good to imitate (1995, 364), or, as in the case of some religious or political ideas, because they come in complexes with other memes that instruct people how to receive them (as the truth, for example). Abujamra does this to a certain extent by stating prominently on his CDs that Karnak is not to be described as "world music."

Dennett's explanation of the varying success of memes at being replicated can help us understand why it was "Chattanooga Choo-Choo" and not a dozen other swing-era tunes that surfaced in Karnak's "Comendo uva na chuva":

Minds are in limited supply, and each mind has a limited capacity for memes, and hence there is a considerable competition among memes for entry into as many minds as possible. This competition is the major selective force in the infosphere, and, just as in the biosphere, the challenge has been met with great ingenuity. "Whose ingenuity?" you may want to ask, but by now you should know that this is not always a good question; the ingenuity is *there* to appreciate, whatever its source. Like a mindless virus, a meme's prospects depend on its design—not its "internal" design, whatever that might be, but the design it shows the world, its phenotype, the way it affects things in its environment. The things in its environment are minds and other memes. (1995, 349) [original emphasis]

Over the years since it appeared, the "Chattanooga Choo-Choo" meme has been copied into millions of recordings and minds. One reason may be the uniqueness of its chromatic ascent, with a syncopation on the fourth note. Its greater fecundity has caused it to spread more widely than other tunes from the same era.

A meme-centered approach to musical creativity allows us to ask to what extent a person is completely in control of the constant flow of musical ideas in the mind. Anyone who has had a tune "stuck in the head" has experienced the ability of a musical meme to promote its own replication. Music is ultimately a biological activity, and the musical mind may be plausibly represented as an environment in which certain musical ideas persist and get passed on while others do not.[7]

Psychologist Susan Blackmore emphasizes the capability of memes to replicate despite the best efforts of human beings to curb their replication, and extends the concept of memes to the point of minimizing or even eliminating the role of the self:

> We may feel as though there is a central place inside our heads in to which the sensations come and from which we consciously make the decisions. Yet this place simply does not exist. (1999, 2)

This suggests what I will call "viral creativity," or a view of creativity based on the acquisition of musical memes from other people, recordings, the environment in general, their selective retention and alteration within the memetic environment of one person's mind, and their propagation in new complexes of memes, which begin the process anew.[8] Blackmore sketches the process this way:

> Where do new memes come from? They come about through variation and combination of old ones—either inside one person's mind, or when memes are passed from person to person. (1999, 15)

Among André Abujamra's gifts is the ability to find, remember, filter, recombine, and then pass on to others a large variety of musical memes. In Dennett's terms, he is a "meme-fountain" (cited by Blackmore 1999, 155). To extend the metaphor further, we could think of the idea for the band Karnak as a meme that Abujamra caught on his world travels, and has been spreading ever since. His use of Picasso's notion of finding (memes) and then seeking (new connections) can also be reconciled with a "viral" concept of creativity.[9]

Although memes are sometimes described as having the "goal" of being reproduced, I do not intend to attribute agency to them in a way that would deny it to the musicians. André Abujamra and his colleagues are highly skilled musicians who make innumerable artistic decisions in the course of composing, arranging, and recording their repertory. Karnak's breadth of musical references could also be theorized in terms of postmodernity, with its emphasis on pastiche. The appeal of the meme concept is that it has the potential to connect current research on consciousness with the way musicians talk about their ideas.

As the understanding of brain function progresses, it may be possible to identify exactly how musical ideas are stored. This may help explain just what happens in the minds of two musicians who know the same tune and why it is that, of the countless sounds we are exposed to, we retain and use only a small fraction. It does not require an assumption of agency on the part of a musical meme to explain why it spreads more widely than other memes. The potential for replication is somehow inherent in that meme's design, and combines with the consciousness and agency of musicians and listeners to propagate the meme. It is another way of talking about the "catchiness" of musical ideas: we catch them as we would a virus, and spread them to others.

One may rightly ask how "meme" is an improvement over such terms as phrase, timbre, melodic pattern, or rhythmic feel. It certainly is less specific. But it can contribute to musical discourse in two ways. First is the three-part analogy with the gene, the organism, and the extended phenotype discussed above. Just as the scientific understanding of DNA enables us to identify common characteristics among groups of people normally treated as distinct, the use of the meme idea makes it possible to identify bits of musical information that circulate widely and are found in musical styles and traditions that are normally treated as distinct. The fact that Karnak uses a sample of Tuvan singing, a reggae time feel, and a sample of big-band swing in one song does not make it music any less "Brazilian," because to be a musician today in Brazil, or anywhere, for that matter, means to be exposed to a highly diverse stream of information. The most Brazilian aspect of Karnak's work may be its sense of humor. In Brazil, Karnak could conceivably fit into such categories as MPB, national pop, and world music. Abujamra rejects the label "world music" for good reason: it would limit his band's appeal and his options for marketing it. Some Brazilian musicians describe their music as *sem rótulo* ("without a label"), in order to frustrate the market-driven impulse to categorize each new musical product.

The second contribution of the meme idea is a model for the transmission of musical information. Musical ideas can be thought of as viruses, which carry in their design something that encourages their replication within a host and their transmission to new hosts. Just as microorganisms can circulate without the knowledge of their hosts, musical memes can enter a musician's vocabulary without a conscious effort to acquire them. This unconscious, "viral" sort of musical transmission supplements more deliberate kinds of musical learning. It is common in musical traditions that emphasize improvisation, for example, for musicians to talk about getting the self out of the way and letting musical ideas happen "on their own." The use of a meme-centered or viral model of musical transmission makes it possible to talk about a transmission of musical ideas that transcends both individual awareness and established categories of musical style. Live musical performances, recordings, direct instruction, and random sounds in the street can all be accommodated as sources of new musical memes.

The ethical dimension of sampling has received much attention in the literature on world music, and the memetic or viral transmission of musical ideas can be extended into this area as well. No musician can be aware of the source of every musical idea he or she uses, but in the case of ideas whose provenance can be established, the obligation remains to acknowledge the source. The fact that some musical traditions are said to be "diluted" or "contaminated" by outside influences is also relevant here. Like genetic information, musical information is constantly being mixed and transmitted widely, and this process has only accelerated with the globalization and democratization of information technology. A memetic view of music takes this constant blending as a given, and considers musical categories to be provisional attempts to identify a consistent set of musical traits. Individual musicians, in this view, remain the principal actors and retain the ethical obligation to respect the sources of their ideas, when they can be identified.

Memes and Karnak

The creative decisions André Abujamra described with the quotation from Picasso, "first I find, then I seek," are compatible with a meme-centered or viral view of musical creativity. Sounds of all sorts find their way into Karnak's recordings because they have found their way inside André Abujamra's mind and secured a place for themselves by replicating and making connections with other memes, and because he and his group chose to include them. The diverse collection of sounds that this band has assembled makes sense because the memetic environment of São Paulo is conducive to such diversity. In Abujamra's words, "we're already mixed." Thinking in terms of memes can also explain why Karnak's music can be moving and interesting for people who happen not to be from São Paulo. The profusion of memetic information in Karnak's music makes it more likely that it will strike a wide variety of listeners as interesting.

The meme idea, ultimately, may be more useful as an analogy than as anything else. It provides one way to understand the intuitive stylistic diversity that is characteristic of the music of André Abujamra and Karnak, and a way to suggest, in its analogy with genetic and viral transmission, a view of musical creativity that gives equal consideration to individual agency and to the interpersonal spread of musical ideas.

Notes

1. Mestre Salustiano (Manoel Salustiano Soares) is well known in Pernambuco and, increasingly, throughout Brazil, as a master performer of *maracatu rural, cavalo-marinho, mamulengo,* and other traditional genres; numerous popular musicians from Pernambuco cite him as a touchstone of authenticity.
2. Sound clips and other information may be found at the band's website, http://www.karnak.com.br.
3. Notes to *Karnak*: "Karnak is not world music! Karnak is a band without precedent!" Notes to *Universo umbigo*: "Mais uma vez repito, nós somos uma banda pop, não somos world music!"
4. Abujamra discovered rock and country and western and developed an affinity for the music of ZZ Top as a high-school exchange student in the Youth for Understanding program in the United States between August 24, 1982, and July 17, 1983. He had asked to be placed in a cosmopolitan city where he could pursue his interests in music and theatre. Instead, he was sent to Kingfisher, OK (pop. 5,000), 45 miles from Oklahoma City.
5. Unless otherwise noted, quotations by André Abujamra are from a telephone interview conducted in Portuguese on April 25, 2000, or subsequent e-mail exchanges. English translations are mine. Lyrics are quoted with permission. The author gratefully acknowledges Abujamra's collaboration.
6. The closest thing I could find to this quotation is the following: "To search means nothing in painting. To find is the thing." Picasso interview in *The Arts* (1923), quoted in Crofton (1988, 142).
7. Two recent publications on music employ the memetic approach: Gatherer (1997), which discusses changes in African-American music in the twentieth century, and Jan (2000), which applies memetic concepts to music of the Classical era.
8. To see whether the phrase "viral creativity" was a meme I had picked up from someone else without realizing it, I searched for it on AltaVista on May 8, 2000; there were no hits.
9. When asked about the concept of memes during our interview, Abujamra was unaware of it but found it intriguing.

References

Alekseev, Eduard, Zoya Kirgiz, and Ted Levin. 1990. *Tuva: Voices from the Center of Asia.* Smithsonian/Folkways CD SF 40017.

Appadurai, Arjun. 1990. "Disjuncture and Difference in the Global Cultural Economy." *Public Culture* 2/2: 1–24.

Blackmore, Susan. 1999. *The Meme Machine.* Oxford: Oxford University Press.

Crofton, Ian. 1988. *A Dictionary of Art Quotations.* New York: Schirmer.

Dawkins, Richard. 1982. *The Extended Phenotype: The Gene as the Unit of Selection.* Oxford: W. H. Freeman.

———. 1989 [1976]. *The Selfish Gene.* Oxford: Oxford University Press.

Dennett, Daniel C. 1995. *Darwin's Dangerous Idea: Evolution and the Meanings of Life.* New York: Simon & Schuster.

Feld, Steven. 1996. "pygmy POP: A Genealogy of Schizophonic Mimesis." *Yearbook for Traditional Music* 28: 1–35.

———. 2000. "A Sweet Lullaby for World Music." *Public Culture* 12/1: 145–71.

Furnald, Cliff. n.d. "RootsWorld: Brazil." *RootsWorld* online. http://www.rootsworld.com/rw/feature/brazil1.html.

Gatherer, Derek. 1997. "The Evolution of Music—A Comparison of Darwinian and Dialectical Methods." *Journal of Social and Evolutionary Systems* 20/1: 75–92.

Gilman, Bruce. 1998. "Guerrilla Sound." http://www.brazil-brasil.com/musfeb98.htm.

Jan, Steven. 2000. "Replicating Sonorities: Toward a Memetics of Music." *Journal of Memetics—Evolutionary Models of Information Transmission* 4 http://www.cpm.mmu.ac.uk/jom-emit/2000/vol4/jan_s.html.

Karnak. 1996. *Karnak.* Tinder Records 42850842.

———. 1998. *Universo umbigo.* Velas 11–V 254.

———. 2000. *Estamos adorando Tokio.* Net Records 0001.

Hermes, Will. 1997. "Global Chop Shop." *Village Voice* (December 30): 82.

Monson, Ingrid. 1999. "Riffs, Repetition, and Theories of Globalization." *Ethnomusicology* 43/1: 31–65.

Pareles, Jon. 1998. "Small World, Many Hats." *The New York Times* (June 25): E5.

Porcello, Thomas. 1991. "The Ethics of Digital Audio-Sampling: Engineers' Discourse." *Popular Music* 10: 69–84.

Slobin, Mark. 1993. *Subcultural Sounds: Micromusics of the West.* Hanover, N.H.: Wesleyan University Press/University Press of New England.

Zemp, Hugo. 1996. "The/An Ethnomusicologist and the Record Business." *Yearbook for Traditional Music* 28: 36–56.

12

Doing the Samba on Sunset Boulevard
Carmen Miranda and the Hollywoodization of Latin American Music

WALTER AARON CLARK

Q: Has this trip changed your views any about Latin America and your policies? Do you see any perspectives differently after this trip?

The President: Well, I learned a lot, because that's what I went to do, is—I didn't go down there with any plan for the Americas or anything. I went down to find out from them and their views. And you'd be surprised, yes, because, you know, they're all individual countries. I think one of the greatest mistakes in the world that we've made has been in thinking, lumping—thinking "Latin America." You don't talk that way about Europe. You recognize the difference between various countries. And the same thing is true here.[1]

To those who know anything at all about Latin American history, demography, geography, and culture, this epiphany exhibits a curious quality. Still, it is easy to understand how President Ronald Reagan, who had spent so many years in Hollywood, might have come to perceive Latin America as a culturally homogeneous region and be surprised to learn, off the set, that the reality was so different. His career as a movie actor coincided with the emergence of one of the most phenomenal screen figures from Latin America and one who, more than any other person, helped create an all-purpose, homogeneous image of Latin Americans, their culture, and especially their music.

Hollywood used the sensational singer and actress Carmen Miranda as a do-all prop in dramatic settings as diverse as New York, Rio de Janeiro,

252

Buenos Aires, Havana, and Mexico. The resulting conflation of costumes, instruments, musical genres, and languages is highly entertaining on one level but pernicious and (at the time) politically counterproductive on another. As Allen Woll observes, the merely partial coverage by U.S. news media of events in South America leaves a gap that is "often filled by fictional representations in motion pictures and television shows. Film, in particular, has played a major role in shaping modern America's consciousness of Latin America" (1980, v).

The purpose of this essay, however, is not primarily to explore biographical or political issues but to focus on the musical numbers themselves to discover the ways in which the music (and its attendant dramatic elements such as language, choreography, costumes, casting, and sets) fosters the creation of a hybrid and fundamentally mythological image of Latin America.

La Pequena Notável

Carmen Miranda, so closely associated with Brazil, was actually born in Portugal, in the village of Marco de Canavezes (Porto), on February 9, 1909. She was baptized Maria do Carmo, though the family came to call her Carmen because she looked a bit Spanish to them (Bizet's 1875 opera had made that name very popular). She later adopted her mother's maiden name of Miranda, and thus, her eventual stage name. Desperate economic conditions in Portugal compelled the family to emigrate to Rio the year after her birth, where Carmen's father found work as a barber. In 1925 her parents opened a boardinghouse, which attracted a number of customers in the entertainment business, including composers, who introduced her to the world of radio and recordings.

While her career was in the embryonic stage, she worked in a milliner's shop designing and making hats (a portent of things to come), while softly singing her favorite songs. Many of the earliest tunes she learned and performed were, ironically, not sambas but rather tangos, in the style of her idol Carlos Gardel. It was not long before Brazilian composers noted her talent and began to collaborate with her. These included such figures as Synval Silva, Ary Barroso, and Dorival Caymmi. Her meteoric rise to fame in the 1930s brought her to the summit of popularity in Brazil, as a recording artist, performer, and even movie actress.

During this early phase of her career, she invented a persona for herself—the brash, liberated, extremely extroverted and showy Carmen Miranda—one quite at odds with her more conservative, retiring, and proper alter ego, Maria do Carmo. This penchant for reinventing herself would be greatly amplified by the mass mediation of her adopted persona. It was also necessitated by the cultural politics of her milieu, as "it was essential that her Portuguesse origin be kept secret because the public might reject a non-Brazilian performer of sambas" (Gil-Montero 1989, 28). Although her physical appearance betrayed European ancestry, she cultivated the *gíria*, or street slang, of her Rio environs, thus masking her true identity. However, her later addition of North American elements to this character would prove controversial in Brazil, where she would be accused of having become "Americanized" and making Brazilians look laughable and ridiculous.

Carmen's devotion to samba came at a time when, under the regime of Getúlio Vargas (president 1930–1945, 1951–1954), a new ideology of national identity was forming, one that embraced blacks and mulattos as distinctive facets of Brazilian society and culture. The samba was the musical icon of this unique Brazilian identity, and the middle and upper classes were now ready for a white woman like Carmen to promote this national art form. In 1930 she signed a contract with RCA Victor and began her ascent to stardom. In that first year she recorded no fewer than forty songs, and by the end of the decade she had recorded 281, with a variety of companies.[2] Half of these were sambas, and the other half mostly Carnival marches, rumbas, and tangos. In 1934 she began working with a Rio group called the Bando da Lua ("Moon Gang"), an association that would last through her Hollywood years. It was during this formative stage that César Ladeira, a Rio radio announcer, dubbed her *La pequena notável*, or "The Remarkable Little Girl." This child-like aspect of hers would take on great significance in the films she made in Hollywood.

One of the major developments of this decade was her emergence as a film star. The most significant of her Brazilian films was the last, *Banana da terra* (1938). Set in Bahia, this film was a collaboration between her and the Bahian composer Dorival Caymmi (b. 1914). Her star turn comes with Caymmi's unforgettable "O que é que a Bahiana tem?" ("Oh, What Does a Bahian Girl Have?"). Caymmi's lyrics clarify what the Bahian girl has that makes her so appealing: turban, earrings, skirt, sandals, and bracelets and other types of jewelry, all adorning a body in seductive movement. Here really was the birth of her Hollywood screen image. But it is important again to understand that this was Carmen's creation, under the inspiration of Caymmi. The Bahian women themselves considered turbans and gaudy jewelry old-fashioned slave attire and rarely wore such things. Thus, Carmen did "not copy the costume worn by the Bahian women [but] took elements from it and then added personal touches" like the strings of beads, bare tummy, exotic hats piled with fruit, and always bright colors (Gil-Montero 1989, 57). Carmen had now assembled all the ingredients that would make her a Hollywood star. All that remained was to go north.

Doing the Samba on Sunset Boulevard

In 1939 the Broadway impresario Lee Shubert visited Rio de Janeiro and witnessed the Brazilian sensation in action. He immediately perceived Carmen's potential and offered her a contract. She jumped at the opportunity, with the proviso that the Bando da Lua accompany her. Carmen was on her way—to Broadway. Vargas himself took an interest in this development. He hoped she would foster greater ties between northern and southern hemispheres and serve as an Ambassadress of Brazil in the United States. This could benefit Brazil economically by increasing its share of the American coffee market. She shared his vision and declared,

> I shall concentrate all my efforts on one objective: to take advantage of this chance to promote Brazilian popular music in the same way I popularized samba in the countries on both sides of the River Plate. What I want is to show what Brazil really is and change the wrong ideas existing in the United States about our country. (cited in Gil-Montero 1989, 67)

It is instructive to bear these words in mind when surveying the actual trajectory and impact of her career. In fact, Carmen and the Bando made their 1939 Broadway debut in the musical *Streets of Paris* singing a number entitled "In South American Way," a rumba instead of a samba (music and lyrics by American pop songwriters Jimmy McHugh and Al Dubin)!

Carmen had the preternatural gift of being in the right place at the right time. Washington was in midst of rehabilitating its Good Neighbor Policy toward Latin America, in an effort to compensate for overseas markets now closed by the Axis and war. This effort was put forth on several fronts, including cultural. Hollywood's assistance was vital in this regard, because it was one of the chief means by which the United States could reach out to Latin American countries and win the hearts and minds of the populace and governments there, enlisting their aid economically and, all too soon, militarily. Hollywood was only too happy to comply, insofar as many of its overseas markets were no longer available, and it wanted to build on the substantial market Latin America represented, with more than 4,000 movie theaters. In 1940 the State Department set up an Office of the Coodinator for Inter-American Affairs, with Nelson Rockefeller as its head. John Hay Whitney was put in charge of the very important Motion Picture Section of this Office. Whitney and Rockefeller worked closely with Hollywood studios, especially 20th Century Fox, to ensure that there would be a steady stream of movies with Latin American themes that could be exported south in the hopes of warming up hemispheric relations. By war's end, Hollywood had produced no fewer than eighty-four such films (Lopez 1993, 69). The greatest luminary in the cavalcade of Latin American screen talent to demand such an effort was Carmen Miranda.

It did not take Hollywood long to notice Miranda's star quality, and her first appearance on the U.S. screen came in the 1940 musical *Down Argentine Way*, which opens with her singing the now trademark rumba she premiered at the Shubert. Several movies followed over the next decade, including such classics as *That Night in Rio* (1941), *Weekend in Havana* (1941), and *Springtime in the Rockies* (1942). Others, like *Doll Face* (1945), *Copacabana* (1947), *A Date with Judy* (1948), and *Nancy Goes to Rio* (1950), are not of the same caliber but nonetheless feature some memorable numbers. (And some were just plain bad, such as *Scared Stiff* of 1953, with Dean Martin and Jerry Lewis, in which Carmen appears as The Enchilada Lady, selling Mexican food and doing a crude parody of herself.) Carmen also recorded many of the selections from her films, and they appeared in sheet music. Harry Warren (the son of an Italian-American bootmaker, whose musical education had come from being a Catholic choir boy, a carnival drummer, and a saloon pianist) and Mack Gordon were the principal composer/lyricist team who wrote for her, although she also did arrangements of tunes supplied by Brazilian composers. It is from the numbers composed by Warren, however, that we see best how the process of Hollywoodization worked, and in one movie above all others.

The Gang's All Here[3]

Critics may differ about the relative merits of Miranda's films; for instance, *That Night in Rio* (*Uma noite no Rio*) is still regarded in Brazil as the best of her Hollywood movies (Gil-Montero 1989, 121–22), while few North American critics would assess it that highly (see fig. 12.1). But *The Gang's All Here* (1943), with music by Warren and lyrics by Leo Robin, directed and choreographed by Busby Berkeley, stands out in my mind as by far and away her best film, and perhaps one of the best Hollywood musicals ever. Originally to have been entitled "The Girls He Left Behind" (in Brazil it is called *Entre a loura e a morena*, meaning "Between a Blonde and a Brunette"), the plot is simple. On his last night on leave, an army sargeant, Andy Mason, falls in love with a glamorous showgirl named Eadie Allen (played by the blonde Alice Faye) at the Club New Yorker. However, Andy is already engaged to Vivian Potter (played by the brunette Sheila Ryan), the daughter of the very wealthy and prudish Peyton Potter, who also happens to be business partners with Andy's father. Andy woos Eadie under an assumed name ("Sargeant Casey"), causing all sorts of problems later on. She falls in love with him and sees him off at the train station the next day. Andy returns from the Pacific several months later, in time for a splashy war benefit staged by the Club's cast at the Potter estate. Dorita (Carmen Miranda) discovers his ploy, nearly ruining Andy's plan to marry Eadie, who flies into a rage

Fig. 12.1. Carmen Miranda performs the Warren/Gordon hit "I, Yi, Yi, Yi, Yi, I Like You Very Much" in *That Night in Rio*. Courtesy of 20th Century Fox.

upon learning the truth. In the end Vivian decides to pursue a dancing career, and Eadie, convinced of Andy's sincere love, forgives him. This is basically a morality play about fidelity in wartime.

Miranda adds a splash of local color to the film that audiences found riveting, even hypnotic. Her malapropisms, gesticulations, facial expressions, and of course her outrageous costumes jump off the celluloid and command our rapt attention. As *Variety* discovered, "Carmen Miranda dominates whenever the cameras rest upon her."[4] The chief characteristic of this picture, however, is its greater emphasis on song and dance than in most of her other films. The music is integrated into the drama through repeated use of some melodic material, and the actual numbers are far more frequent, elaborate, and extended. Indeed, the slender drama serves as an armature to support the music and dance.

The opening is memorable. From total blackness appears a singing head, that of Aloysio de Olveira, the guitarist in the Bando da Lua. Although he is not playing his guitar onscreen, it is heard in the background accompaniment. He sings the then enormously popular "Brasil" by Ary Barroso, an evocatively wistful serenade meant to instill in the audience a longing for (an imaginary) Brazil, a zone of tropical splendor and insouciant languor, for escape from the terrors and trials of the present moment. "Brazil—the Brazil that I knew / Where I wander'd with you . . . Lives in my imagination." The exotic effect is heightened by his singing in Portuguese.

The text's romantic nostalgia for someplace far away and long ago is reinforced in the music. The initial melodic gesture in the song is an ascending major sixth, an interval that has an enduring history signifying longing and desire, for instance, in such disparate examples as the Prelude to *Tristan und Isolde* and the folk song "My Bonnie Lies Over the Ocean." Moreover, the elastic rhythm and lack of a strong beat intensify its rhapsodic quality. A thickening of the orchestration and jazzing up of the harmony coincide with a gradual quickening of the tempo as the camera pans left to survey the ocean liner *S.S. Brazil*, disgorging passengers and cargo at dockside in New York. The song suddenly metamorphoses into a very upbeat samba played by the Bando da Lua, who appear intermingled with the passengers.

Of greatest visual significance now are the sacks labeled "sugar" and "coffee." Here was the Good Neighbor Policy in operation. Brazil was not only a zone of escapist fantasies but of natural abundance. It is precisely at this moment that the camera surveys a large net full of fruit, panning slowly downward toward the predictable elision of the net's cornucopia with the tutti-frutti hat of Carmen Miranda.[5] She takes up the song in its new incarnation, gyrating in trademark fashion while perched on her platform shoes. In the background one now hears a female chorus singing wordlessly in the manner of sirens from the zone of seduction. The association of the wordless female voice with mystery and exoticism is a powerful one, for example in *Tannhäuser* and Holst's *The Planets*, or more recently in the theme song of the original *Star Trek* series from the 1960s.[6] All this precedes a new encounter.

Phil Baker, the bandleader now acting the part of representative of New York's mayor, appears in a car accompanied by a marching band playing "A Hot Time in the Old Town Tonight." Here is the musical emblem of North America, and its brazen bombast effectively interrupts the Brazilian music. Baker immediately asks if Carmen has "any coffee." The quizzical look on Carmen's face and exchange of apparently disapproving glances among her and the Bando are accompanied by an interrogative flourish in the woodwinds that underlines her gestures musically. Here was a moment of self-reflective irony in the context of Good Neighborliness. The greedy, acquisitive *norteamericano* is oblivious to Latin modes of social conduct, courtesy, and transaction. Significantly, Carmen does not answer his coffee question and proceeds into the next tune, a paean to the glories of New York. It represents the full Hollywoodization of Brazilian music, as they are completely inundated by the jazzy strains that flow in a resistless stream from the unseen ensemble.

At this point it is also clear that this is a play within a play, and that the real setting is not at dockside but rather in a nightclub, the Club New Yorker. Only at the end of this number, which introduces Alice Faye as one of the showgirls in the act, does Carmen relinquish the coffee she has withheld to this point. That is, the question highlighted in the woodwinds before is now answered, but only after an appropriate interval of musical introduction. Of course, the action in this scene reproduces the actual journey that Miranda herself had made only a few years earlier. Yet, all of this takes place in a kind of mythic dimension, as there are absolutely no blacks in this number, the one group without whom there would be no samba or jazz! This mythological dimension of Miranda's persona finds its most potent expresssion in the next scene.

"Did you tell her about me dancing with that South American savage, that gypsy?" The drama's resident puritan, Peyton Potter, has been dragged to the Club New Yorker by his business partner, Andrew Mason, *père*, and now worries that his wife will learn that he got caught up in an audience-participation dance with "Dorita." His humorous neurosis represents a view of South America as a realm in which savages and gypsies are indistinguishable, a view perhaps shared by many in the movie theaters of the time. The characterization of Brazil as a zone of natural luxuriance inhabited by natives living in peaceful, if primitive, accord with their environment is reinforced by the ensuing song and dance.

The floor show at the Club New Yorker continues with Miranda's most celebrated number, "The Lady in the Tutti-Frutti Hat." It opens with organ grinders in white suits and real monkeys capering about them and in the trees, in search of bananas. The music evokes the characteristic sounds of the *organillo*, mimicked in the orchestra using a "wrong-note" technique that simulates the misfiring valves of an organ grinder's instrument. This serves to establish the comical, madcap ambience of the number. The music here is simulated in the orchestra rather than reproduced live, and does not accompany a song. The trumpet plays the melody, and the accompaniment in the strings simulates the strumming of a guitar.

The camera pans across a generically tropical "landscape" of a little "island" dotted with "palm trees," and among these there is a generous assortment of leggy, nubile young maidens in bare feet wearing shorts and halter tops. Each wears a scarf tied around her head, the basic design of so many of Miranda's headresses and one that we recall she herself adapted from the costume of the *Baiana*. Their skimpy *ensembles* are in banana shades of yellow and green. The numerous pairs of long, clean-shaven legs—which the camera thirstily drinks in—were no doubt a welcome sight for woman-hungry GIs on leave, and that is the major part of their appeal. Of course, few of the young women actually look different from the girl next door in Peoria—if more shapely and glamorous, perhaps—and not a one of them is at all dark, or black, despite the obvious references to an equatorial region (most likely Bahia in north-eastern Brazil) in their costumes, locale, and the samba music. But the symbolism behind their voiceless capering in this number is more elusive than their sheer commercial appeal.

As the scene opens, the women are all lying recumbent on their little island, apparently in a state of customary tropical torpor. They are roused from slumber, however, by the approach of: The Lady. From the back of the set she emerges on a bullock cart drawn by bare-chested young men (whose subservient, eunuch-like status does not change during the number and who do not interact with the women at all). Miranda sings, in English, a stylized samba full of references to supposed amorous encounters. But there is something very odd going on here. The fecundity of the region is suggested not only by the scantily clad females cavorting about the set but by the Freudian image of the banana itself (as well as of strawberries), huge models of which are carried about by the maidens. (At one point in the choreography, they form a vulvaesque circle and heft their bananas up and down in repeated simulation of coital penetration, at least that is what we are thinking, even if the censors would have excised anything quite so explicit. In fact, this thinly veiled sexuality caused the number to be censored in Brazil.) Yet, Miranda's hair, unlike theirs, remains concealed under her enormous hat of fruit, except for a little bit of bang. Her hat possesses as a result a curious symbolism in this context. The fruit tells us of her estrous fertility, but the nun-like concealment of her hair declares her unattainability. (It comes as a great surprise in her later movies actually to see her hair.)

With her arrival on a rustic bullock cart drawn by males, surrounded by what appear to be vestal virgins, and by virtue of her unattached/uninvolved status throughout the picture (except for a tenuous and apparently platonic relationship with Phil Baker, the bandleader), Miranda's character takes on a symbolic dimension, a sort of blend of the Virgin Mary (Our Lady) with some tropical fertility goddess (these are common in the Afro-Brazilian cults that gave birth to the samba, especially *Candomblé*). Moreover, she appears as a child-woman speaking fractured English, one who has gotten into mommy's closet and jewelry box and made herself up in a ridiculously incongruous assemblage of baubles, bangles, and beads. The prattle of her lyrics suggests something of childlike naiveté and simplicity, combined with an elusive sexual appeal:

> Some people say I dress too gay
> But, every day, I feel so gay
> And when I'm gay, I dress that way
> Is something wrong with that?

All of this is consistent with her natural persona as The Remarkable Little Girl. These lyrics contain several direct or indirect references to the virginal, unavailable status conferred by her hat:

> Americanos tell me that my hat is high
> Because I will not take it off to kiss a guy.

And further on:

> Brazilian señoritas they are sweet and shy
> They dance and play together when the sun is high
> But when the tropic moon is in the sky, ay, ay,
> They have a different kind of time
> *And even I forget that I'm*
> *The Lady in the Tutti-Frutti Hat.*[7]

The Bando provides visual backup, but they are almost inaudible due to the prominence of the orchestra. The strings especially play an important role in this number, with the occasional highlighting from flutes or trumpet. In fact, to audiences at the time, the trumpet more readily connoted Mexico or Cuba, in the context of Mexican mariachi or Cuban *conjunto*. In any case, its augmentation of the melody exhibits a rhythmic simplification that reinforces the primitiveness of the setting. Miranda's melody is a very stylized

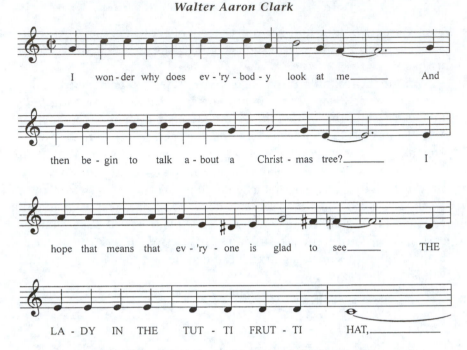

I won-der why does ev-'ry-bod-y look at me_____ And

then be-gin to talk a-bout a Christ-mas tree?_____ I

hope that means that ev-'ry-one is glad to see_____ THE

LA-DY IN THE TUT-TI FRUT-TI HAT,_____

Ex. 12.1. Warren/Robin, "The Lady in the Tutti-Frutti Hat," *The Gang's All Here.*

and simplified samba, if compared to recordings she made in the '30s in Brazil. It is in straight quarter notes, all on the downbeat, with only a bit of syncopation at the end of the phrases. The flat (Johnny-one-note) melodic contour suggests an atavistic simplemindedness. This monotone character is repeated at the larger level of the phrases themselves, which are highly repetitive. Also, the melody is very diatonic, contained within a one-octave C-major scale, with only a hint of chromaticism in the third phrase. In fact, it all sounds a bit childish, which is exactly the effect intended (see ex. 12.1).

The virginal, child-like quality of this number taps into a deeper preconception of Latin America in the European and U.S. psyche, that is, that of a virgin region awaiting consummation by the superior, masculine European culture, and of a child who needs the guidance and tutelage of the Protestant, industrial, democratic northern hemisphere.

Miranda's choreography, always the same in every movie she made, includes a spin at a make-believe marimba, made of bananas, of course. The version of the melody she plays is full of "wrong notes," and is thus highly comical, the musical counterpart of her malapropisms. The xylophone, of African origin, has nothing to do with Brazil, and is associated with southern Mexico and Central America. Indeed, this entire number is essentially a

musical fantasia, a series of extrapolations on the theme that parallels the visual fantasy onscreen. The lush string sound that accompanies the banana choreography leaves the samba completely behind, while the worldless female chorus expresses a siren-like rapture that words could not hope to convey. The string and vocal arranging suggests tropical luxuriance, tending toward a swoon. The "wrong-note" technique is amplified at the end of Carmen's song by a "wrong-chord" arpeggio in the highest register of the harp that emphasizes her bats-in-the-belfry comical nature (she glances upward when this chord is played, as if it had emanated from her head). After she leaves the stage, the maidens return to their slumber, legs conspicuous, and we again see the organ grinders with their monkeys.

From this example, we can extrapolate some general categories of (mis)representation, which in turn merit further exploration by citing examples from others of her films. These categories include: 1. suppression of negritude; 2. incongruity of context and confusion of type; 3. racial and gender stereotyping; and 4. stylization and simplification of music and text.

Suppression of Negritude

The suppression of negritude, or "blackness," served a very real commercial purpose. A striking testimony to racial animus, and Hollywood's self-conscious need to pander to it, surfaces in the following letter from Zella Richardson, of the City of Atlanta Board of Review, to E. J. Mannix at MGM, dated January 8, 1944.[8]

> My dear Friend: . . . I had the real pleasure of sitting thro the very pleasing picture THE GANGS ALL HERE and of enjoying the MANY comments such as— "At last the Producers have realized that white people CAN be entertaining without having to inject Negroes" and "Thank the Lord one picture without niggers"—Yes, I'm quoting.
>
> . . . We cannot understand the desire to exploit these people [negroes] . . . who to us represent paganism at its height, when they are doing their natural things, and the acts of monkeys when they are aping the white folks. That's the way we feel . . . so I will just continue to cut out the most objectionable parts, and WALK OUT with hundreds of others on the rest.
>
> . . . I have to be fair and say that . . . this IS causing trouble among the races—that this trouble will some day reach a climax not to be desired . . . we will just swallow those things which offend us so, and wait till our boys come home to right them.

Despite her sensational claims concerning incipient race war over Hollywood's "exploitation" (an interesting word choice) of negroes, her sentiments no doubt enjoyed broad currency during that period, and similar

suppression of negritude can be found throughout Miranda's movies. For example, *That Night in Rio* begins with a memorable song-and-dance number featuring Carmen and Don Ameche along with several chorus girls in Miranda-style garb. The setting is the hills of Rio during Carnival, and the samba number is clearly meant to establish the atmosphere. But the cast is totally devoid of a single dark-skinned person, despite the large black population of Rio and its central presence in Carnival celebrations. Once again the music is similarly whitened, absorbed into a lavish Hollywood arrangement with the heavy percussive quality and dense rhythmic layering of Afro-Brazilian Carnival samba largely expunged.[9] But even scenes like this did not go far enough to please some. A critic for *Cue* complained: "I'll never know why Miss Miranda insists on making herself up so she looks like an African witchdoctor's nightmare."[10] Consciously or not, audiences and reviewers did not want negritude.

One hastens to point out, however, that Carmen's own opinions on race did not conform to the racial prejudice that was so obvious in her movies. She addressed this topic frankly and directly when she said, "I never had racial or religious prejudices. I dealt well with blacks, Japanese, and Jews" (Consiglio 1986, 58; trans. Sarah Hamilton). She could credibly claim an absence of anti-Semitism insofar as she had married a Jew, David Sebastian. Her collaboration and friendship in Brazil with black *sambistas* like Synval Silva also suggested a lack of racial prejudice.

This was, however, not merely a strategy for placating the racist sensibilities of white moviegoers in the United States, but in Latin America as well. In Miranda's first Hollywood movie, *Down Argentine Way*, the Nicholas brothers make a brilliant appearance in a dance-club scene doing one of their trademark gravity-defying tap numbers. The Assistant Commercial Attaché to the American Embassy in Buenos Aires reported to Fox the reasons that Argentines objected strenuously to this (along with so many other things in the movie). Basically, he explained, it added "to the Argentine impression that all Yankees think they are Indians or Africans. . . . A colored person is seen in Buenos Aires as often as a Hindu in Los Angeles" (Gil-Montero 1989, 97). In fact, Afro-Argentines, who often worked as gauchos, made important contributions to Argentine song and dance. But this did not accord with the national self-image the ruling elites in government and culture were striving to cultivate.

Despite the demographic differences between Argentina and Brazil, similar attitudes existed in the former Portuguese colony as well, and this merits closer examination. William Rowe and Vivian Schelling explored racial attitudes in the context of Latin American popular culture and traced the attitudes through several stages. This evolution perhaps allows us to under-

stand the wider cultural significance of Miranda's persona, especially in light of repeated references in the press to her as "savage" and "primitive." In late nineteenth- and early-twentieth-century Brazil:

> ... the attempt to extirpate the unsightly "barbarian" elements—forms of social life and culture connected to blacks, mulattos, Indians, peasants, illiterates—from the fabric of Brazilian society is manifested in a set of ideas, policies and state actions. (Rowe and Schelling 1991, 38)

Among these "state actions" was a deliberate policy of encouraging European immigration (like Carmen's father), in order to improve the overall racial stock of the country.

But a shift in attitudes came about in the 1920s and '30s, especially as a result of the modernist movement, which "called upon the intelligentsia to 'discover Brazilian reality,'" that is, to embrace the various native and African elements in the country's demography and culture (Rowe and Schelling 1991, 41–42). The centerpiece of this ideology was *mestiçagem*, a belief that the racial "melting-pot" was beneficial and not negative. This became "a key feature of a populist programme of national integration" during the regime of Getúlio Vargas, one of Carmen's biggest supporters; nonetheless, there persisted "the widespread notion that Brazil's racial problems were being resolved through ethnic integration, whose goal remained white civilization" (Rowe and Schelling 1991, 42). Here is a possible parallel between Carmen's Bahia-inspired costumes to the blackface of an Al Jolson: a white person posing as a black. Perhaps the Euro-Brazilian Miranda represented the *mestiçagem* identity in her appropriation and "sublimation" of black dress and music, thus fulfilling the national goal of "ethnic integration" with the retention of privilege by those of European ancestry (an inherently contradictory and consequently unrealized ambition). It was through this process that "[p]opular cultural forms became important sites where ... traditional, ethnic and local identities were articulated by the state within the project of national integration and development" (Rowe and Schelling 1991, 44).

Miranda's Hollywood numbers certainly constituted one such "site." Still, there were those in Brazil who rejected this program and Carmen's projection of Brazilian identity. When she returned to Brazil in 1941, some critics expressed the belief that "Brazil was not well served by a Portuguese who promoted 'vulgar negroid sambas'" (Gil-Montero 1989, 101). But Hollywood was at pains to try to avoid this reaction. In terms of the Good Neighbor Policy, the American producers felt it necessary not to feature any aspects of Latin America—either in race relations, religion, poverty, or politics—that might be offensive to the middle classes and ruling elite. That

Carmen was of European origin, and the Moon Gang was solidly middle class, was advantageous to this policy. This makes it easy to understand why, "in their second trip to the United States, [the Moon Gang] left behind the only member married to a black" (Gil-Montero 1989, 115).

Incongruity of Context and Conflation of Type

It is not at all unlikely that a Brazilian entertainer would have been appearing in night clubs in Buenos Aires or Havana, doing sambas. Miranda herself had become popular in Argentina as a star of stage and screen, performing her Brazilian routine, although she actually got her start singing tangos in Brazil. Still, there is a colossal disconnect between reality and Hollywood in terms of the contexts in which her numbers appear. Take for instance the number "Ñango" from *Weekend in Havana*. In an internal document entitled "Vital Statistics," by publicist Harry Brand, the claim is advanced that the "Ñango" was based on a "voodoo rhythm of Afro-Cuban origin."[11] Even if such a dance actually existed, that voodoo is associated with Haiti and not Cuba was a detail that either eluded Brand or was considered of negligible importance. He elsewhere claimed that "[b]efore writing the number, the song writers (Warren and Mack) secured from Cuba acetate recordings of the jungle rhythms which they have incorporated into the song." [12]

But Carmen's big numbers are done in the Club Madrileño scene, where she sings "Rebola, Bola" (a Brazilian *embolada*, or tongue-twister), composed by Aloysio de Oliveira, in Portuguese, despite the fact that her character's name is Rosita Rivas. Moreover, in her choreography there is absolutely nothing to suggest Cuban dances such as the rumba, conga, *danzón*, or anything else appropriate to the locale. She uses her trademark strutting, undulating, and wriggling, which served her equally well in any setting Hollywood desired.

Still, one has to give *Weekend in Havana* some credit. The music is suffused with boleros, rumbas, and typical Cuban rhythms, especially 3+2 clave. Alice Faye's enchanting number "Tropical Magic" utilizes the beguine rhythm, and as Roberts points out, the beguine is essentially a rumba (and a Cole Porter trademark) (1999, 83). Some trouble was also taken by 20th Century Fox to get the scenery right, and there is actual footage of Havana, including Sloppy Joe's, made famous by Hemingway. In fact, according to more "Vital Statstics" internal documents, again by publicist Harry Brand, Dr. Oscar Presmanes, Los Angeles Cuban Consul, paid a visit to the set of the movie and, after approving the script, had these words of approbation for the film: "This is the first picture that has been made about my country that does justice to its beauty and charm."[13] But this was mere diplomacy, and the Cuban critics panned the film as a gross misrepresentation of their island home.

The biggest offender, however, was the first movie Miranda made, *Down Argentine Way*. Astoundingly, there was not a single tango in the entire film (if you want to hear a tango, you have to watch her second movie, *That Night in Rio*). Instead, the signature number is a rumba, sung by Betty Grable (who also does a conga), while Carmen sings sambas: "The film received bad reviews in Brazil and was forbidden in Argentina because 'of wrongly portraying life in Buenos Aires.' . . . the setting [was] a confused mixture of Brazil, Mexico, Cuba and Argentina" (Barsante 1985, 18). According to the *Examiner*:

> When "Down Argentine Way" was shown in Rio de Janeiro it was hissed off the screen. What made the customers especially bitter was not so much Don Ameche's corny characterizations of a South American, but because Carmen Miranda, cast as an Argentinean, is a Brazilian and does not speak Spanish, but Portuguese.[14]

Don Ameche, however, does his bit for anti-Americanism, as he performs "a rhumba [*sic*] in Spanish with castanets and talks about orchids, as rare in Argentina as in New York." Moreover, there is "a fiesta with mantillas and Spanish combs. One of the songs ends with the Spanish expression 'Olé,' which is never used in Argentina" (Gil-Montero 1989, 97–98). At one point in the film, Don Ameche spreads out his arm in a sweeping gesture, amid scenery that with its old-style mission architecture evokes Mexico and not Argentina, stating, "Here you have the authentic Argentina." The assembled peasants and town folk proceed to dance to—a Mexican *zapateado*!

And yet, the North Americans just did not get it. U.S. reviews of the movie were ecstatic. Without a hint of irony or self-consciousness, *Variety* breathlessly enthused, "The Miranda personality and her swift-tongued song recitals in Portuguese *give an authentic Argentinian note to substantiate the title of the picture*" [emphasis added].[15] Hollywood's utter incomprehension of the probable political consequences of pictures like this is beautifully encapsulated in the following assessment by the *Hollywood Reporter*: "In it is a timely and intriguing spirit of good will between North and South America."[16] Even Carmen herself participated in the propaganda parade, proclaiming that "for the first time, the true imprint of the Brazilian popular soul was portrayed in a Hollywood film as it really is" (cited in Gil-Montero 1989, 103). *Down Argentine Way* complicated the Good Neighbor Policy in Argentina, where there was already considerable sympathy for the Axis, and alienated both the public and officialdom from the United States and its war aims.

In fact, Hollywood never really caught on. In one of Miranda's later films, *Nancy Goes to Rio*, her signature number, "Tico, Tico" (a *choro* by Zequinha de Abreu), was fitted out with "special lyrics" by Earl Brent and Georgie Stoll. The conflation of Brazil and Spanish-speaking realms, especially Cuba, is again on display:

I know I'll meet myself a couple caballeros
And maybe learn a couple of sambas and boleros.
I'll be so happy down in Rio de Janeiro
With my maraccas and a rose in my sombrero.[17]

Adding insult to injury, in this same movie Nancy is feted by her cast mates, who sing of her impending trip to Rio—by singing her an *habanera*! In *A Date with Judy*, Carmen appears as the rumba instructor Rosita Conchellas, whose task is to teach Melvin Foster (Wallace Beery) to rumba. In one scene, the old man practices his dance steps at home, clearly grunting out the conga rhythm—while holding a book on how to rumba!

Racial and Gender Stereotyping

Savage, torrid, witchdoctor's nightmare, jungle music: these are some of the ways the press and industry publicists often referred to Miranda and her numbers, revealing attitudes about Latin America in general. Consistent with this role, she always has something "torrid" to sing, never anything lyrical, slow, or sad. "Jungle music" elements were clearly associated with blacks but not presented directly as such. Her public clearly craved upbeat songs and dances, and her handlers were determined to provide them, even against her will. The Brazilian magazine *Manchete* quoted her in 1954 as saying that she had once tried to introduce a slower Brazilian song into a movie, but the director refused, stating, "Carmen, here you have to play the kind of music which Brazilians, Americans and Europeans like. If you could please only Brazilians you wouldn't be here" (Gil-Montero 1989, 173). In fact, in early 1946, she stated in an interview that:

Even before the Brazilians disapproved of my films, I was upset. Many times, as soon as I had seen a new picture at a private showing, I would go to the executives to complain about the kind of repetitive roles of limited range and say that very soon the Brazilian public would dislike me. (cited in Barsante 1985, 119)

And things did not really improve over time. "Despite all our efforts, Americans cannot tell samba from other rhythms from Latin America," Carmen complained (Gil-Montero 1989, 173). Xavier Cugat had stated along the same lines: "Americans know nothing about Latin music. They neither understand nor feel it. So they have to be given music more for the eyes than the ears. Eighty percent visual, the rest aural" (Roberts 1999, 87). But Miranda never seemed to understand the central role she had played in perpetuating that confusion, precisely because she had supplied the crucial visual dimension that rendered unimportant any attempt at musical authenticity.

If money alone had been her object, Carmen would have had little to complain about, as she was the highest-paid entertainer in the United States by 1945, with an annual income of $200,000, more than Bob Hope, Errol Flynn, Bing Crosby, or Humphrey Bogart. But she was an artist whose creative impulses needed a better outlet. Sadly, they never got one. She was making lots of money off of these films, but the studios were making even more money off of her, and they were not about to fix a money machine that was not broken.

Time and again, Carmen Miranda and other Latin actresses were described as "torrid." Consider the case of Lupe Vélez, a Mexican actress of the 1930s, and '40s, who starred as Carmelita in a seemingly endless succession of (now forgotten) "Mexican Spitfire" movies for RKO.[18] The series came to an abrupt and tragic halt in 1944 when the actress took her own life. The archetypal Latin female was:

Non-Anglo-Saxon, sexually aggressive, unable to speak proper English, possessive, illogical, jealous, highly emotional, regarded as a sex object, temperamental, and hot-blooded [and] usually native to a tropical, exotic climate. "Hot Tamale," "Firecracker," and "Wildcat" are some of the other names applied to her. (Walters 1978, 61)

In many ways, Lupe Vélez was to Carmen Miranda what John the Baptist was to Jesus. She paved the way and actively participated in creating a stereotype of the Latin female that Carmen then took to outrageous, even campy, heights (or depths). Words like savage, torrid, primitive, barbaric, fiery, tempestuous, and volatile came to be used in an almost unconscious, offhand, and yet very revealing way in U.S. press notices about Carmen's films. They reflect a certain ambivalence, that is, that she is a threatening presence sexually, but her mangling of English and her comic outfits somehow diminish the danger.

The Los Angeles *Herald Examiner* described Miranda as "outfitted in smart, barbaric colors, waving articulate hips and rollicking through the most fun of her Hollywood career."[19] Washington, D.C.'s *Evening Star* entitled its review of *That Night in Rio* "Torrid Carmen Miranda Brightens New Musical" and observed:

> The way of progress is indicated clearly. All the boys need to do to improve their contributions . . . is to teach this *torrid tamale* from South America more and more broken English until she has a vocabulary larger than those of the other members of Mr. Zanuck's musical stock company.[20] [Emphasis added]

Variety found that "Carmen Miranda . . . chants and dances and wears her bizarre attire with a savage grace which spreads excitement around her in widening ripples to color every scene she plays.[21] The *Hollywood Reporter* said of this same film, "[Miranda's] performance in English is . . . vivid, fiery and tempestuous."[22] In regards to *Springtime in the Rockies*, *Variety* later declared that Miranda was:

> colorful, arresting, exerting her forthright, primitive charm through her staccato chanting, her energetic dancing, the way she displays her bizarre costumes, and, above all, her volatile sense of comedy from which all her other manifestations spring.[23]

All of this formed a much less flattering image of Latin America than what audiences and critics in the southern hemisphere were comfortable with. Indeed, the Uniao Cultural Brasil-Estados Unidos wrote to Will H. Hays, President, Motion Pictures and Distributors of America (and notorious film censor), on January 2, 1942, to remind him of "the great need for teaching the average American citizen the following facts about Brazil," which included its size (largest in South America), language (Portuguese and not Spanish), urbanization (São Paolo is comparable to Chicago), and culture and science (as important as that of the United States), and so forth.[24] To be fair, the studio did run the script and music for *That Night in Rio* by the Brazilian Embassy in Washington, D.C.[25] But the stereotyping continued unabated throughout Miranda's career, and beyond.

Stylization and Simplification of Music and Text

Miranda's torrid stereotype required a commensurate distortion of the musical and textual materials used to create her character. Again, to be fair, Miranda's movies represented a quantum leap over what American audiences had previously experienced in the way of Brazilian music from Hollywood, especially in *Flying Down to Rio* (although that movie was remarkably sensitive in other ways, including its use of blacks in the song-and-dance numbers and generally favorable depiction of Rio as a modern metropolis). Miranda was the leading performer of samba, backed up by her hand-picked Brazilian musicians, occasionally, at least, singing songs written by Brazilian *sambistas* (e.g., the samba "O tic-tac do meu coraçao" by Alcyr Pires Vermelho and Walfrido Silva in *Springtime in the Rockies*), many for her personally. But the truth is that most of the numbers in her movies were written by Americans possessing only a superficial acquaintance with the genre, and the songs were composed to appeal to a U.S. audience that, at least as far as samba was concerned, was completely unsophisticated. *LA Weekly* certainly saw this many years later when it remarked on "the pseudo-sambas of Tin Pan Alley tunesmiths Harry Warren and Mack Gordon, and [the replacement of] her soulful Portuguese lyrics with pidgin doggerel like 'Chica Chica Boom Chick.'"[26]

Mirabile dictu! In fact, internal documents give us some genuine insight into the genesis of this number, which was one of the big hits from *That Night in Rio*. According to Harry Brand, Mack Gordon had this to say about its text:

> Harry [Warren] had the basis of a great tune—we played it over on the piano and I hummed it with him. But I wanted to get the rhythm down so I could take it home with me to work on the lyric. To fix the rhythm in my mind, I hit upon a group of syllables which exactly fitted the music. I sang them out loud. The syllables were "Chica, Chica, Boom, Chic-." "Sing that over again, Mack," suggested Harry. So I did. "That's great, Mack, you've got the title—let's call the song 'Chica, Chica, Boom Chic.'" So, that's what we call the song—it's a perfect jungle chant![27]

Despite its dubious association with the jungle, we must remember that the Brazilian embassy was shown the script and song texts in advance. Thus, it seems incredible they acquiesced to the rest of the lyric:

> Come on and sing the chica chica boom chic,
> That crazy thing, the chica chica boom chic,
> Brazilians found the chica chica boom chic,
> They like the sound of chica, chica, boom, chic,
> It came down the Amazon,
> From the jungles,
> Where the natives greet everyone they meet
> Beatin' on a tom tom.[28]

That "chica chica boom chic" was more closely situated to the Mulholland aquaduct than the Amazon River and that Brazilian Indians do not play "tom-toms" were fine points of ethnography that the composer and lyricist knew full well would not disturb the sleep of American moviegoers. Moreover, this was conceived as a rumba, not a samba, and therefore has little relation musically to Brazil. In fact, Aloysio de Oliveira had to modify both this rumba and the conga "I, Yi, Yi, Yi, Yi, I Like You Very Much" with elements of samba and *marchinha*, respectively, in order to enhance their Brazilianness (Gil-Montero 1989, 120).

What so distressed Carmen's countrymen, however, was that through her active participation in this kind of thing, her art had become Americanized. As we have noted, Carmen complained bitterly that she was never given an opportunity onscreen to sing slower, more lyrical songs. The studio executives believed that only her hyperactive numbers had any box-office appeal and that the subtleties of Brazilian popular music would be lost on American audiences. For instance, nearly all her movie numbers are in major keys, while in fact many of the sambas she made famous in Brazil in the 1930s—for example, "Diz que tem" by Vincete Paiva and Hannibal Cruz, or the bewitchingly melancholy "Coraçao" by Synval Silva[29]—are in minor keys and exhibit some poignant lyricism. Like so much Brazilian popular music, they convey *saudade*, a sort of wistful nostalgia. But the happy escapism of Miranda's Hollywood movies, and the kind of role in which she found herself frozen in every film, demanded that anything elevated, serious, sophisticated, or reflective be completely expunged.

Ambassadress of the Samba?

Carmen's expressed feelings about her role as a representative of Latin American culture in general and Brazilian music in particular are somewhat contradictory. On the one hand, she was pleased with her role as a symbol of Latin America and the "proof" that symbol provided of amity between the northern and southern hemispheres:

> It is comforting to know that a simple popular artist like me could have been used as a political weapon. But if I didn't have talent and this charisma they attribute to me, I would not have survived, right? (Consiglio 1986, 19; trans. Sarah Hamilton)

However, she was vehement in rejecting the notion that she was "Latino-americana":

> I detest this expression, as it is so generalized. I like to be called a Brazilian, not from South America or Latin America, for I have nothing to do with the descendants of Spain. After all, we Brazilians are the only citizens of Latin America that speak Portuguese, and we really are different. (Consiglio 1986, 61; trans. Sarah Hamilton)

This statement is highly ironic, because as we now know, her admixture of diverse elements from Mexican, Cuban, Brazilian, and Argentinian traditions created a hybrid that often obscured the Brazilian character of her art. She actively participated in the creation of a mythological, pan-Latin stereotype that incensed South Americans to the same extent it entertained—and misinformed—moviegoers in the United States. But, as Ana Lopez has pointed out, this "hybridization [is] potentially inherent to all national cinemas" (1993, 6).

We close with another quote from Roberts's seminal book, one with which this author cannot agree. He states that Miranda's movies "made no statements about Latin music, and to object to their stereotyping is about as valid as objecting that *Oklahoma!* gave a false impression of American farmers" (1999, 106). One may or may not choose to object, but the stereotypes possess an importance that transcends mere nitpicking about authenticity. In fact, her movies constitute a very important statement about Latin American music, demographics, politics, women, and culture in general. It is simply that, as many have observed, the statements are misleading. As Shari Roberts proclaims, "Miranda's parodic text works undeniably to reinforce regressive stereotypes of Latin Americans and of women, and to support racist and sexist conceptions" (1993, 19). The music plays a key role in such stereotyping.

Yet, we need not view the situation as uniformly sinister. In their promiscuous miscegenation of musical types, choreography, and costumes, Carmen's movies could be viewed as a phenomenon nearly half a century ahead of its time. The "ethnofusion" that now drives the popular-music industry exhibits at times bewildering combinations and permutations of styles not only from Latin America but the world at large. Carmen was, in fact, a prophetess of the musical global village that had not yet fully arrived in the 1940s. Her Hollywoodized eclecticism has a postmodern quality, and we can find meaning, significance, and (yes!) entertainment in it outside the highly political context in which it emerged, whether of Brazilian nationalism under Vargas and his regime of racial reconciliation, or of the Good Neighbor Policy in the midst of a world war.

Miranda revivals have taken place at periodic intervals since her death in 1955. In the 1960s, *tropicália* film-makers in Brazil were fascinated and deeply influenced by her Hollywood movies.[30] The 1990s witnessed another resurgence of Miranda-mania, especially as a result of the brilliant 1994 documentary *Banana Is My Business*.[31] Succeeding generations will almost certainly continue to find much in her art that is compelling, relevant, and joyful. To assert anything less would be to diminish her stature as the creative genius she truly was.

Notes

1. This exchange occurred during a press conference on December 4, 1982, in the early going of Reagan's presidency. I am extremely grateful to archivist Diane Barrie of the Ronald Reagan Library for tracking down the precise quote and source for a statement I only dimly recalled from so many years ago.
2. For a thorough discography, *see* Barsante (1985, 230–35); *see also* Cardoso Juniór (1978) for lyrics and further recording information.
3. The soundtrack of this movie is available on CD: *The Gang's All Here* (Sandy Hook Records, S.H.2009, 1978). Other CD compilations of her U.S. recordings include *Carmen Miranda: South American Way* (Jasmine Records, JASCD 317, 1993), and the *Carmen Miranda Anthology* (One Way Records, MCAD 22124, 1994).
4. In a September 21, 1942, review of *Springtime in the Rockies*. Unless otherwise stated, this and all other reviews cited below are found in the press files for each film in the Margaret Herrick Library, General Collection [MHL/GC], Academy of Motion Picture Arts and Sciences, Hollywood.
5. The banana possesses considerable symbolism on many levels. It is not only psychological, even Freudian, but also has resonance in the sphere of business and politics. The United Fruit Company had extensive interests in Central America and made its contribution to Good Neighborliness by establishing a Middle American Information Bureau in 1943 to encourage inter-American understanding. The following year, it introduced a Miranda-inspired logo, Chiquita Banana. The feminist dimension of the banana's political economy, using Carmen Miranda as a point of departure, is the topic of Enloe (1990, 124–50).
6. See Austern (1998, 26): "From the travels of Odysseus to the voyages of the starship *Enterprise*, the Western mind has been called to vicarious adventure in distant lands of pleasure and danger through the voice of an exotic woman."
7. These lyrics were obtained from a typewritten document in the MPAA Production Code Administration file on this film, in the Margaret Herrick Library, Special Collections [MHL/SC].
8. Ibid.
9. Shari Roberts (1993, 13), points out that this process of "whitening" the *samba de morro* had begun in Brazil, and the mellower variety was popularized by Miranda and others in the 1930s. One should keep in mind, however, that many of the composers of this newer type of samba were, in fact, black.
10. In a review of *Nancy Goes to Rio*, dated April 8, 1950.
11. MHL/GC, press file on *That Night in Rio*.
12. In an e-mail message to this author of May 20, 2000, ethnomusicologist Peter Manuel, an authority on Caribbean music, could not identify the *ñango*, except to speculate that perhaps "the word in question is ñañigo ... a member of the abakua secret societies, derived from the Carabali people. They have distinctive music and dance. But it's not a religion per se, and there is no spirit possesssion (as there is in voodoo)." Perhaps this was the inspiration for Brand's explanation.
13. MHL/GC, press file on *Weekend in Havana*.
14. Review dated July 17, 1941.
15. Review dated October 2, 1940.
16. Review dated October 2, 1940.
17. Lyrics from MHL/SC, MPAA Production Code Administration file on *Nancy Goes to Rio*.

18. Walters (1978, 106) provides a sampling of titles: *Mexican Spitfire* (1939), *Mexican Spitfire Out West* (1940), *Mexican Spitfire at Sea* (1941), *Mexican Spitfire's Baby* (1941), *Mexican Spitfire's Elephant* (1942), *Mexican Spitfire Sees a Ghost* (1942), *Mexican Spitfire's Blessed Event* (1943).
19. Review dated October 24, 1941.
20. Review dated November 7, 1941.
21. Review dated March 7, 1941.
22. Review dated March 7, 1941.
23. Review dated September 21, 1942.
24. Letter in MHL/SC, MPAA Production Code Administration file on *That Night in Rio*.
25. According to internal documents, MHL/GC, press file on *That Night in Rio*.
26. Review dated October 2, 1998, MHL/GC, file on Carmen Miranda.
27. MHL/GC, press file on *That Night in Rio*.
28. Lyrics from MHL/SC, MPAA Production Code Administration file on *That Night in Rio*.
29. Both numbers are available on *Carmen Miranda: The Brazilian Recordings* (Harlequin HQCD 33, 1993).
30. For an insightful look at the relationship between *tropicália* musicians and Miranda, see Veloso 2001. He speculates that "her great vocation for the finished product, her ability to design extremely stylized samba dancing as though creating a cartoon character, might . . . have been the decisive factor in her popularity [in the United States]."
31. Directed and narrated by Helena Solberg; produced by David Meyer and Helena Solberg. International Cinema production in association with the Corporation for Public Broadcasting, Channel 4 Television, and the National Latino Communications Center. Fox Lorber HomeVideo FLV1211.

References

Austern, Linda Phyllis. 1998. "'Foreine Conceites and Wandering Devices': The Exotic, the Erotic, and the Feminine." In *The Exotic in Western Music*. Edited by Jonathan Bellman. Boston: Northeastern University Press.

Barsante, Cássio Emmanuel. 1985. *Carmen Miranda*. Rio de Janeiro: Europa Empresa Gráfica e Editora.

Cardoso Júnior, Abel. 1978. *Carmen Miranda, a cantora do Brasil*. São Paulo: Cardoso Junior.

Consiglio, Dulce Damasceno de Brito. 1986. *O ABC de Carmen Miranda*. São Paulo: Companhia Editora Nacional.

Enloe, Cynthia H. 1990. "Carmen Miranda on My Mind." In *Bananas, Beaches & Bases: Making Feminist Sense of International Politics*. Berkeley: University of California Press.

Gil-Montero, Martha. 1989. *Brazilian Bombshell: The Biography of Carmen Miranda*. New York: Donald I. Fine.

Lopez, Ana M. 1993. "Are All Latins from Manhattan? Hollywood, Ethnography and Cultural Colonialism." In *Mediating Two Worlds: Cinematic Encounters in the Americas*. Edited by John King, Ana M. Lopez, Manuel Alvarado. London: British Film Institute Publishing, 67–80.

Roberts, John Storm. 1999. *The Latin Tinge: The Impact of Latin American Music on the United States*. 2d ed. New York: Oxford University Press.

Roberts, Shari. 1993. "Lady in the Tutti-Frutti Hat: Carmen Miranda, a Spectacle of Ethnicity." *Cinema Journal* 32/3: 3–23.

Rowe, William, and Vivian Schelling. 1991. *Memory and Modernity: Popular Culture in Latin America*. London: Verso.

Veloso, Caetano. 2001. "Carmen Mirandada." In *Brazilian Popular Music and Globalization*. Edited by Charles Perrone and Christopher Dunn. Gainesville: University Press of Florida, 39–45.

Walters, Debra Nan. 1978. *Hollywood, World War II, and Latin America: The Hollywood Good Neighbor Policy As Personified by Carmen Miranda*. Master's thesis, University of Southern California.

Woll, Allen L. 1980. *The Latin Image in American Film*. Rev. ed. Los Angeles: UCLA Latin American Center Publications.

Contributors

María Susana Azzi is a cultural anthropologist at the Universidad de Buenos Aires, professor and board member of the National Tango Academy, and a board member of the Astor Piazzolla Foundation. She is the author or coauthor of four books on tango, including a critically acclaimed biography (with Simon Collier) of Piazzolla for Oxford University Press.

Walter Aaron Clark is an associate professor of musicology at the University of Kansas. He is the author of *Isaac Albéniz: Portrait of a Romantic* (Oxford) and *Isaac Albéniz: A Guide to Research* (Garland), in addition to the chapter on music in *Latin America: An Interdisciplinary Approach* (Peter Lang). He is currently writing a book on Enrique Granados (Oxford).

Philip Galinsky is a visiting assistant professor of ethnomusicology at UC Davis. He has taught at Hampshire College in Amherst, Massachusetts, and in 1998 he was a visiting scholar at the Joaquim Nabuco Foundation in Recife, Pernambuco, Brazil, in the Department of Anthropology. His research has been published in *Latin American Music Review*, *Ethnomusicology Yearbook for Traditional Music*, and *The Beat* magazine. He is currently preparing his dissertation for publication (Routledge).

John Koegel is an assistant professor of music history at California State University, Fullerton. His research has appeared in numerous journals, and he is presently editing *Mexican-American Music in the Lummis Wax-Cylinder Collection* (A-R Editions). He is also completing the bibliographic study *Sources of Spanish Colonial, Mexican, and Mexican-American Music in the United States: A Bibliography, Discography, and Inventory* (Harmonie Park Press).

John Murphy is an associate professor in the Jazz Division of the College of Music at the University of North Texas, and taught previously at Western Illinois University. He is working on a book on Brazilian popular music, globalization, and cultural politics, and his recent publications include a chapter in *Brazilian Popular Music and Globalization* (University Press of Florida, 2001).

Javier Barrales Pacheco teaches music and is chair of the music department at Sequoia Union High School, Redwood City, CA. He has also taught courses on Latin

American music at San Francisco State University and Berkeley. He has served as board member, publicist, archivist, musician, and multimedia specialist of Raíces de México (dance school and company of East Palo Alto) since 1993.

Raúl R. Romero is executive director of the Center for Andean Ethnomusicology at the Catholic University of Peru in Lima. He is the author of *Debating the Past: Music, Memory and Identity in the Andes* (Oxford) and numerous articles in academic journals and encyclopedias. He is also the editor of the ongoing series of recordings *Traditional Music of Peru* (Smithsonian Folkways).

Melinda Russell is an assistant professor of music at Carleton College in Northfield, Minnesota. She is coeditor (with Bruno Nettl et al.) of *Community of Music: An Ethnographic Seminar in Champaign-Urbana* (Elephant and Cat) and (with Bruno Nettl) of *In the Course of Performance: Studies in the World of Musical Improvisation* (University of Chicago). Her doctoral dissertation examines musical life in an Illinois city between 1990 and 1996.

Deborah Schwartz-Kates is an assistant professor of music at the University of Texas, San Antonio. Her research focuses on the symbolic construction of identity, the Interrelationship of Argentine musical repertoires, and the application of ethnomusicological ideas, methods, and approaches to historical musicology. She has published her work in *Latin American Music Review, Yearbook for Traditional Music,* and *The New Grove Dictionary of Music and Musicians* (2d ed.).

T. M. Scruggs is an assistant professor of ethnomusicology at the University of Iowa. He has done extensive fieldwork in Nicaragua and other parts of Central America, and his research has appeared in print, audio, and video publications. He is also a performing musician and founded the steel-pan ensemble at the University of Iowa.

Pablo Semán is a professor of sociology and anthropology at the National University of General San Martín. He has published widely in Argentina, Brazil, and Venezuela. He coauthored an article on Pentecostalism in the Southern Cone in the *Journal of the International Sociological Association* (2000), and his chapter "Brazilian Pentecostalism Crosses National Borders" will soon be published in *Pentecostalism and Transnationalism: Africa/Latin America* (Hurst).

George Torres is an assistant professor of musicology at Grinnell College, where he teaches courses in European and Latin American musics, and directs the Latin American Ensemble. He previously taught music at St. Lawrence University, where he was also director of the Caribbean and Latin American Studies program. He has delivered papers at national meetings of the American Musicological Society, the College Music Society, and the Society for Seventeenth-Century Music.

Pablo Vila is an associate professor in the Department of Sociology at the University of Texas, San Antonio. He researches music and identity in Argentina (especially *rock nacional*) and has published articles about the topic in Argentina, Mexico, the United States, Canada, the United Kingdom, France, and Spain.

Index

Index

Index

Index

Index

Index

Index

Index